Georgina Lawton is a twenty-something journalist, travel writer and host of Audible's DNA podcast, *The Secrets In Us*. Georgina has been a weekly *Guardian* columnist, with her work also appearing in the *Independent*, *ipaper*, *Stylist*, *gal-dem*, *Travel + Leisure*, *VICE*, *Time Out London* and many more.

Follow Georgina on Twitter @GeorginaLawton and on Instagram @georginalawtonwri

GEORGINA LAWTON

raceless

Exploring race, identity and the
truth about where I belong

SPHERE

SPHERE

First published in Great Britain in 2021 by Sphere
This paperback edition published by Sphere in 2022

1 3 5 7 9 10 8 6 4 2

A CIP catalogue record for this book
is available from the British Library.

ISBN 978-0-7515-7937-6

Typeset in Garamond by M Rules
Printed and bound in Great Britain by
Clays Ltd, Elcograf S.p.A.

Papers used by Sphere are from well-managed forests
and other responsible sources.

Sphere
An imprint of
Little, Brown Book Group
Carmelite House
50 Victoria Embankment
London EC4Y 0DZ

An Hachette UK Company
www.hachette.co.uk

www.littlebrown.co.uk

For my parents and my brother

Contents

1

The Secret

Being loving does not mean we will not be betrayed.
Love helps us face betrayal without losing heart. And
it renews our spirit so we can love again.

BELL HOOKS, *All About Love*

I was born into a secret. But before I even knew this, before
it became my secret to hold, it belonged to my parents.
And before that, the sole owner of the secret was my mother.
Allow me to explain. My parents' story, so far as it concerns
me, began in 1989, at the Charing Cross Hotel in central
London. They worked, catering to the whims of tourists,
moments from city attractions like Trafalgar Square and the
National Gallery. He was twenty-eight and a chef out back
in the kitchen; she was twenty-seven and on the front desk, at
reception. Both were the last of their siblings to meet someone
and settle down – he one of three, she one of eight. Although
they were from very different rural backgrounds, they were
the only ones in their families to settle so far away from home.

My dad's parents saw he was smart and so thought sending

him to a boarding school at the age of ten was the best thing, and soon after, the family relocated to Shropshire, a soporific county of green sandwiched between the city of Birmingham and the Welsh hills. He hated boarding school, returned home to his family every holiday until he was eighteen, but found himself keen to leave again as soon as school was done. He went to Wolverhampton Polytechnic after flunking his exams and learned to love the burgeoning punk music scene, teaching himself bass guitar, joining a band or two, and making friends who would later attend his wedding. He studied Economics at the poly, and despite never attending lectures, scraped a third and had an entry-level traineeship at an accountancy firm lined up for him upon graduation. When they called to check if he still wanted the position, it was his father who confirmed that yes, of course, he'd be there to start on Monday. But my dad had found the whole number-crunching thing mind-numbingly boring at university and turned the opportunity down – much to his father's disapproval. He retrained as a chef, like his mother, and revelling in the fact that he could go back to the student life for a couple more years, he moved to London.

My mum grew up in West Ireland, the second youngest of a very Catholic, very strict household where weekly mass attendance was a precondition for youth club admittance on a Saturday night and many school lessons were taught in Irish. Her parents were hard workers but not well off; they farmed cattle and raised their own pigs and chickens in muddy green fields surrounding the house, fetching turf from the wet raised boglands nearby for the constantly roaring hearth in the main room of the house. They never went without, but there was little time for frivolities like bedtime reading, playing board games, or learning to swim – despite the drama of the Atlantic waves crashing on to the rocks just minutes away. Mass, schoolwork and chores were the all-consuming bedrock principles to an Irish childhood; there was little time for affection, or ruminating on feelings. And as soon as you could, it was expected that you would move away to make something of yourself, in Limerick, or Dublin, or London. She started in the first and ended up in the last by 1988, skipping a stint in her country's capital, unlike her two eldest sisters who settled there.

At the Charing Cross Hotel my mum and dad were acquaintances at first, then friends, and then they started dating. She lived-in at the hotel but would often stay over at his bedsit in Notting Hill. It was small and cramped with a shared bathroom and kitchen, and the man who lived on the top floor often rambled to himself, which was scary when my dad wasn't there with her. When they got married, in 1990, it was in her local parish of Cooraclare, in County Clare. Dad had thrown himself into the Irish culture: he loved the music, the people, the craic and the rebellious nature of it all, and she loved that he loved it. Over a hundred people attended their wedding. Her father – 'Dada' as he was known – gave them £1000 (an awful lot of money back then) towards it all, which they used to pay for the hotel reception. They cut a three-tier fruit cake from a bakery in Ennis – the nearest town, which was 25 miles away – and danced to 'I've Had the Time of My Life' for their first song.

They had moved out of the bedsit and into a tiny top-floor flat in Shepherd's Bush by the time their first child arrived. My mum had friends in the area, people she knew from West Clare; Dad had started working at a school in Hammersmith. He got two weeks' paternity leave, which was good back then, helping with the feeds in the night, hands-on from the beginning, doing what he was supposed to. It was a long labour. I was a large baby, weighing 9½ pounds, which was a lot for my mother's petite 5ft 4in frame to handle – there were many stitches afterwards, the pain of recovering from those worse than actually giving birth. After all the sweating and panting and pushing and crying that took place in Queen Charlotte's Hospital in Hammersmith on the afternoon of 12 November, a baby girl was born. There were no difficult words exchanged on the day, no heated discussions, no angry tears. There was no questioning of my mother's fidelity, no dramatic hospital walkout. There was simply a new family.

But it was not the baby they had been expecting: they both could admit that privately, although not to each other. As she gazed down at the gurgling bundle in her arms, a cocktail of emotions – mixed up with the hormones and drugs for the pain – swirled through my mum's body and made her dizzy. She was floating on a cloud of euphoria, but as she came to, she could see that the actions of her past had invited themselves into her present, and now they were here to stay. She saw the baby in her arms, with her mop of charcoal-black hair and huge brown eyes fanned by thick dark lashes, and she just knew, she just *knew* straight away. The baby was not his. That night nine months ago – it was just one night – had led to this. *What was she going to do? What would everyone think?* She had a healthy baby girl, thank God, but the baby was not her husband's. On what should have been a totally joyous occasion, thoughts of life as a single mother flashed before her. She knew all too well how they treated women like her in Ireland. After all, it was only during her mother's generation that they had banished unwed mothers to brutal institutions run by nuns, snatched their babies and stripped them of their social rights. The legacy of those stories was buried deep within her country's national fabric. And it wasn't spoken of; you never spoke of such things. *What would everyone think?*

That night. That one stupid, selfish night that she had

long since pushed into the deepest crevasses of her mind, was something she had not admitted to anyone, much less herself. It was a secret she had kept under psychological lock and key, but now here was this baby, a living, breathing reminder of that fleeting encounter with a man she had wanted to forget, in a place she would not allow herself to return to. And she would have to look at the evidence of that encounter for the rest of her life, the memory haunting her now, and for ever, through her baby. Here was her daughter staring back at her with such innocence and expectation. She couldn't talk – yet – but there would soon come a time when she could, and what would she tell her then? She didn't know, she couldn't think. But she was relieved when her husband took the baby in his arms and showed no visible sign of distress, of rage. He was elated – a daughter! He cooed and cuddled and accepted her without question. But terror hovered above her in that delivery room, an invisible cloud, and who knew if, or when, it would start to rain? She was unsure of what to do, what to say, whether to address the issue right before their very eyes. She panicked, she commented on the baby's features – how dark they were, and with all that thick hair too! And then the midwife, whose face she can still remember to this day, offered her a lifeline that would anchor the story into the bedrock of their lives. The nurse said, so she did, that the reason this beautiful baby was so irredeemably brown-skinned was possibly down to a *throwback gene* from a distant lineage, a link to a far-away, forgotten land – because wasn't my mother Irish, and hadn't there been lots of mixing on the west coast, what with all the Spanish and the Portuguese around there? My mum was born close to a town called Spanish Point, so-called because it was where many of the ships from the storm-dispersed Spanish Armada were wrecked in the late sixteenth century, darkening the gene-pool of West Clare as a result, or so it was said. And Dada was olive-skinned with dark features too – his skin was olive and leathery, not *really* white. And so the story stuck. It placed the baby into a (spurious) section of mythologised Irish 'history', tying it together with her grandfather's appearance and sealing up the remaining gaps in a badly kept secret no one else ever challenged. If my mother willed everyone around her to believe it too, then it could be. And when her husband didn't ask for any more details, when he continued to coo over the child and make plans for their return to the flat, the silence between them was co-signed and codified. The secret set like concrete. It was done.

In allowing what was obvious to remain obscured that day in the hospital, they made an unspoken promise to each other not to dwell on the history or heritage of their baby girl; to raise her lovingly, without another word on the matter from that day forth. The seeds of their family tree were planted by that nurse in November, and it would grow into a narrative that spanned decades and countries, a narrative that each of them would cling to in order to maintain the secret around their child's identity.

It was a story my mother would repeat again and again and one that I would learn to recite hundreds of times, in a tone that began apathetic but slowly morphed into something more defensive with each passing year. The absurdity contained in that nurse's suggestion offered my parents an escape from addressing a tricky topic in their marriage, leading to a joint decision to overlook my heritage as a way of accepting it. But I was raised in love. And when the time came many years later to pore over everything I had ever been told and search for the answers on my own – after I had worked through the rage and sadness – I tried to put myself in my parents' shoes. I thought about how scared Mum must have been when I was born; how my father must have wrestled with the decision of whether to stay or go all by himself, before choosing to stick around and stay with his new family. When, later, I got lost in my thoughts, and anguish and alienation walked hand in hand through my head, I wondered if my mother regretted not being more careful, if she regretted *me*, if my father had stayed out of obligation or guilt. I lost sight of who we were, and searched for a lie in the love that came from my home. I searched for a prickle of detachment or discontent between me and my father over the years. I wondered if I'd been blind to it, if I'd missed something in the minutiae. But I could not find it. After revisiting our life together, I realised that such a feeling had never existed between us. The secret I inherited was, at times, a lonely gift. But destroying it – *blowing that shit wide open* – was the most transformative, educational thing I have ever done.

2

Restarting

The world does not deliver meaning to you. You have
to make it meaningful ... You have to live; you can't
live by slogans, dead ideas, clichés, or national flags.
Finding an identity is easy. It's the easy way out.

ZADIE SMITH, *On Beauty*

On a brilliantly hot Caribbean morning in March 2017, as the first of the day's sunshine poured through the shutters of my tiny beachfront apartment and spread across the floorboards like warm golden syrup, I received the results of my third DNA test in a year. I looked out of the window at a sparkling sea moments from my building. I was seconds away from giant palm trees, crystalline waters and powdery white sands on Nicaragua's Corn Islands, 3241 miles away from my old life on the outskirts of London. But that morning I had to confront my past and everything I'd left behind. And I had to tell my mum of my genetic news. I didn't know how she'd react.

Down a surprisingly clear FaceTime link to London, I said, 'I've got the test results back.'

What followed was a long stretch of silence. Then, finally, a response. 'Oh. So, what did it say?'

'Well ... I'm Nigerian.' Another pause.

'Forty-three per cent actually. And the rest of me comes from Ireland, which we know since that's from you ... ' I trailed off.

'Right ... ' Everything went quiet once again. 'Well you're still more white than anything aren't you?'

I closed my eyes and breathed in slowly. Parrots chirped outside my window.

'What do you mean by that?'

'Well, I'm just saying the percentages ... ' My mum stopped, sensing that she had said the wrong thing. 'Oh don't worry.'

I decided to ask the question that was on the tip of my tongue, but which I knew would obliterate the conversation in a matter of seconds. To toss the verbal grenade I had in my pocket.

'So, do you think my biological father could be Nigerian?' I asked flatly. 'Is this maybe jogging your memory at all?'

'I don't want to talk about this.'

Boom. Detonation complete.

'Mum, we need to—'

'I don't have anything else to say, Georgina.'

The rage came quickly, I was somewhat surprised at its potency, even though I was so far from my mother's physical presence, I could feel it practically radiating off my body, vibrating through the phone. How could she not understand? How could she not tell me?

'Well you need to try harder because this issue isn't going away,' I hissed. 'I want *answers*. I think I deserve them at this stage.'

Another pause. 'I've got nothing else to say.'

It's safe to say this was not the reaction I'd been hoping for. I'd only waited my whole life to put a name to the country responsible for my appearance; I'd only been trying to piece together my identity on my own for over two decades, straddling the borders of a racialised existence outside my family and a non-racialised one in their presence, all the while dealing with projected ideas from strangers about what I looked like, who I resembled, what I was. I'd just found another piece of the puzzle, I'd worked it out on my own, but there was no support from the one person I needed it most from. My mum refused to hear me, to understand why this was so desperately important.

Our conversation ended after another pregnant pause, which morphed into a frustrating silence before I was forced to hang up. This was a practice that was now totally routine for the long-distance conversations we'd had since I left home months earlier. I'd learned that if my mum didn't want to talk – about the cataclysmic series of events that had left us separated by thousands of miles less than two years after Dad's death – then she would simply become mute. I'd lost track of the number of conversations that had been stifled by silence.

Who my biological father was, how I was brought into the world, my ancestry – all of it was off-limits. In those moments, the emotional chasm between us far exceeded the physical distance.

I was starting to realise that this absence of discussion had been something of a recurring theme throughout my childhood. And so when I felt the nothingness creeping into our call again that morning, I chose to leave before the fury took hold of me once more. It was only 9 a.m. I couldn't fight – I hadn't even had breakfast.

That morning I'd been woken up by a heat so heavy it felt

like I was wearing it, a second skin. A dampness coated my back, and my throat was dry as I had processed my DNA test results and called my mum to discuss the truth about the heritage of the daughter *she* had raised. It felt all the more surreal calling from Nicaragua, a chaotic, colourful country that couldn't be more different from the smallness and safeness of my home town basically. It was a mad phone call, a mad time, but this madness was far more bearable than the one which had defined so much of my life before. I realised that I couldn't escape who I was; the compulsion to uncover the truth had followed me halfway round the world. But, I thought to myself as I looked out of the window again, there were definitely worse places to be in the throes of an early-life identity crisis.

I had grown up cushioned and comfortable, with two loving parents and a brother three-and-a-half years younger than me, in a home that was stable and secure. I was loved, cared for, doted on – a Daddy's Girl. I was a high achiever. A netball player. A keyboard player. I was – and still am – constantly late for everything, an avid reader, outgoing, talkative, moody, generous. I am someone who eats their feelings and detests celery. I was the leader in my friendship group and a natural thrill-seeker. I was not a child who was shy or withdrawn, but one who was unafraid to assert herself, yet eager to be liked. I was many great things, and a few bad things too. I was a part of my family. But I was also different from everyone around me – because everyone is white, and I am not. This simple, yet bewildering, difference was highlighted to me a handful of times outside my home as a child, then as I grew older, with increasing frequency. But it was never really explained by the two people who held the key to all the answers: my parents. In fact (and I know it sounds implausible), *everything* race-related went largely unacknowledged between me and my mum and dad, between my brother and me, and between my parents and their families and friends – until I started asking questions. I was an inquisitive child with an anti-authoritarian streak that would rear its head at inopportune times, but which was probably linked to the fact that my very existence was contradictory and nonsensical. I was looking to find my place in the world around me. And, so, naturally as I grew older, my questions became plagued with urgency, because when I was born, my mum and dad simply introduced me to everyone without explanation – as if it were the most normal thing in the world for two white parents to produce a black child – and continued this way all their lives, until I began to disrupt the silence. As a result, there were many situations that were almost comical in their inanity. Dave, my dad's best friend and former best man, once told me that he remembered my parents cooing over my baby photos when I was barely a year old, and my parents saying that I looked just like my fair-skinned father, Jim – 'I was thinking, erm, no she doesn't! But we just went along with it because no one had told us the story. Strange times.' Indeed.

And this sort of thing went on for approximately oh, say, another twenty-two years.

As a child I spent a very long time trying to work everything out for myself before eventually becoming invested in upholding the story my parents told me: I was theirs and that's all that mattered. It was none of anyone's business where I was 'from'. But race didn't care about my family lore, or my parents' inability to discuss our differences. Race was dogged in its desperate pursuit of me; it could not be ignored, it was inescapable. And as much as I tried to brush it off, as much as I tried to believe what I was told, race attached itself to me, a little more, year on year. I first became cognisant of my role as the perpetual outsider at the age of five, when a classmate showed me a nifty little skin-scratching technique to temporarily turn myself lighter. Soon, strangers would ask me to qualify my ties to all these white people around me – parents, cousins, my brother, my friends: who was *I* to *them*? I staunchly defended my story and myself (as I had been taught by Mum), and believed her when she occasionally said I was white, like her. Why? Well because children have no choice but to believe in the world defined for them by adults – it is natural, instinctual and self-preserving. If my parents had told me the colour of the sky was pink, or that unicorns were real, I would have believed that too until I was old enough to find evidence to the contrary, simply because I trusted them and relied upon them to help me descramble the mysteries of the world. For many years I didn't know anyone else who looked like me and who might have nudged me closer to the truth, and I certainly didn't have the understanding required to challenge my parents, because well, you know – *I was a child* – and so I took refuge in our story, because belonging is everything. It is paramount to our happiness as human beings, it places us in a story, a history, and colours our lives with purpose and meaning. But the story, like a swirling sink-hole, would drag others down with me, making us all look utterly mad. I remember many a friend or cousin being roped on board to dutifully explain the odd nature of my family set-up too – 'It's true, it can happen – she really does have white parents.' (Shout out to my real ones.) We were kids. And they believed what I had been told to believe. (God knows what their parents really thought, lol.)

By fourteen or so, I was a bit more cynical and had grown tired of playing Head Lecturer and Chief Storyteller with every new person I met, my voice weary from the weight of it all. I'd moved away from 'I'm white like my parents' to 'I think I'm mixed-race but I'm actually not sure what I'm mixed with?' – progress – albeit minuscule. I wanted answers, but I didn't know how to get them. Even though it was never affirmed, I felt on some level that asserting myself could result in upheaval, heartache, disruption and as a child that's a terrifying prospect to contend with – the notion that your very existence poses a threat to the established order, that your questions could change everyone and everything around you. I wanted things to stay as they were, I loved my family, I loved our life, our routine, our dinners and days out. What child would choose to belong anywhere other than the home in which they were loved?

Before everything changed, all I'd known was life with my mum, dad and younger brother, with visits to family in Shropshire, and annual summer holidays to County Clare, Ireland, which is home to my mum. I saw Clare in sprawling landscape photographs on the DNA-testing homepage that morning, a smorgasbord of grey and green cliffs jetting out into the Atlantic Ocean and glossy fields like the ones I had run through on my childhood summer holidays. I remembered wet and windy family memories built on annual summer pilgrimages to the tiny town of Doonbeg, close to where Mum was born (and where Donald Trump now owns a golf course). I could smell salty sea and stale alcohol, the silage in the fields, and the lingering whiff of smoky turf in the evening air. I could feel the hay beneath my heels as I leapt from bale to bale. I could see my parents getting ready for a night out, myself and my brother tucked up in the bedroom my granny slept in, watching wistfully as my mother applied lipstick and my father chastised her for taking too long. I could hear my mother singing 'The Fields of Athenry' as I ate a bag of Taytos in the cracked, red leather booth of a smoke-filled bar, as a red-faced man with an indecipherable accent slipped me a Euro. I knew Ireland almost like I knew Britain, and these were my only two cultural identities, despite what my outward appearance might have suggested.

And then everything changed. In 2014, a series of destabilising events uprooted us all: my dad died of cancer, aged fifty-five. And a year after his death, when a callus had not yet formed over our grief, a series of DNA tests proved what I had always imagined, and what I had always feared the most: that one of my parents was not my own. My Irish mum and English father could not have produced me, a brown-skinned, curly-haired baby. Finding this out without my dad around turned my home into a hellish matrix of what it once was; a parody of everything I used to love. The aftermath propelled me from the familiar spaces I knew as home with jet force. I left in the hope that I could peel off all my layers and find who I was really meant to be, at the very centre. That third DNA test which told me of my ancestry followed on from two family DNA tests (one paternity, one sibling). Navigating the confusing results from all these (more on this later) shattered my segments of self, built up over two decades, into nothingness. I left home to escape, to rebuild, to breathe.

That morning in Nicaragua when I clicked the link to my DNA test results, fear gripped me by the neck. I had grown tired of trying to shrink myself into the confines of an identity that didn't make any sense but I was still scared. I thought of my father, whether what I was doing was somehow disloyal. Dad's love for all of us was gargantuan – there was not enough time in the world, not enough grains of sand on a beach to accurately measure its scale and force; it was a love that was constant and absolute. But after cancer stole him, the world became colder and harsher. A desperate need to know who I was and where I belonged occupied a space in my head which previously had been filled with my father's gentle reassurances and the warmth of his presence in my life. Now that he was gone, it was harder to mute the voice in my head which had told me I could live with not knowing, that I was asking for too much, that my real racial identity didn't matter, that I was being ungrateful for even pursuing the truth. I know now that voices like these arrive when we are scared; they exist to keep us cocooned in the safety of our comfort zones, and if we were meant to settle for a life that was mediocre, we would never fear drowning out that voice. If our lives were meant to be half-known and half-lived, we would give in to that voice which keeps us safe and small and stops us from making monumental changes. I was most definitely done with having half a story, half an identity, and in many ways, half a life. So I ignored that voice and decided to sacrifice softness and safety in my search of answers. And of course, there is always a better life waiting for you beyond your comfort zone.

When I opened up the results from the DNA-testing company that morning, I focused my attention on the 'Ethnicity Estimate' section of the site. It was here, the accompanying email said, where I would find the country breakdown which would finally reveal where in the world my blackness was from. A lifetime of being adrift between two islands without a clear anchor to either was about to end – and boy, was I hyped! Terrified as well, that was to be expected, but truly excited to uncover more. As I rested my laptop on my knees I could just about catch sight of my reflection in the screen. I saw copper-coloured skin, a deeper shade of red after months in the sun, dark shoulder-length curls of many textures that you could lose both hands in, and a large wide mouth with slightly crooked teeth that I planned to fix. I was, indisputably, a brown-skinned girl. I had always been that way, yet I had lacked an explanation for that simple fact my whole life.

I scanned the digital map under the 'Ancestry Estimate' section, goosebumps rising on my forearms and reminding me that this was far from a normal situation or a normal day. The regions where my ancestry lay were highlighted in teal and burnt orange. But hang on just a second, there were only two areas blazing in full colour: Africa and Europe. I zoomed in. West Africa and the west coast of Ireland, in fact. I let out a gasp: I hadn't expected such a straight split, or origins in *West* Africa. Over the years I'd lost track of the number of times I'd been asked if I was Eritrean or Ethiopian or mixed with Indian – and so my best guess had been hinged on a country in Africa's eastern region, or a complete hodgepodge of places. I'd grown used to the ambiguity having had no choice but to settle in it, yet according to this site, which had processed my DNA in a lab far away from Nicaragua many weeks earlier, most of my black ancestry originated from just one spot – Nigeria. Forty-three per cent of *me* was from *there*. My genetic make-up had been decoded, my blackness was laid out in front of me, the region boldly highlighted before me. *Nigeria*. It had always been within me, I thought, I'd just never been able to access it. All of a sudden, I had a racial identity which was my own: I was apparently from West Africa, whatever that actually meant. It was almost everything I'd wanted to know and yet it was a stark departure from my former life. I didn't know how to feel. Should I have been happy? Relieved? Instead I felt properly sorry for myself, and started to cry. Big tears dropped on to my bare toes and fell between the gaps of the creaky wooden floorboards beneath me. I went to the open window, allowing the sea breeze to dry the tear tracks on my face.

Dad. I need my dad. I want my dad.

These results were indisputable proof, once again, that we were totally different in biological make-up, and the fact that we'd never spoken of that when he was alive made it seem, that morning, as if he was light years away, as if we had existed as father and daughter in another galaxy altogether.

I realised that I had virtually no sense of my own blackness, no knowledge of a cultural identity and history that had manifested itself in my skin, my hair and my ancestry. The shock and relief was at once compounded by an unshakeable sense of loss. I thought about all the weirdness that had come my way, after existing amongst whiteness without ever knowing why, of trying to force myself into many spaces that were never built with my comfort in mind. I thought about fighting all the nay-sayers about my family lore, how they were right – 'your mum fucked the postman' – of carrying the burden of a secret I did not understand, nor ask for. And what would I lose now, by embracing this part of me, I wondered? Could my mum ever see me, fully? Would she accept me as I worked to undo a psychology birthed from whiteness? And could I really identify as half Nigerian if I knew nothing of its people, its languages, its culture? How could I still call myself my dad's daughter with this newfound genetic knowledge? *I need you, Dad, I miss you.* I sat on the edge of my bed staring at my screen. The laptop felt hot and heavy on my legs and my mind whizzed with disparate thoughts. *Dad, I miss you so, so much.*

Nigeria. Now that was a place that felt mysterious and far away; all my life I had been told Africa was not mine to claim, and as such I had no immediate sense of contentedness with the revealing of this knowledge. But in recent years I'd been trying desperately to piece together an authentic identity that made sense, in place of any actual explanation for my blackness. I'd become politically minded; I had started to write articles about identity and inequality. I'd begun to seek out the stories of women who looked like me, desperate to see myself in them. But it had been hard to walk with my head held high when the origins of who I was had remained obscure; it was impossible to know what I wanted to be, what I really stood for, when a large part of me had gone unacknowledged by my family. The years of heavy silence had rooted in me a sense of not wanting to be African, and for that I also felt deeply ashamed. I realised that not knowing my heritage, being discouraged from identifying as black, had layered me in anti-black thoughts, and even with the immediate impact of these incredible DNA test results, this would not dissolve quickly and without concerted effort.

Ethnicity and race have long been conflated in our societies. Science has concluded that neither have any sort of genetic basis, but both have played a huge role in formulating the human condition. Ethnicity is based around cultural and social identities and, as such, is largely interchangeable – religious customs, language and culture all connote a person's ethnicity – but race is the idea that we can group people by distinct physical qualities. Society works in that you can be part of many *ethnic groups* but only, really, of one *racial group* (mixed-heritage individuals will almost always find themselves categorised by their minority background. I can be Irish, Nigerian and British, *ethnically*, but I will always be black, *racially* (and first and foremost for that matter). Assumptions around the cultural identities of minority individuals are frequent, but in many ways to be expected. Knowing where to 'place' an individual helps us relate to them, creating a sort of cultural short-hand that we lean into, so we can communicate. But migration and mixing is shaping a multicultural world, and a richness of cultures, ethnicity, races and customs means it is no longer easy, nor acceptable, to successfully locate a person's ethnic or racial identity based solely on what you can see.

The idea that different groups have immutable and inherited differences coded into their genes became popular in the first half of the twentieth century and is known as biological determinism. The belief that those racial categories have core essences that determine character and behaviour is known as genetic essentialism, or racial essentialism.[1] These ideas have been used to justify the subjugation of black and brown people during the colonial period of global expansion, where whiteness also become synonymous with social relations defined by class, ownership and property rights. It has largely been accepted that race is an invention, a method of social control, and a creation that will always benefit and prioritise whiteness. And even though racial essentialism has long since been disproved, the boom in consumer DNA testing (which is explored in more detail later on) is giving rise to genetic racism once again. This 'scientific' discourse around race is helping ground harmful stereotypes, but that's not to say that race has no meaning in our lives. Race *is* real, simply because we have attributed meaning to it. Race is real because we perceive it to be. It impacts our life trajectory, shaping the paths we follow, the neighbourhoods we live in and colouring our every interaction with one another. But constructing race has been done to benefit the position of the white majority, and enacting racism for the very same reason. Because whiteness has functioned as the normative standpoint for most of humanity, white people, up until very recently perhaps, have not had to think about race in the same way as everyone else and in many ways have functioned as raceless individuals. This goes some way in explaining how I saw myself as white, or raceless, as a small child in a white world. Largely, I was not aware of what race meant or that I was in possession of any sort of racial identity, least of all one that was different to my parents'.

I was thinking about all this in Nicaragua that day as I took myself for a walk along a secluded beach alone, wondering if my parents had hoped that our shared ethnicity – the bonds forged through British and Irish customs – would somehow mitigate my race. What was so bad about acknowledging my blackness? Had they meant to erase it? Overlooking it had not just been encouraged, it was entirely *de rigueur* while growing up, and so the task of somehow altering the fabric of who I was, and what I believed, felt entirely Sisyphean. It was 2016 and so the internet was not yet awash with the plethora of 'Finding My Blackness' personal essays that would soon befall every online millennial magazine – to say I could have used a little inspo was an understatement: where to begin, I wondered as I kicked off my sandals and let the warm water cover my feet.

After the disastrous call to my mum, I decided to contact the friends back in London who knew I was awaiting ancestry test results. The first was Abi: we'd become firm friends during my first term at the University of Warwick, having met working in a part-time campus job in the alumni relations team. During our shifts (when we'd call up former students and sweet-talk them into donating money to our institution) I was always wowed by Abi's skills as an orator – the girl can quite literally charm the birds from the trees – and her words have also soothed my soul in many a crisis situation over the years. Abi is second-generation Nigerian, one of four siblings who grew up on the outskirts of south-east London. Our upbringings are markedly different; she told me of early years in council estates and parents preoccupied with making ends meet, but where a celebration of heritage was intrinsic and automatic. Abi has also faced her fair share of family issues but chooses not to lead with her trauma when she is among others, instead listening and offering up advice and wisdom that only hints at a life lived beyond her years.

Anyway, I got a rapturous reception when I called – 'welcome to the club, G. Aha, now we're even more like sisters than before! You know, I knew it would be Nigeria, didn't I say?' She laughed and I laughed.

'Yeah you did actually. I'm just happy that I finally know. But it's weird . . . like what am I supposed to do now?'

'How do you mean?' I heard the rush of the city and the hum of the traffic as she walked through a Boots in London Bridge on her lunch-break, a world away from where I was.

'Well, I don't know how to *be* Nigerian, in the same way as you, do I?' I began. 'I already feel like a fraud, I don't have the cultural knowledge, the details . . . I don't know how to tell people that half of me is from there . . . but that really, none of me is from there, because I don't know a thing about it. And everyone will expect me to know stuff. You lot are so proud.'

'Listen, it's not that deep. To be honest you'll probably always have the ethnic identity as the one you've grown up with. But now you have a country of origin for your black side, you can start to do more of that cultural research many black people have by default, growing up with black parents. All this does is give you permission to start more confidently exploring that side of you. This knowledge is useful, it's the start of a meaningful journey, I promise.'

'I know, I know. But I thought the results would be different. I actually thought I would be from somewhere else . . .' I trailed off. What I'd wanted all my life, I suddenly wanted to give back. Was I disappointed? Perhaps a little. For over two decades I'd been nestled in a narrative that was nebulous and nonsensical, but at least it was mine. That narrative had placed me within my family, and I'd been able to fall back on that each and every time it was called into question by others. But although I'd doubted it as I got older, I never knew what to replace it with and so I'd never really, truly stopped believing it – until I got those results in Nicaragua. How was I expected to love my newfound Nigerian-ness if I didn't know it, if I couldn't feel it?

'Don't put pressure on yourself to have this Nigerian pride thing down right now,' Abi said half-laughing. 'You haven't grown up with any real positive affirmations of blackness around you. It's really not your fault. And I think there's something of a scale of black identity anyway.'

'How do you mean?'

'Well, there's a link between your experience and others in the diaspora, like African-Americans who don't know shit about their heritage because of slavery. You know that. You've just been there.'

'Yeah, true.'

'Anyway there's *always* cultural learning to be done. People who grew up in Nigeria are further along the scale than those who grew up here and who are Nigerian-British like me. You're a lot further out, seeing as you haven't had any of that knowledge by default, but you can get there if you want. I'm still learning food, languages and customs. I kind of know some, but not everything. And you grew up in a white family, no one will expect you to know any of this unless you really want to learn. Hey, actually if you want – we can go for Nigerian food in Peckham when you're back.'

'Yes mate!'

I wanted to try Nigerian cuisine but I still felt late to the party; like I'd rushed into a room of people playing musical chairs only to find everyone else already comfortably settled in their country-marked seats. My identity had been crafted slowly over the years, and I had grown used to the missing pieces. The idea of suddenly labelling myself as Nigerian felt utterly clumsy and disingenuous. Abi was a close friend but as far as I knew (and weirder things had happened in my life thus far) we were *not* related. And plus, there was only so much cultural learning that could be done with a mate. I thought of the innate pride she took in her Yoruba ancestry, and how she, like everyone else I knew, thought so little about forging a personal identity. To anyone looking in at my life, my family battles growing up had been few and far between; I had never worried about if we were rich or poor, or lived in a crime-ridden area. I had never gone to bed hungry, or hurt. I had never witnessed violence in, or outside, my home – in fact, my parents barely rowed at all. There had always been food on the table, sweets in the cupboard, bouncy balls, board games and water pistols in the garden to play with. But beneath all that joy, there was a permanent sense of disorientation, which I now realised was linked to a lost heritage and a family-wide secret that I had been forced to carry. It had brewed in me, I think, a feeling of anxiety and restlessness for many years, as a result of trying to work out what was true, and what was not. And so I can forgive 24-year-old me for feeling uneasy, even disappointed, with the result she had waited all her life to receive. The secret had wrapped itself around me like knotweed over many years, thriving in a quiet, silent shade and springing up to stifle my sense of self. In other words, I had internalised some *serious* anti-blackness.

To fix this, I realised, would require epic unlearning via a series of tasks that would need to be performed across a large expanse of time and largely alone. Then, of course, I would need my family to get up to speed, which would be even more arduous. Demanding them to see and hear my race, in order to see and hear me, was not asking for too much, I already knew this. But my race and its meaning had been wilfully ignored by them all for years, until it had swelled into something so large, it was almost untouchable, insurmountable. I'd left home to start on this solitary quest by myself and living in and amongst communities of colour after so long felt urgent and right; it was giving me time to reflect, and most importantly it was helping me make up for lost time. As an English Literature graduate with a keen interest in Sociology and Politics, my first love has always been fiction, and so it only felt right that I began searching for stories and studies that reflected some of my own experiences back to me as I began my journey. I was transfixed by books that explored cross-cultural and transnational family issues such as *Nervous Conditions* by Tsitsi Dangarembga, *Brick Lane* by Monica Ali, *Homegoing* by Yaa Gyasi, and *Americanah* by Chimamanda Ngozi Adichie, the last of which was recommended to me by a friend while I was in Nicaragua and still is one of my favourite novels. In Adichie's work, I found that I resonated greatly with the sense of dislocation that comes with the main character Ifemelu's move from Nigeria to America, and with it her first encounter with race, that places her, an African immigrant, squarely at the bottom of society. Where she admits that 'race was not embroidered in the fabric of her history; it had not been etched on her soul', I saw stark parallels with my own family life because Ifemelu's thoughts are not race-focused in Nigeria, negated as they are by life in a black-majority country. Similarly, I also led a life largely undisturbed by race as a young child, living in a world where my race and its impact remained ignored. I realised both upbringings resulted in a serious impediment of racial understanding, a sort of racial handicapping if you will. And once I began to understand that things beyond my little community were racially hierarchical and shaped by the forces of inequality, like Ifemelu I was completely unprepared for the impact of that. I lacked the knowledge and understanding of how to move through a world where whiteness is prioritised. I was not equipped with the appropriate response to the ubiquitous 'where are you from?' question, which many know roughly translates to mean 'why are you black?' (I literally didn't know why) or 'which parent is the black one?' (umm – neither?). I was unable to clapback to the insults of 'nigger' and 'paki' (I was unsure which one, if either, actually applied to me). And where was this unknown, mysterious country to which I was encouraged to 'go back' on more than one occasion when growing up in Sutton? Did they mean Ireland? Sure, I'd be going back in the summer by ferry! Like Ifemelu, when I finally stepped far beyond the people and places I knew, I was forced to confront centuries-old systems of oppression and ugly, racist stereotypes that had been constructed long before my birth, to keep me and the many who came before me, feeling inferior and inadequate. Adjusting my mindset to catch up with how the rest of the world had always seen me without any help or explanation from those around me would be tough to say the least, but it was absolutely necessary so I could finally move through the world with a sense of dignity.

Personal identities are not built in solitude; they are formed through social interactions within our families and communities to help make us who we are. They are not subjective or biological. We absorb the stories, customs, rituals and norms that we grow up with; the greatest mark on who we are is created by those who love and care for us. But for mixed-heritage individuals and any people of colour living among white families, there also exist the specific challenges around living between contrasting cultures and navigating loving, affectionate relationships with family members of different races. Discussing privilege, identity and discrimination with the people you love is a precarious balancing act if you are the only minority, or the first person in your family to look different (as is the case for many first-generation mixed-heritage individuals and any transracial adoptees). In trying to preserve these relationships, while deducing how to assert your own identity, in a world that only sees in binaries and in a family that may not fully see you, there is a risk of rejection, isolation and mental instability. Standing out as the only non-white face can leave you at a strange intersection of feeling loved yet not fully understood, seen but at the same time not seen. It can be maddening. Often there is a perceived power in possessing racial ambiguity; in being able to pass as one thing or another, in code-switching and bridging gaps like some sort of magical, racial chameleon. But that too is exhausting, living in the bits in between, because you will still, always, be expected to 'pick' one side over another, while your very existence is still lauded as representative of a new era of understanding. If, like me, you don't know your heritage, that adds another level of complexity. There is far less literature, far less nuanced discussion, around issues of misattributed identity or identity erasure and almost nothing on how to navigate messy conversations about race and inequality in our interpersonal relationships. In the past few years I've searched for writing on all this – most of it has been academic and of a sociology ilk which has been incredibly informative – but there have also been some exceptional personal writings and films that have greatly aided my understanding. The 1929 novel *Passing* by Nella Larsen depicts the entangled lives of two light-skinned black women in twentieth-century America and is a gripping examination of the psychological toll associated with passing one's self off as a member of more than one racial group. The contemporary collection of American essays called *Wear the Mask: 15 True Stories of Passing in America*, edited by Brando Skyhorse and Lisa Page, also taught me that passing also comes in many forms and that an individual can be unwittingly passed off as something they are not. I watched the Amma Asante-directed film *Belle*, about a mixed-race heiress in eighteenth-century Britain, as well as an incredible documentary by filmmaker Lacey Schwartz called *Little White Lie,* depicting her own life story which is strikingly similar to my own, only set in Brooklyn. In digesting many of these stories, I have learnt that they are threaded with shame, love, embarrassment and forgiveness when a white space has been 'disrupted' with an identity that is unexpected or taboo. Each passing perspective or transracial tale is deserving of its own nuanced discussion, and as our towns and cities continue to become melting pots of diversity, we must get better at having tough conversations about race and privilege with one another. Many of us don't even have the language to describe what we mean, the terms to denote discrimination or othering in our closest interpersonal relationships, or even the descriptors for families like my own. Take transracialism for example. Since the 1970s, the idea of being transracial has been applied within adoptive circles and refers to an upbringing where a child of one race is adopted by a family of another – usually children of colour and white parents. I realised a few years back that I have had a transracial family experience – only without the adoption part. Yet I only came across the word after it was hijacked in 2015, by an American woman who became known for identifying and passing as a black while working for the Spokane branch of the NAACP, and who was found to have no verifiable African ancestry. (Don't make me name her.) After that, the dialogue around transracial identities in the mainstream media became focused on the stories of white individuals who suddenly demanded that their right to identified as black or brown be respected, completely missing the point about a racial identity being a little more than just a 'feeling', an affinity with a music or food from a certain culture, or shared oppression (that is, class). Being transracial is real, but the damage done by the media circus in 2015 erased a very legitimate discourse for many people who had been raised within white families. In reading beyond the headlines and into the transracial experiences of others I've noticed that a culture of silence around how we are raised remains. There is also an expectation to be 'grateful' for an upbringing that could otherwise have taken place in a backwards, far-away land, which often prevents many from vocalising their experiences for fear that they may 'rock the boat', upset their caregivers and end up sent 'back' to the hellhole from which they came. There also remains a pressure to absorb the cultural identity around you without question, or risk being ostracised from both the ethnic background in your home, as well as the one that may be expected of people who look like you.

These feelings are often espoused by Brits of African heritage who experienced childhoods that were both transracial and transnational. The private, unregulated fostering of Ghanaian and Nigerian children in Britain, often known as 'farming', began after both countries achieved colonial independence (in 1957 and 1960 respectively). While their biological parents worked or studied for professional qualifications, mainly in London, West African children were placed in the care of white, working-class families in Sussex, Surrey, Kent and the surrounding Home Counties. By 1968, *The Times* estimated that five thousand African children were being privately fostered in Britain each year, at a cost of around £3 per week[2]. Thoughtful cultural representations of this experience have sprung up in the last few years: Adewale

Akinnuoye-Agbaje's 2018 film, *Farming*, tells his own story
of survival within a racist Essex gang, and *The Last Tree* from
2019 is a beautifully shot, semi-autobiographical film by
Shola Amoo, depicting a Lincolnshire childhood lost to the
concrete jungle of south London and a life cleaved in two.
You could draw parallels between my life and those of farmed
children, yet I have not been caught in the cross-fire between
two lives, two families, one black, one white. I do not know
of the pain and the pressure associated with recalling lost
cultures or customs when in the presence of black family
members, and cannot pretend to understand the complexities of being pulled through an unregulated care system. I
have always had a loving white family and I am mixed-race.
My largest concern lies with piecing together what has been
obscured from me, and working out why. I can, however,
certainly relate to the complexities of integrating into black
communities when you lack any sense of a black cultural
identity, the bemusement that ensues when others realise
your life does not fit neatly into a prescribed box, and the
internal dislocation which comes with always standing out.
As put by the British Nigerian writer Derek Owusu, who was
farmed as a child, 'Late discoveries about identity are very
common among black children raised in foster care by white
families ... I was eight years old when I first realised I was
black'.[3] And as Tobi Oredein, the British-Nigerian founder
of *Black Ballad,* notes in her powerful 2016 *Buzzfeed* essay
on being farmed: 'While I was obviously black, I didn't feel
Nigerian. I looked Nigerian, my name was Nigerian, but I
wasn't Nigerian culturally. I didn't have any sense of how it
felt to be Nigerian. Looking back, it's clear I felt I was merely
"passing" as a Nigerian.' These accounts, and many others
have helped legitimise what I spent years feeling, but was
unable to vocalise.

The fear of rejection is often heightened for adoptees and farmed children who must live with the constant reminder that they were given up by their birth mother, but this can also take hold of any child who is minoritised in a white family. When that child also doesn't know *why* they stand out, or suspects that their existence is shrouded in secrecy, that is, their parentage or identity is not explained to them, things grow ever more complex. Dealing with any of that will have a profoundly destabilising effect on your mental health (as I later found out – spoiler). The damage to identity and self-esteem will find expression in self-loathing. I have learned that not all transracial upbringings lead to identity erasure, but when they are devoid of open, healthy dialogues around race, it also works to maintain tensions at the heart of the home, preventing families from being close to one another.

While I certainly have a lot to be grateful for, a cosy, cul-de-sac childhood in which my creative expression was nourished and cuddles came quickly, it was also underlined with much frustration as I tried to work out if my life was what I thought it was, and later on, a deep-rooted melancholy-cum-anguish related to uncovering a tornado of truth all at once. In the past few years I've tried to make sense of everything by speaking to others like me and asking some difficult questions. When a personal identity has been wrongly constructed for you, even if accidentally, how do you start again? What do you do when something integral to who you are, such as your parentage, or your heritage, has been obscured and overlooked? How do you discuss race in your most personal relationships? When I left home and realised the scale of what lay ahead of me, the piecing together of things I'd need to do in order to become whole, I felt overwhelmed. I didn't want to be angry. But the secret needed to be de-centred from my life. I didn't want DNA test results to eradicate the connection between me and my parents, yet I wanted to embrace the part of me that had been denied. But where to begin? The Nigerian-Irish, English-Guyanese sociologist Dr Jayne O. Ifekwunigwe, who writes about mixed-race identity, suggests that for individuals unable, or unwilling, to break with their white familial ties, a method of 'additive blackness' is both a survival tactic and political strategy. She explains that building on a familiar social foundation can create a synthesised identity, or a fusion,[4] that is more logical than any concept of exclusion. For someone like me who was socialised in a white setting, that would *not* mean rejecting ties with my family, but adding knowledge and understanding that would connect me to all parts of my lineage. This would be the synthesis.

In 2016, I was totally unable to locate home within myself and so I decided that a process of learning and unlearning through reading, writing, travel and therapy, beyond the only community I had known, would help me understand how I could grow into a more comfortable, more conscious future. I would also need to confront the past of my parents in order to understand the silence around my identity. If I could do that, I could grow into the woman I knew I was destined to become.

3

Don't Make a Fuss

Was she never to be free of it, that fear which
crouched, always, deep down within her, stealing
away the sense of security, the feeling of permanence,
from the life which she had so admirably arranged
for them all, and desired so ardently to have remain
as it was?

NELLA LARSEN, *Passing*

If I close my eyes, I can see my old Catholic girls' comprehensive school, St Philomena, in Surrey, like a dramatic still
from a music video. I remember rolling up ankle-length kilts
the colour of melted truffles, chocolate-brown and cloudy-
cream; the too-heavy brown wool blazers that absorbed every
droplet of dew in winter and left you sweating in summer. I
remember drying off in warm autumn sunshine after grim
swimming lessons in our murky school pool; swapping
weekend stories beneath the shade of towering oak trees at
lunchtime and watching friends French-plait each other's
flowing golden hair; hiding from teachers' sight amid tall

sun-bleached weeds; lessons taught in an eighteenth-century manor house that overlooked a sprawling tapestry of green we were forbidden to walk on simply because it was 'The Holy Lawn'. I remember favourite hymns ('I Watch the Sunrise' – absolute banger), getting the giggles when the priest ashed up my forehead each year on Ash Wednesday, and someone always fainting during outside masses in hot summers. During the only detention I ever received, which took place on a Saturday, I can clearly recall riding a penny farthing bicycle around the sprawling 25-acre school grounds, past the tennis courts and the drama room, for some unknown, inexplicable reason. There were teachers there who imbued me with a lifelong love of learning – and one or two shit ones too, during whose lessons I would text Aisling, my best friend, across the room on my orange Sony Ericsson Walkman phone (superior to the Motorola Razr *by far*).

Others thought good grades came easy, but I worked hard. I worked hard in the hope that no one would notice that I didn't really fit in anywhere; I worked hard to overcompensate for standing out in every social space I occupied. If I absolutely had to be the only non-white girl in my primary school year, in my friendship group at secondary school, in all family photos, and during all my holidays to Co. Clare and Shropshire, I'd better be the book-smart black girl who was an overachiever – *that* would become a defining aspect of my identity, papering over the bits I didn't know about.

My school had a sixth form, and at sixteen I stayed put with all my friends, most of whom I'd known since primary school, which was situated in the same grounds. Sixth-formers were granted the long-coveted privilege of being allowed to shed the horrific school uniform, and I revelled in being able to choose my own clothes each day (leggings and bare shoulders were banned for Catholic girls, though) while studying English, History and Politics for my A Levels.

One autumn afternoon in the first term of the year, before I had turned seventeen, I was in the middle of a mock essay exam on the UK's first-past-the-post voting system and its main drawbacks (there are several) and benefits (none). I was halfway through the test when my teacher broke the silence and called me to her desk. She was studying the class register intently, and frowning, as if I had done something awful.

'I just wanted to ask,' she said, still looking down at her folder, 'why your ethnicity is marked down on the school system as ... *white?*'

As the teacher met my eyes, she pointed to the second page of the register where next to each pupil's name were contact information and personal details. Sure enough, beside mine were the words 'White British'. It was my turn to frown, and even though I was sitting up straight, in a chair beside her, I felt a ball of tension rise from my stomach to the tops of my shoulders and push down – it was an instinctive desire to shrink myself, to become weightless and take up less space. The words I wanted to say were stuck in my throat, as if I'd swallowed something cloying and sticky, and even though the class was small and everyone's heads were bowed, I knew it was in imitation of completing this test. No one was actually writing any more.

Miss wanted answers. 'Well, is it a mistake?' (She was barely whispering at this point.)

'I don't know,' I began. I didn't feel like recounting my life story with the class listening in, even though most of them were my friends and had long been aware of the colour of my family. 'Both my parents are white, and that's all I know really ...'

'But that doesn't make *you* white, does it?'

It did not. My mum had referred to me as white as a child many times before, but it had become apparent to me in my teens that this was a label which did not apply to me. Even so, it was impossible to claim my blackness when it was never named at home.

But I resented my teacher's obtrusiveness, the way her head was tilted in mock sympathy, the disbelief dripping from her voice.

And then, out of nowhere, she went for the jugular.

'Do you think there was some mistake, at the hospital, when you were born?' she asked. 'Were you adopted without being told? Or perhaps there's been an affair? I'm just wondering how this could have happened ...'

I heard a gasp from Emilia, my other best friend, across the classroom. We briefly met each other's gaze, frozen in time for a needle's-eye of a second, both of us screaming silently with our expressions while everyone else was also fully tuned into this conversation. Heads were up and pens were down – obviously this was way more interesting than voting reform.

I told my teacher all I knew; that this was the first time I'd been made aware of this, and that as far as I knew my parents weren't lying to me. But what I really wanted to say was: *Can you keep your voice down and mind your own business please, Miss?* My teacher didn't seem even slightly satisfied with my answers, but spared me the humiliation of asking me to elaborate further, and let me return to my desk. I felt the force of fifteen pairs of eyes lasering in on the back of my skull as I made my way back to my desk. I picked up my pen and completed the test as if nothing had happened.

A few days later there was a school assembly in our hall. I was sitting high up in the foldable seats, looking down on the rest of the school, as the sixth-formers did, when my friend Maria and I became aware of a group of older girls from the year above whispering quite obviously about me. Maria and I had known each other since primary school; our friendship had been cemented in the Year 6 production of *Grease*, where I played Rizzo and she stole the show as Frenchie. She was one of my oldest friends and fiercely loyal.

'George,' Maria said, using the nickname that only my oldest school-friends do, and nudging me in the ribs, 'I think they're talking about you.'

Emboldened with Maria by my side, I tapped one of the girls on the shoulder.

'What are you saying?' I asked, suddenly bellicose.

'It's nothing.'

But seconds later I saw hands cupped over mouths and heard barely suppressed giggling, so I leaned forward again.

'If you have something to say to me, just say it.'

'Miss told us you're the one with the white parents,' one girl said quickly.

And before I could think of anything to say in response, before I could decide what emotions were coursing through my body, the girl had turned back round. What else was there to add when this was all I knew? Maria's expression was one of sympathy, she squeezed my arm in a show of support as the first hymn of the morning started up.

That evening at home I told my parents about the laughing and the questioning. My mother was seething. Smoke billowed out of her nose like a dragon as she puffed on a Marlboro Light in our back garden.

'That nosy old cow, how dare she!'

My father was sitting at our dining-room table after returning from work at 6.30 p.m. as normal, flicking through the *Sutton Guardian*, our local paper, and nibbling on a leftover Peperami stick from my brother's lunchbox (he couldn't abide food waste). When I told him about my teacher, his dark, fluffy eyebrows furrowed above his large silver metal-frame spectacles and he shook his head.

'It's just not on,' he said. 'I'm going to that school to speak with the headteacher about this.'

'I think we should write a letter,' my mum chimed in from the patio step where she was sitting.

I asked them once again if I was theirs, if there was anything they needed to tell me, anything that I could then tell others. But the well-worn likelihood of me being a 'genetic throwback' was reiterated again. The reassurances and hugs followed after. But the conversation stopped there.

While on some level I appreciated my parents' staunch defence, there was little in the way of explanation as to *why* they were adamant that Caucasian was the correct label to apply to their black daughter. I didn't know which of them had been responsible for ticking the ethnicity forms that had gone to my school all those years ago and stayed unchanged throughout my time there, but maintaining the story was evidently a joint decision. At sixteen years old, I was starting to see that upholding this narrative was nothing short of insane – what had started out as blind acceptance, then polite endurance from other kids, was now morphing into total scepticism and ridicule from adults. But Mum and Dad reassured me, as they had done for years, that I was loved. I knew this. They loved me. And I loved them. The blame was shifted solely onto the teacher. It was her fault for intruding on our business, popping our protective bubble of security, disrupting our secure family.

'Let's just leave it, I don't want to make a fuss,' I told them over dinner that evening.

A quiet, internal part of me wanted to bury the whole thing and bristled at the embarrassment of defending a story my teachers thought stupid, but my parents insisted on contacting the school, and a week later after class, my teacher offered a sincere apology for 'making me uncomfortable'. We never discussed it again.

I usually enjoyed Politics, even though this teacher was a raging Tory who often told us her husband was in the country's top 1 per cent of earners (gross, and also irrelevant) and did little to hide her own political leanings. But looking back, I still believe she overstepped the mark in publicly policing the identity of a child in her care, a child who was fighting a battle she had neither created nor understood. And when she went one step further and informed other students of my family dynamic, she marked me out as a spectacle, causing me further humiliation. I've since tried to understand how my parents didn't take any of this into consideration, why challenging the teacher took precedence over addressing the issues my blackness was creating, why this episode didn't shock them into swift action, or initiate a tricky conversation between them both. It is pretty difficult to imagine they were oblivious to the impact this family-wide refusal to address my race was having on me. As the American writer Zora Neale Hurston once put it: 'I feel most colored when I am thrown against a sharp white background.' And that was my life, at all times. Everywhere I went I was the permanent outlander without the most basic explanation for my appearance. Everywhere I went I stood out like a dark stain on a white cloth.

My teacher's methods were most definitely trash, but that day she taught me a valuable lesson about race, in that she let me know that whiteness is a wholly exclusive racial category based around notions of racial purity, and as such would never allow admittance to anyone like me. Despite my white family and my Anglican name, whiteness beyond my cultural upbringing would never want me. And when my teacher realised that I was without explanation for my heritage, my claims to whiteness were also magnified in their absurdity; without confirmation that I was the biological offspring of at least *one* of my parents, my blackness was seemingly more obvious, the ties to my community more tenuous – and with that, more of an affront.

This specific type of othering – being forced to pick a side or having one picked for you, as my teacher did that day – is common for those of mixed-heritage backgrounds, and in writing this book and talking to others I've realised that this fact alone can induce an identity crisis at some stage. When you add the fact that I lacked what is known in adoption circles as a racial mirror (that is, someone who looks like you, and reflects and affirms your experience of being part of that ethnic group) and was carrying the weight of my mother's shame in the form of a secret around my identity, you can see why an identity crisis of epic proportions mixed up with a cocktail of depression was very much in the post for me. Research shows that mixed-race people of black and white heritage in the UK are more likely to be racialised by their minority background[1] – and this is a global trend. In 2015, the Pew Research Center found that 69 per cent of mixed black and white American adults reported being racialised as black, whereas most biracial white and Asian adults stated they were read as white, as did the vast majority of those with white and Native American heritage.[2] Another study, from Harvard University, found Asian-Americans who are one-quarter white (so, likely with a white grandparent) are attributed a white racial identity more frequently than one-quarter-white African-Americans.[3] It seems to me that a more pertinent set of identity challenges exists for black individuals, because blackness functions as a consistent, inescapable marker of racialisation as does no other racial identity.[4] This can sometimes create a feeling of choicelessness for those who may otherwise feel equally aligned with all parts of their heritage, although I do of course know many who embrace the minority (black) identity that has been ascribed to them all their lives, and reject any and all associations with their majority (white) background, simply because they find it easier to do so. One study, of mixed-race black Americans in Atlanta, went as far as to argue that identifying with one's racial minority heritage equates to 'passing', in the same way that light-skinned African-Americans historically passed as white to escape bondage and a life of brutal oppression. They argue that because traditional racial passing involved deception and concealing one's heritage, mixed persons who identify as black are engaging in a type of 'race performing' otherwise known as 'reverse passing'.[5] Now I don't agree with this. Mixed individuals simply align themselves with the part of their racial heritage that so often demarcates their lived experience, the part that the world can see. Also, it isn't 'performative' to identify with your socially constructed racial category (boo). Let's not forget that the term 'mixed-race' is problematic in and of itself, suggesting that there is such a thing as a 'pure' race (black or white) and that you as a mixed person represent a muddying of genes, a blurring of racial boundaries. But these racial boundaries are nonsensical, have no inherent biological meaning and were constructed by European powers to consolidate power and wealth and justify the subjugation of the black 'other'. As a mixed person, you are still a part of this 'other'; mixedness has always been of blackness, not of whiteness. And although it is quite possible to identify as both, historically the notion of being mixed-race has been a way to reify race while consolidating neo-liberal ideology. I accept that this is how I am viewed in some contexts but I also recognise the toxic racial hierarchy that has birthed these constructs and given us colourism as a by-product, a racial hierarchy *within* black and brown communities that is based largely on skin shade, but which also works to preference looser, straighter hair and facial features that resemble a European aesthetic. So the irony of this study coining the term 'reverse passing' for biracial black Americans, when racialisation is very much a social construct that US systems of power have worked to uphold at all costs, is not lost on me.

Of course that day in sixth form, isolated as I was from black communities and culture, I was not aware of my position of relative privilege because I had not been socialised in any black environment where lighter skin and looser curl patterns were celebrated. I was the only person I knew who looked like me among all my family and friends, the reasons for which were unbeknownst to me. And so in my world, my appearance did not hold any cultural cachet, rather, it was actually a deep source of shame. Against my white backdrop I also began to realise in my teens that my blackness was hyper-visible as well as inexplicable. And my teacher's behaviour was part of the agonising, awkward catalyst for change. She unwittingly nudged me a little further along the path to self-acceptance by reminding me that the world would never view me as my family did, but that I shouldn't want it to either.

During that same stretch of time in sixth form at school I spent my weekends learning to drive, or clubbing in various sticky-floored establishments across Clapham and Croydon (shout out to the old Tiger Tiger). This period of my life was busy with university applications, driving lessons and tests, exams and social events, but also tense with severe anxieties about my appearance: I loathed my hair, weight and skin, and was constantly on a diet. I felt highly conscious of avoiding the sun on holidays, and bleached my hair to match a straw-coloured weave which I had installed every six weeks in a misguided attempt to emulate Beyoncé. Outside of my house I'd started reluctantly identifying as mixed-race whenever anyone asked. But when probed for more answers to what exactly I was mixed with, I quickly learned how to morph into a highly adaptable racial chameleon. I'd place the onus on the person doing the asking, demanding that they guess a country combination that I would select at random, just to buy me some time, really. Brazilian and Scottish, Jamaican and Iranian, Irish and Eritrean – whatever, didn't matter – if I liked it, I'd inform them that their guess was correct. It was the social equivalent of spinning a globe with your eyes shut and travelling to wherever your finger lands and my friends became adept at knowing when to play along and when to steer the conversation elsewhere.

But it was extremely destabilising and lonely enduring these regular rituals of othering outside the home, while trying to understand where I belonged, and how my genetic make-up was at odds with that of my parents. I didn't look like either of them, I could see that; I wasn't white, I could see that too; but their promises of our ties to one another assuaged my fears, their love kept me close to them. It was their way of doing the best they could but existing in a mind-bending vortex of contradicting realities, living with the baggage of a racialised identity while being encouraged to ignore race and its impact for fear of somehow upsetting the status quo frequently turned my world upside down, complicating things where they should have been simple.

Luckily, school was (mostly) a haven and distraction. Emilia and I were made deputy head girls in the Upper Sixth – a privilege that actually came with a staggering amount of additional pressure around exam time, what with the expectation of organising a school talent show and leavers' ball with the Catholic boys' school in Purley, Croydon – a school my brother attended, where my mother worked as a receptionist and where I also met my friend Patrick (Pat) who was another esteemed deputy. When we were left with a large amount of money after the sale of the ball tickets (even after investing in fancy cupcakes for the tables), we were at a loss of what to do with the money. 'Keep it,' the former head girl told us over Facebook. 'There's always loads left over.' The new head girl at the time said this was not compatible with her morals and refused, but it was definitely compatible with mine. Emilia and I spent our share on a boozy Ibiza holiday with Aisling, while Pat (my bougiest friend) bought a designer leather jacket. 'I don't think you should be doing that,' my mother had frowned at the time. 'What if someone finds out?' My father, who never cut corners but loved to stick it to the man when he could, disagreed. 'Colette, her time isn't free,' he grinned. 'They've worked hard, they deserve it.' After school my evenings were spent playing netball, running up the house phone bill talking with mates about the day's events during three-hour calls, or with my dad, who regularly took me out driving to decrease the likelihood of me failing my driving test for the second time. I wanted to leave it and pick it up after exams, or maybe even after university, but Dad encouraged me to persist, knowing that I wouldn't bother if he didn't push me.

He'd take on this melodramatic tone each time I wavered in my conviction. 'Keep goooing! Don't put off until tomorrow what you can do today.' I offered weak protests but climbed into his black Fiat 500 anyway. At night when the roads were still and the sky was black, Dad drove to an empty warehouse estate behind the back of a giant Tesco. We would switch seats, he would turn his radio off, and I would receive instruction on how to reverse around a corner and parallel park like a pro. Every time I got it, the pride on his face lit up the car beneath the phosphorescent glare of the street lamps. My wins were his wins. Before finishing school, I passed my driving test on that second attempt, and my parents decorated the house with a banner and some balloons to celebrate.

At sixteen I also landed my first job, at a National Trust café, alongside Emilia. There are few jobs more quintessentially British than working at a National Trust property, I think, other than perhaps teabag-sealing at Tetley's, or grooming the Queen's corgis. The National Trust is Britain personified, the apex of Englishness. Its properties are the crumbling castles and historic homes that form the backdrop to period dramas such as *Downton Abbey*, amid sprawling country hills and glittering coastlines, deer-dotted woods in which couples and grandparents happily amble around on their days off (or reluctantly get dragged to, depending on your type of family), where we take children for mud-splattered Easter-egg hunts in April and let dogs bound freely at the weekends.

I loved working there with my best friend by my side. We swapped shifts to suit our jam-packed social lives while frosting sponge cakes, prepping tuna sandwiches and stacking piles of warm, soft scones with clouds of clotted cream. The best shifts to be had were in the summer; one of us would often get posted in the ice cream parlour situated in the park grounds (much to the other person's annoyance as you'd be stuck under the boss's nose in the main kitchen). You'd enjoy a shift of relative solitude, the only thing to contend with being the foot-stomping revulsion from the customers when you ran out of Calippos, or ice-cold water – 'well that's not very good on a hot day like today is it?' 'No, I suppose not, really ...' When Emilia was posted in there, she'd sometimes use the assigned radio to make fake requests for more stock so I could go visit, or communicate with me as to when we could co-ordinate our lunch-break or make after-work plans – 'Mate, I need more lemon drizzle cake ... Over.' Many a leftover lemon slice was stuffed into backpacks to scoff at home, and we mastered the art of disguising a hangover while serving on the till. It was also the first time we'd ever had our own money. Once we'd saved up enough we immediately booked a week-long, gloriously tacky holiday to Kavos, Greece, which my mum very much disapproved of, and which Aisling was forbidden from joining. The café was the place where my universe widened dramatically. I'd had nearly all the same friends from primary school through to sixth form, and my cultural experiences had been shaped by my family, but when I entered the world of work, in a park a few miles closer to central London, I was surrounded by people of different back-grounds and many of them wanted to know my story, where was I *really* from? What was my *mix?* These interactions I had at work were further reminders that I could not pass, in the same way I passed within my family, my blackness could not be excused here, yet I found myself defending what I knew all over again because there was no alternative – the tedium of which was starting to crush my spirit.

'You habesha, yes?' a tall, slender man with shiny black curls and dark brown skin asked me excitedly one Sunday morning as I prepared his latte during the morning shift, with my back to him. I shook my wavy-weave instinctively, even though I didn't understand the question or have a clue what that meant.

'No?' He leaned over the counter, his eyes scanning me quickly.

'You sure?' He sounded dubious yet disappointed.

The problem was, I wasn't sure. I'd lost track of the number of times I'd been told by strangers that my Britishness and Irishness wasn't markedly visible in the shade of my skin, the kink in my hair and the contours of my muscular, curvy physique; that when people looked at me they couldn't see high tea or Irish dancing but something altogether more 'exotic'. Flirting with a new set of country predictions felt alienating but also slightly alluring; each one offered me a passport to an exciting new world, a ticket to a far-away culture, one that might be mine and that was possibly coded into my genetic make-up. But accepting this possibility would mean rejecting all that I knew, and so I stayed wilfully in racial no-man's-land, although looking back these formative years probably piqued my interest in travel and travel writing. At seventeen I didn't quite know how to find that part of myself without disrupting my family. I had picked up on the fact that I should stay silent for my parents' sake, but although I was curious to know where I belonged, I was not desperate to be the source of disruption, which I had begun to realise I would be. At this weekend job my particular skin tone and hair texture brought about certain benefits in a way I hadn't noticed in all-white Sutton. Black male customers flirted with me and told me I was pretty – I was the object of male attention for what felt like the first time ever, because I was seen. (The irony of this happening on the terrain of what most would consider the whitest, most British of cultural institutions is not lost on me, but our National Trust Café was at the end of the Northern Line, in London's Zone 4.) After what felt like an entire lifetime of being picked last in the white circles I had moved in, this was all too welcome and entirely flattering for an insecure teenage girl. I had shied away from showing an interest in boys for the most part of my early life and never dated anyone; I wasn't ready because I didn't know myself and the white boys hadn't wanted me anyway. And for me to date someone who looked like me would have first required the mammoth task of unlearning years of internalised self-hatred, and this did in fact take *years*.

After work that day I Googled the term 'habesha' and learned it was originally used to describe anyone originating from northern Ethiopia and is now commonly attributed to those from Eritrea too. If that region of the world was within me, I thought after my father picked me up from my café shift that Sunday, it would mean one, or perhaps both of my parents were not my own. Maybe my teacher had been right – what if there had been a mix-up of epic proportions at the hospital on November 12? Later I trawled the Google image results, and in the tiny cross-section of East African women displayed on the search page I could see similarities. We had the same large dark eyes and thick curly hair, but . . . were these my people? Had this part of the continent, with its vast mountainous plains and brown and beautiful women, bequeathed me my looks – if so, how?

Shortly after the habesha day, a new boy called James started at the café. A year older than me and Emilia, James was in his final year of sixth form. He had sandy-blond hair, friendly brown eyes, and reminded me a little of a very smiley, if not slightly irritating, Labrador. He had a crush on Emilia, and whenever we were all on shift together he'd tease her about her hair or mock her somewhat low voice in a transparent attempt to maintain her attention. But James had extraordinarily bad chat. And so Emilia wasn't sure if she was on it. And once we all got comfortable around each other and details about my family background surfaced, James began to direct his jokes at me, and they quickly took on a racialised tone. By now the narrative around my family story had swollen to a size far bigger than me; all my friends were well accustomed to telling it to others, taking up the mantle of chief defender whenever I was weary. But there was only so much they could do, and sometimes it came between us. In my first job, surrounded by new people and fresh introductions, the news of my heritage spread like wildfire around the kitchen and became the central joke whenever I was on a weekend shift with James, who had zero filter.

'Your parents are white? Yeah, mate and I've got a Chinese mum,' he would scoff as he fell into the stock cupboard laughing, before adding something about having a 'Jamaican dad' as I threw a packet of all-butter shortbread at him in feigned protest. Emilia would promptly tell him to fuck off and I'd quip something back, but then find something else to distract myself with. But existing on a knife edge between the private me and the public me, where simply claiming my family without them by my side meant fighting a battle I did not sign up for, was getting oh so draining.

One weekend when my parents were away (and for reasons that truly escape me now), I invited Emilia, Aisling, James and his tall friend with a flippy emo fringe round to mine. I was in possession of that rare gem of recreational time when the stars align your calendar with that of your parents, and the entire household becomes a kingdom bequeathed to you, a mere adult-in-waiting: I had a free yard. I promised to protect the house at all costs and forgo takeaways, alcohol and visitors, but inevitably ended up hosting a four-person 'gav' (short for gathering). The evening went fairly well: we ordered food, watched films, and all the beer cans were disposed of afterwards so as to avoid parental detection – I'm fairly sure there was some kissing too. What I do remember clearly, however, is the side-splitting laughter when James saw my family photos hanging on the wall of our living room; the pointing and dropping of jaws.

'Oh, wow, OK! That's your family then?'

'Yeah.'

'That is fucking funny, mate.' He scoffed and brought his silly fringed friend over to peer at the pictures. 'I thought you were joking before but ha ha! This *actually* is your family!'

The images that were the source of such hilarity still hang on my wall at home. In the first, I am not quite four years old, sporting a fluffy head of curls and wearing a white and navy striped dress with a collar. I'm grinning, the first pearls of baby teeth just on show, as I hold on my lap my po-faced baby brother, his eyes wide, blue and unblinking as if he has just seen the Big Bang. There is another photo of me being held by my parents as a baby which hangs above our sofas, Mum wearing a questionable shoulder-padded beige blazer jacket, Dad beaming in a grey suit. They look happy. Every time I go home I still enjoy looking at those photos, which came to be defiant symbols of who we are as a family, but also, admittedly, a confusing contradiction in terms for anyone looking in from the outside. That weekend when I had friends over, I joked that the photos wouldn't look out of place in a national anti-racism campaign, or a government advert for adoption in multicultural Britain, and of course everyone laughed along.

During the weekly Sunday roast dinner – which my father would spend hours preparing, while my mother ironed our school uniforms for the week ahead, and I and my brother completed our homework on the dining table, despite Dad's music blasting out of our computer speakers – I thought about how our family unit appeared to others. As we ate, and my brother and I battled it out in our weekly Crispiest Roast Potato competition, I broached the topic once again.

'Mum, someone said I looked Ethiopian at work the other day.'

'Mmm?' she responded as my father ploughed his fork into his food, silently.

'And the other day, a friend asked why I don't look like anyone. Are you sure – like, really sure – that there wasn't a mix-up at the hospital? That, you know, I'm *actually* yours and Dad's?'

'Tell them it's none of their business,' my mother sniffed as she poured herself a large glass of wine. 'Of course you're ours. I remember carrying you.'

4

Wearing Someone Else's Face

One ever feels his two-ness, an American, a Negro;
two souls, two thoughts, two unreconciled strivings;
two warring ideals in one dark body, whose dogged
strength alone keeps it from being torn asunder.

w. e. b. du bois, *The Souls of Black Folk*

I'd first started to get to grips with how I had come to exist
at the age of five, when I made a valiant attempt to scratch
off my skin, at the suggestion of a classmate.

'Look, if you want to be white, try *this*.'

Libby Thompson, a brown-haired girl with an upturned
nose and cockney accent, clawed at my forearm with her nails
and turned a small section a temporary shade of chalky white.

'Wow, it works!'

I was elated, and proudly surveyed my ashiness in the
school playground. But of course, it didn't last. And there
was no way I could scratch my whole body to match Libby,
whose skin was the colour of a creamy vanilla milkshake. I
knew I didn't exactly want my skin separated and removed

in its entirety from my body (even as a young child I realised that this would be a somewhat terrifying prospect), but I thought that if it were somehow lighter, whiter, just a little bit more like that of everyone around me, then surely my life would be easier. All the boys fancied Libby, who was a year older than me and the most popular girl in my class. I can't remember what preceded her suggestion (though I must have been complaining about the unsavoury darkness of my own body to warrant such an intervention), but I do remember her tone: precocious, matter-of-fact, but with no trace of malice. She was simply trying to help a brown gal out! I can still distinctly feel how sharp Libby's fingernails were as they dug into my flesh, how genius I thought her plan was (even though it hurt), and how much in that moment I wanted to look like her, the other girls in my class, and my mum. The memory remains vivid in its intensity, playing out in my mind's eye as if it happened last week. I see my difference in high definition that day, chalked out on the playground before me in brilliant white, like a game of hopscotch. I could see my difference back then, but I couldn't quite work out what it meant. My parents didn't look like me, but nobody had explained it. Nobody told me I wasn't white too.

Shortly after the skin-scratching incident, I remember asking my parents if they'd had another baby because they wanted their next child to be white, like them. I posed the question on the way home from school one afternoon, as my mother pushed my younger brother in his buggy and I held on to the handle, trying desperately to keep up the pace because my mother was, as she would say, 'flyin' it' down the road, trying to make it home in time for her receptionist shift at a holiday booking company around the corner from our house.

'Did you want my brother to see if he would come out brown too?' I asked.

'No, of course not,' my mum smiled down at me. 'We always wanted two kids and that's what we got. Two great kids.'

I can't remember the first time my parents explained the throwback story to me, or whether it came from the mouth of my mother or father first, but I do know that I started to wear that narrative like a protective shield – at first reluctantly – telling anyone who asked that I was a genetic miracle, a one-in-a-million type of girl, born to white parents with a white brother against all odds. The story anchored me further into the bedrock of my family and justified my place there – it gave me purpose and belonging. But as I think back now to how often I was demanding answers from the adults around me, and how my younger brother's arrival had me even more worried and confused about our contrasting appearance, I can see that even at five I was already starting to feel unsettled and unsatisfied with what I was told. My brother was a small, gurgling toddler with wispy blond hair where I had a head of dark curls; his tiny hands and feet were prawn-pink where mine were nut-brown.

To understand how this code of silence was maintained for another twenty or so years, you first need to get properly to grips with the spaces I spent most of my early life occupying. The infant and junior schools my brother and I attended (which shared the same grounds with the Catholic girls' secondary school I later graduated to) were situated in sprawling fields within the village of Carshalton, a sleepy, suburban slice of the capital which is part of the London Borough of Sutton (the debate with others as to whether or not my home town constitutes 'real' London still rages). Carshalton and Sutton are within the county of Surrey, home to flat, verdant fields of protected greenery and the annual piss-up which is Epsom Derby horse races. Carshalton is famous for its historic buildings, World War Two memorial plaques, crumbling antique shops, artisan bakers – and a large duck-pond that is one of the sources of the River Wandle, and where you're not actually allowed to feed the ducks any more. Despite the double-deckers and overpriced coffees, it still feels more like a rural escape in the countryside than a borough within the UK's capital city. Its inoffensive quaintness is somewhat incongruous when compared to its more lively urban neighbours of Merton (the borough of the Wimbledon tennis championship) and Croydon (birthplace of Stormzy and dubstep). Sutton and Carshalton revel in being uneventful – that is their USP – so much so that in 2014, Sutton was chosen as the borough in which to trial a new benefits service after a senior civil servant declared it 'the most normal place in Britain'. According to data from the Runnymede Trust, in 2011 the white population of the London Borough of Sutton stood at 70 per cent. In 2001, when I was eight years old and not yet fully cognisant of my identity, the percentage of black and ethnic minority residents in the borough was 16 per cent[1]. Living within this little pocket of whiteness, within the most ethnically varied place in the country, wasn't something I really thought about until I reached my early teens, but now this life between country and city, chaos and order, big and small, seems a fitting setting for a young child occupying a position of racial liminality. I would become adept at swapping worlds and switching codes with a moment's notice, never quite sure of why I was doing it, but only feeling as if I should. As far as I can remember I was the only black child in my infant school, and the only one in my year when I progressed to junior school other than a boy named Nicholas who was in the year above. I distinctly remember ascribing Nicholas a race – I knew and recognised that he was black – while in comparison, I happily remained white or without a racial identity, and fiercely protective over my parents and our home. In my favourite books I was not searching for faces like mine simply because they did not feel familiar. When my father read me Enid Blyton, Roald Dahl, or J. R. R. Tolkien before bed, I remember feeling elated at the incredible, dramatic voices he'd adopt, enthralled to be brought into these fantasy worlds which my dad controlled. Race was not on my agenda, I was living in blissful ignorance of who I was and this meant I wasn't really looking for people like me or evidence that something was truly wrong. Thinking about it now, of course, I can see I stood out everywhere: not just at home but at every class birthday party at our local leisure centre; in each school play, swimming lesson and keyboard lesson I took part in; during every trip to the doctor or dentist with my mum, and every visit to the local Tesco with my dad. Looking back, I can't really see myself anywhere in those early years in Sutton and Carshalton. Racial discomfort penetrated the white haze coating my world only every few months, when someone new made a comment which unsettled me, or experienced racism from a stranger on holiday, or kids at school. But these feelings were not legitimised by anyone around me, and so were not enough to rip from me the soft womb of whiteness that was my life. And a child cannot fully express themselves and their worries around their identity if they are constantly told it is in their head, that their race is not something that concerns them.

At the heart of my life on the humdrum borders between Surrey and London was my parents' love, which kept me cushioned from the reality of dealing with our differences; their support system enabled my protective context to remain intact and ensured that everything stayed the same. For eighteen years I walked the same pavements back and forth, passed the same red-roofed 1930s-style houses, crossed the same quiet roads, and had many of the same friends, all of whom accepted me and my story without question. Naysayers will declare me crazy; debates have raged in many an online comment section on why I simply didn't just 'look in a mirror' or 'go to Specsavers' to realise I was black. But their time would be better spent reflecting on the smallness of their own childhood worlds, the control over which rests with our parents, and acknowledging how all of us are totally psychologically susceptible to our caregivers' teachings. As children our world is limited; the parameters of life barely extend beyond school, home, the houses of our friends, and the odd extra-curricular class. I'm grateful for the steady continuity that was maintained in my life during my early childhood, but I also recognise now how this inadvertently contributed to the erasure of my racial identity. The dull roar in the background reminding me that things were off-kilter slowly became a persistent buzz at the back of my brain as a teenager, and later, after I moved away to university, a deafening scream that I could no longer ignore. Only when I moved into more diverse spaces in London and beyond, could I look back on my life and think how bizarre it had been to try to blend in and to have tried to force my appearance to become something altogether more artificial in a desperate attempt to fit in.

But other than the racial trauma caused by the denial and secrecy around who I was, my childhood in Carshalton was generally quiet – it was a peaceful place to live, I made friends for life and found solace in schoolwork. Growing up there was like balancing on a precarious see-saw in a sunny park, the highs shaped by the love between me and my family and the treats and rewards at school, and the lows defined by the indescribable burden of living a lie I could not unpack.

My upbringing was somewhat unusual but my childhood

racial awareness was actually not. Children pick up on the power dynamics and social cues within their little world without clear explanation from adults; skin colour and gender can be detected from just six months old, and racial conceptualisation occurs between the ages of three and five. A child's universe is defined in part by a complex web of social norms that are set in schools and absorbed from toys, examples in the mainstream media and the world around them. It's actually very normal for ethnic minority children within white settings to endure similarly alienating moments of reckoning as I did at the age of five. One study in which children were asked to complete a computer task that measured implicit responses towards images depicting people of different races found that non-black minority background children showed a pro-white bias from the age of just six years old.[2] Another found that white children identify their racial identity up to three years faster[3] than their ethnic minority counterparts, which suggests an early awareness of the perceived value attached to whiteness. The message that whiteness is preferable, beautiful and desirable is inescapable for a child, even when not deliberately enforced by parents or family. For mini-me, even though I had evidence of my value and worth at school and in the social circles I inhabited, the ubiquity of whiteness and the lack of explanation of its meaning in relation to who I was caused me a profound amount of stress which quickly manifested itself in how I presented as I got older.

I was deeply self-conscious (although I wouldn't let on) and experienced the destabilising effect of feeling very watched and very visible at all times. I was in these all-white spaces, while simultaneously being told that I wasn't actually black – that was hella awkward at times! In Ireland each summer, right up until I was around fourteen or so, I would be informed that my posture was appalling. My auntie's instruction to 'Stand up tall, will ye?' came regularly, her words fired at me like bullets in her thick West Clare accent. I walked like a hunchback in an attempt to take up less space wherever I went, and Clare, a farming county that is homogeneously white, most definitely magnified my colour – my blackness walked into every room before I did. Desperate as I was for it to go unnoticed, desperate to inhabit someone else's body, desperate to blend in, I tried walking like Quasimodo. This – unsurprisingly – produced the opposite effect to the one I was seeking, and at eleven years old I was already 5ft 6in and the only person I knew who looked like me. Inconspicuousness would not come easily. The checking of my posture remained relentless from my mother too, right up until my mid-teens, when suddenly, I was viewed as a sexual object by men and going unnoticed became altogether impossible – so I stopped trying.

In Ireland, while I often felt a desperation to be lighter-skinned, I noticed all my cousins yearned for a tan. I never understood the obsession, the near-hysteria each time the weather topped 15°C – 'It's a scorcher, lads!' – but I loved the mad rush to the beach, my dad packing up the car with buckets and spades to take me, my brother and my cousins around the rock pools, pointing out all the tiny crabs and translucent creatures, lying horizontal on the dark sand to build us giant forts which he would dramatically topple over himself each time the tide came in, shouting 'Retreat! Retreat!' In Ireland I stood out, but in this impossibly friendly, heat-starved country the sun was not strong enough to alter my appearance and turn me darker, so I played for hours in the soft beams against a muted backdrop of grey and green. But on our overseas trips during Easter holidays, my deep-rooted fear of standing out was reignited. My parents took my brother and me to Spain (which I loved) or France (which I enjoyed considerably less) for a week or two each year, holidays that were filled with adventures, poolside playtimes with our parents, beachfront restaurants and the usual family stressors: my dad tearing his hair out trying to get us to the airport on time, my mum making us turn the car around for the second time to check if she'd turned the straighteners off, my brother mooning a police car out of the back window (at my encouragement) and my dad going apoplectic with rage because he thought a nearby police car was going to pull us over. The usual stuff. We always rented a car abroad and my parents would ensure all family activities were suited to me and my brother; if we weren't at the beach, we'd spend a day at a theme park or waterpark. I am a natural thrill-seeker and always wanted to try out the biggest slide or ride with Dad, who would offer weak protests at first but always accompany me in the end, gripping my hand during the biggest peaks and loops while my mum looked on from below. I loved these family days out, but I hated the new layer of othering that came with being abroad. Back home everyone knew our story, but on holiday with new friends I had to explain it all over again. I'd get mistaken for a child of the black family in front of us in the airport queue and have to field questions from new friends around the pool on whether I was adopted, or if that was really my brother. In these sunnier climes, I also detested how my appearance would change after a week or two in the sun. This was not Ireland, so let me tell you: I went *dark*.

It's not as if I avoided the sun entirely – as if vitamin D was some sort of poison that would lead to a premature demise – but I bristled at my mum's fascination with this sweltering heat, her need to tan her small freckled frame under the baking hot sun, turning golden brown like a piece of toast under a grill. Her sun-worshipping tendencies had everything to do with growing up on Ireland's most westerly tip, the country's first point of call for drizzle blown in across the Atlantic. Although she had left in her mid-twenties, she carried with her a serious case of what I have long diagnosed as Sunshine Deprivation Syndrome. It left her permanently chasing summer and planning most of her days around the sun with a devotion matched only by her dedication to her Catholic faith. While my parents sunbathed, I would play in the water for hours with my brother, both of us lathered in sunscreen beforehand. But I resented the sun's influence on our holiday. I hated our daily dance around its schedule, how activities were plotted to ensure maximum heat exposure. I didn't get why sun loungers by the pool were painstakingly rotated around the clock every few hours, the tutting and fretting which ensued if the sky were anything other than perfectly cloudless, or worse, if the German family in the villa above had beaten us to the best spot! Most of all, though, I disliked the way the sun illuminated my difference. I yearned for the same treatment my family received under the penetrating glare of this incandescent ball in the sky. I would have *killed* for a generous dusting of freckles like the ones my mother and brother received on their arms and noses. I wanted to share in the family glee of obtaining a tan, and take part in the nightly ritual of applying After-Sun. I didn't envy my brother's burn after a day of shirking my dad's re-application process, but I did want the sun to treat me the same it treated everyone I knew. To my dismay, the rays simply turned my nut-brown skin almost a deep shade of mahogany, marking me out as even more of an outsider.

At seventeen, a week-long trip to Tenerife turned into a near-month-long adventure when a volcano erupted in Iceland and a huge ash cloud spread over Europe, grounding all flights for weeks and sending airlines into panic mode. EU law dictated that anyone stranded abroad had the right to be fully reimbursed by airlines, so our family trip was extended – for free. My dad grinned gleefully as we watched the news unfold in our little villa apartment before he quickly switched back to organiser mode, calling his work and then my school to ensure that I was set a politics essay to write by the pool (boo!). A month stuck in Tenerife meant I returned home about three shades darker, and although once again I brushed off all the jokes about my new look – 'Georgina's changed races', 'She looks kinda Indian ...' I vowed mentally to do a better job at staying obscured by shade. I saw the darker version of myself as less attractive, sure, but more than that, I saw a tan as disrupting my sense of place within the home. I craved the ghostly pallor of the people around me, because performing whiteness was easier if I looked a little more suited to the part.

A fascinating study suggests there are real-life health implications when you are misidentified. A study on healthcare outcomes and race carried out by the University of British Columbia found that participants who reported higher incidences of racial identity mismatches were more likely to suffer with poor general health. 'People who considered themselves to be white but believed others tend to think they are something else, perhaps that they were of mixed-race, for example, were at a higher risk of high blood pressure and poor mental health', one of the researchers noted. Being perceived in a way that does not match with our own internal view of ourselves is a trauma that is deep enough to leave emotional and physical impacts on the body that can negatively alter health outcomes.[4] I feel this acutely when I look back on the abuse I inflicted on my own body. Being a visible other coupled with the general instability of a girl's teenage years, created fertile ground for a part-time relationship with bulimia. It's a hidden disease which can thrive only in total secrecy, and at fifteen I was fully committed to a vicious cycle of bingeing and purging at the same time as I poured myself into my school work and my grades soared.

Truth be told, I enjoyed the covert process of stocking up on doughy white bread, shortbread biscuits, Cadbury's Dairy Milk bars and Mini Cheddars before dinner, shovelling everything inside me until I felt I would pop, then deflating my bloated stomach by bringing up a softer, mushier version of what had once been solid and firm. It was addictive, it was terrible for my body, and it lasted almost a year. Bulimia grows from just one single seed of insecurity and multiplies like crazy when fed a diet of repugnance and self-loathing, but I expertly masked my illness with a gregarious nature and a laser-sharp focus on school life. Studies show grim bulimia phases like my own are actually typical of black teenage girls. In fact, we are 50 per cent more likely to suffer from bulimia than our white counterparts as adolescents, and far less likely to receive treatment.[5] But of course we don't fit into the popular media discourse around eating disorders: waif-thin, doe-eyed white girls, with raucous friends and monied parents who can fork out for expensive treatment (see Blair Waldorf in the TV series *Gossip Girl*, Ellen in the Netflix film *To The Bone*, and Daisy Randone in the film *Girl, Interrupted*). Black girlhood is rarely depicted in popular media, and when it is, we are denied vulnerability. There has been much written about the real-life dismissal of black pain throughout every level of the healthcare industry. And a lack of visibility when it comes to our experiences with eating disorders means that if we are unseen, then our pain remains unseen too.

Me? I was rumbled by my mother. She has a nose like a bloodhound and eyes like a hawk and she detected vomit on

our toilet after a while. But we still didn't link my unhealthy
habit with any affiliated, deep-rooted psychological issues
relating to body image or racial anxiety. Like so much in
our family, it remained unmentioned after one conversation
in which I dutifully promised both parents I would never
purge again. I recognise that I was lucky – most sufferers of
bulimia battle with the disease for decades, but the habit was
certainly hard to break and I remember fighting an internal
compulsion instructing me to rid myself of fast-food meals or
fatty snacks while at university. I definitely slipped up a few
times in my late teens but my stopping entirely eventually
correlated with a series of private promises I made to myself
to start uncovering the truth about my racial identity.

So much of our perceived attractiveness is tied to feeling
confident in ourselves. You cannot present the best version
of yourself to the world if you do not truly believe it to be so.
And I think being unable to articulate whether I was African
or Caribbean, mixed with Indian, Spanish, Ghanaian or
Ethiopian, or even whether I was in fact adopted, prevented
me from claiming my own beauty narrative with conviction.
It wasn't until I was transported into more diverse spaces,
that I stepped into a whole other spectrum of desirability
and found that here, with a new set of rules that dictated
who was beautiful and who was not, the odds were stacked
in my favour. And hey, I wasn't mad about it. The first time
I realised this was at my father's work when I was around
six. Whenever my school had an Inset day and my parents
couldn't find childcare, I was brought into my father's work-
place where I was exposed to a whole range of faces, cultures
and accents I wasn't used to. Dad had kept the council job
he loved in Hammersmith and Fulham even though we'd
moved to Sutton when I was almost three, first working as a
head chef, then an area manager alongside a range of largely

female workers. He fondly called them his 'kitchen ladies' and sometimes, on these exciting days off, I got to meet them. I would join my father's forty-five-minute commute from Sutton to Hammersmith on these rare and fabled mornings, departing with him at 7 a.m. to beat the traffic. We crossed Albert Bridge, illuminated like a Christmas tree in the cold and purple mornings, my head barely grazing the dashboard of our blue Rover car. I'd arrive at a ginormous school kitchen and be fawned over by dinner ladies in long white coats and colourful nails while enjoying unlimited access to a delectable treasure trove of sugary, salty, additive-laden goodies – crisps, cookies, cereal bars, sweets and chocolate galore (all pre-Jamie Oliver, obvs).

'Oh, she's so beautiful, she's so tall – she should be a model,' exclaimed one of the kitchen ladies in an accent I now recognise as originating somewhere in, or close to, Ghana. Now I had neither the bone structure nor the confidence of a model, and at six I certainly didn't know what a model really *did* as such, but I knew it felt good to receive compliments relating to my looks because it meant they were finally being named. But why was it only these smiling dark-skinned women who called me pretty? For many years I was quite ashamed of how I looked; I could not make sense of my reflection in the mirror, but these ladies placed a premium on my appearance, naming my features as beautiful; before that, what had remained unsaid had influenced me far more. It wasn't until many years later that I tried to recall my dad's reaction that day and I could see his face; smiling, holding me close, but offering nothing in the way of elaboration on our differing appearance. Without anyone ever telling me so, and like many other children of colour, I had become acutely aware that I was at the bottom of a beauty hierarchy that positioned light skin, blue eyes and straight hair as the most desirable of physical characteristics. Now, I'm grateful for those sporadic, early encounters with other black people which reminded me of my visibility as a young black girl, letting me know that I too could be seen as pretty, nudging me ever closer to claiming the truth about my identity, and teaching me that being black, and being attractive, were not mutually exclusive.

Before these early racial encounters with strangers, my parents actually told me *they* received lots of compliments about my cuteness as a baby. Perhaps it was when I began to talk (and complicate matters) that the topic was resigned to off-limits. I was – if I may say so – pretty gorgeous as a newborn. I had huge brown eyes fanned by long lashes, and a heart-shaped face and wide smile. The stories I have heard about my cuteness include how once, my mother was advised to enter me into a baby modelling competition by a scout who approached her in west London; and how – wait for it – the guitarist of Queen, the legend that is Brian May, commented on my gorgeousness as she queued with me in a pharmacy in Holland Park. I have since asked Mum whether these positive comments relating to my looks ever led into discussions about my heritage, or questions as to who my father was; she has always claimed that no one asked her outright if she had been unfaithful or why I was black – not one of her three sisters or her many friends back in Ireland, her work colleagues or even her neighbours. Now, this absolutely blows my mind. If ever Aisling or Emilia gave birth to a brown-skinned baby I can't imagine that I would tiptoe around the issue of paternity, such is the closeness of our friendship which has also been calcified within a demographic cohort (millennials) known for our predilection for over-sharing. But my mum claims she's never had questions from anyone despite those reactions from strangers both positive and incredulous. Whether this perceived lack of engagement to do with my race was a feat of incredible mental fortitude, or blind ignorance, I am still not sure and there is no way of truly knowing.

Many of my family experiences mirror those within the transracial adoption community. The challenges transracial adoptees face are complex and varied, each one demanding nuanced discussion. Transracial adoptees sometimes navigate a world without knowledge or access to their birth parents and culture, and as a result lack the emotional and social tools to navigate racism. They may find themselves rejected from groups with which they share physical similarities for exhibiting the cultural norms associated with those who brought them up (that is, they may be accused of 'acting too white'). These existential struggles can be applied to anyone from multiple-heritage backgrounds or households: lacking racial representation, or an understanding of how to navigate racialised experiences, can produce near-comical scenarios when you come into contact with others who expect you to be in possession of a different identity, or worse, accuse you of performing an identity which to you is perfectly normal and leave you afraid to assert yourself around others who look like you.

Many of us also battle with the idea that our very existence also represents a crossing of boundaries, a disruption of the most widely recognised narratives around kinship and belonging. As Professor Gina E. Miranda Samuels, herself a transracial adoptee and researcher on this topic, notes in her essay 'Being Raised by White People':

> The daily lives of transracial adoptive families and multiracials are riddled with questions from strangers (e.g., 'What are you?' 'Is that your mother?') requiring public defenses or declarations of one's racial ties, authenticity, and allegiance within single-race communities ... (Dalmage,

2000; Register, 1990). Transracial adoptive families and multiracials are perceived by some as actual or potential racial 'traitors' while being revered or idealised by others as the hope or proof of ending racial division (Dalmage, 2000; Samuels, 2006).[6]

Racial socialisation in families usually occurs between parents and children who share the same racial background. But when you are of a different race to your family, or raised without a full understanding of your heritage, it is up to you to make sense of it all alone.

Cultural socialisation within interracial or transracial families is therefore vital. As a parent or caregiver, this means promoting racial or ethnic identity development, teaching the child how to navigate a racially hierarchical world, ensuring the child is exposed to diverse communities, and balancing the family's dominant culture with the child's racial background. In cases where this is not followed, it is normal for the child to try to resemble those around them. One American study found that 36 per cent of Korean adoptees identified as white while growing up, but as adults, this figure dropped to 11 per cent.[7] We don't know details around the childhood of these Korean adoptees – whether they were culturally socialised or not – but studies like this underscore the intrinsic need to connect with, and be a part of, the people who raise us. Children who self-identify as white are not deliberately deny-ing their roots or trying to shed their cultural identity, it's just that for most of their lives that *is* the only cultural identity they have known. This is hardly their fault! Self-identifying with an ethnic identity that does not 'match' with what is expected, is simply an attempt to settle into the families who have them and underscores the fundamental human need to simply belong. As Maya Angelou so beautifully articulates in the fifth of her seven autobiographical works, *All God's Children Need Traveling Shoes,* 'the ache for home lives in all of us, the safe place where we can go as we are and not be questioned'.

One way we find our tribe is through visual comparisons. Constructions of community and kinship in families help us settle in the world, imbuing us with a sense of pride and cementing our membership in various groups. We enjoy rattling off the visible characteristics we have inherited from Mum or Dad, who in the family has bestowed us those muscular legs, a wonky nose or a prominent chin, that keen sense of adventure. Professor Gina E. Miranda Samuels, in the same essay, emphasises how important these cherished family narratives are: 'The dominant frame for legitimizing kinship ties is through one's resemblance to other family members in physical and personal traits. Through "resemblance talk" (Becker, Butler, & Nachtigall, 2005), of whom one "looks like" in the family, we authenticate our sense of self, familial belonging, and very existence.' The 'resemblance talk' that took place in my home was a bit of a stretch to say the least. We used to say I had my dad's crooked teeth and long, kidney-bean-shaped head as well as a smaller version of my mum's straight, angled nose. But looking at our photos you would not immediately guess that I belonged there. I have always lacked a visible resemblance to anyone in my life; the stories I heard from my parents about where I'd got this or that were told to soothe and make sense of the illogical, to bury the ticking grenade at the heart of our home. Looking back now, I see this placating came from love. I still think about my dad's face when we made those comparisons, his warm, reassuring smile as he hugged me close and told me I was his 'baby', his 'doll-face'. These conversations and comparisons were my parents' way of showing me that they loved me, but they did not quell my latent fears about not belonging within my family.

I remember how Aisling and I discussed body shapes during one of our bloated three-hour, after-school phone calls on the landline that usually preceded a marathon MSN chat session too. 'What do you have to talk about?' my dad would ask. 'You've been with her all day.' But post-school conversations were reserved for more personal topics – the stuff that couldn't be whispered in Maths, and Aisling and I could talk *for hours*; she is the friend who knows me better than I know myself. And at around fourteen, the Gods of Femininity had bestowed upon me a rather generous chest and this, I felt, gave me some much-needed bonus points on the attractive scale. I gladly leaned into this part of my identity: everything I wore was low-cut, dresses and outfits had to show off this part of my figure. 'Just because you have all the goods in the shop doesn't mean you have to put them all out for display,' my father said one evening as I headed out to a club in a plunging black, feathered dress when I was eighteen. It wasn't as if I had started puberty earlier than many of my friends, but I'd always been the tallest and biggest, and when we started to fill out and *my* boobs ballooned faster than everyone's around me, I didn't feel like such an oddity.

'Your mum doesn't have boobs that size, does she?' Aisling asked, as we discussed the excitement of our first bra-fitting at M&S. I was holed up in the spare room where my parents couldn't hear me. 'Where do you get them from?'

'I got it from my Mama.' I started to sing the 2007 semi-hit by will.i.am and Fergie. 'Nah, actually scrap that – I didn't, did I?'

I laughed. But at the centre of that conversation was a barely conceived despondency related to the fact that I didn't look like anyone else, and so I was convinced that being lighter, in terms of both skin and weight, would help me.

'At least I have my mum's nose though,' I added happily.

My nose. I was obsessed with it. At fourteen, much to my mother's total abhorrence I had it pierced. It became another thing that I was asked to fix by way of removing the tiny sparkling gem from my face entirely. I'd had it inserted at a chemist's in Sutton one Saturday afternoon – a standard act of teenage rebellion which my father always overlooked ('Let her keep it, Colette'), but it was also a means of reclaiming a part of my identity I had no control over, by highlighting one of my most Eurocentric features. During one summer visit to Clare, a cousin had told me that I had 'a touch of the Gallagher nose' (my mother's maiden name). Now, nearly all the Gallaghers have a large, bumpy, angled feature at the front and centre of their faces and in all honesty, it is nothing to covet. But because I couldn't change my skin colour, and altering the curvature of my figure was an impossible feat, the nose obsession was a direct link to mother and to my Irish heritage. But resemblance talk in the context of conversations on feminine beauty reminded me that not only did I not look anything like my family, but that my admittance to the hierarchy of beauty would only be permitted via my proximity to whiteness, when my most Eurocentric features were seen and celebrated by others.

Today, whenever white mothers worried about discussing race with their children ask me for advice on Instagram, I firstly remind them that I am very much child*less* and should *not* be relied upon for tips relating to keeping another human alive and healthy, when I can barely prevent a houseplant from dying in my care. Then I might tell them that before they start any difficult discussions, they should simply focus on ensuring that their home is a safe space, where conversations about difference and inequality can be held in a judgement-free zone and where their child feels able to be their authentic self. That a cultural education which informs the child of who they are is vital, as is disclosing all known information around the child's parentage and heritage. Offer help and encouragement (without centring your own thoughts and feelings, boo!), and when your child comes to you with questions about their background, endeavour to answer them honestly. Obscuring the truth will lead to dire and far-reaching consequences for all involved and is generally more emotionally devastating and psychologically damaging the longer you leave it. There is no reason why white people raising black or brown children cannot provide all these things, but it is important to remember that love, on its own, isn't always enough.

In 2017, two years after my dad's death when I was still desperate to make sense of my childhood, I met Chrissie Rose, whose story mirrored my own in parts. Chrissie was born in 1971 to a black father and white mother in Brecon, a south Wales town with a population of eight thousand. His life began as the only brown face for miles, after his father left when he was a baby. Then, from the age of six, the skin condition vitiligo began to strip him of his brown pigmentation, leaving Chrissie at a strange mid-section, being both visibly black and white, with contrasting patches all over his body. He finally transitioned to being totally pale-skinned at the age of twenty-six. After moving out of Wales and living all over the UK and South Africa, Chrissie was able to trace his black father – but at a stage when he was no longer visibly black himself.

'I've been a brown kid and a white adult,' he said to me over a beer at the back of Pop Brixton, the open-air food court and event space on Brixton Station Road. We were sitting outside and I was freezing. 'I remember being in school and playing rugby and a kid saying, "Would you rather be black or white?" But it was out of my hands. If I could reverse time and go back to what I was, I would be mixed-race because it was me. *This* isn't me.' He gestured towards himself, and I allowed my eyes to cast over him. Chrissie was slight of build and wearing a dark green bomber jacket, with dark hair that showed no sign of curl or wave, and very pale skin. 'This is like me wearing someone else's face,' he said as he held my gaze.

Does it still feel like that now, I asked, at the age of forty-six?

He nodded.

I hadn't recognised Chrissie at first. I'd also gone to the wrong spot as he'd asked to meet by the 'train entrance', and like many Londoners who use the words 'train' and 'tube' interchangeably I forgot that some people actually take the Overground out of choice. I'd been waiting by Brixton tube. On a misleadingly cold afternoon in May – the sun shining but providing no actual warmth, duping me into leaving my coat at home – I eventually found Chrissie underneath the railway arches by the corner of Electric Avenue and Coldharbour Lane as he was mid-message to me, typing on his phone. As egg-yellow beams of sunlight hit the side of his face, the first thing I wondered was, am I meeting the right person? He didn't look like any of his photos. I thought back to the Facebook profile picture taken when he was eighteen, a black-and-white portrait in which he was sporting a wide smile and nape-length hair, and a seventies-style curtain fringe. It was hard to see any signs of his mixed-race heritage there. But then during our correspondence Chrissie had also sent a photo of himself as a teenager in which he had curlier

hair and glasses. In that photo, though, what really stood
out for me was his in-between complexion. I remembered
the patches of brown and peach tones all over his face – the
vitiligo was taking hold and his visible mixedness was fading
away. 'The colour was lost from my hands and the bulk of my
face,' he explained when we sat down and I brought up that
picture again. 'My natural complexion was receding back to
my neck at that point.' He was fifteen then. But the man in
front of me looked nothing like either of those images. The
man before me was totally and indisputably white. 'I'm too
pale now,' he conceded in his broad Welsh accent, smiling
sadly. 'I am always the whitest person in the room.'

Chrissie was twenty-eight when he traced his black
father through an agency, locating him in Thornton Heath,
Croydon – which, in another strange twist of parallel fates,
is just a couple of miles from where I grew up. I couldn't
quite believe that by the time Chrissie managed to access the
cultural knowledge and build the father–son relationship
he'd been deprived of for so long, he was no longer visibly
black and looked nothing like his new relatives. It must be
like waiting all your life for a delivery of the right-sized shoes
after years of wearing ones that are too tight, or too large,
only to find that your feet have shrunk by the time your
new ones arrive. Chrissie reconnected with his dad and his
extended Jamaican family but the lack of any sort of physical
resemblance left him feeling like an outsider. He described
to me the feeling of bewilderment when he was introduced
to family friends.

'I go around to my dad's house and now I feel like the white
sheep of the family,' he said. 'When people say "This is my
brother Chris" their friends have this weird look on their face
and say nothing. I feel like part of the family, but because I
don't look like them ... it's annoying. I have the photos of

how I used to look, as a kid, and that's how I *should* look. It would feel more of a natural ... family. I grew up with my mum, I didn't look like her and now she's dead. And now I live a couple of miles from my black family and now I don't look like them. I feel like I've been cheated both ways.'

Chrissie's heritage was also obscured in that his mother never disclosed his father's identity, or attempted to imbue him with any sort of cultural knowledge as he grew up in a totally white town with a white family. 'There was one Chinese family in Brecon but that was it. Everyone else was white, and no one in the family ever told me I wasn't white too,' he said. I asked Chrissie whether he thinks this silence around his own heritage was due to feelings of bitterness towards his father, who had left the family, or whether his mum felt shame at becoming a divorcee with a black child in seventies Wales. Chrissie thought it was a combination of both.

'My mother was called Val and there were lots of Vals around, so it was like, "Oh, is it Val who was married to a black man?" That was sort of always at the end of her name.'

I nodded emphatically, seeing myself in him. I told Chrissie that my mum and I had spent a lot of time discussing her feelings of shame around having an affair with a black man she now couldn't remember, that we had just started counselling after I'd returned from a year of travels, and that it was all painstakingly complex. I didn't unpack how a parent's shame could dim your own light. I didn't need to; we had both lived it.

Chrissie continued. 'I also remember being eight years old and having a boy at school ask me if I was black. I told him in all earnestness I didn't know. When I got home, I asked my mother if my father was black. She said, "He wasn't black, he was just dark-skinned." I was satisfied, and so was my friend the next day. I got called a lot of names growing up, like "wog", and my friends would stick up for me, but when I started changing colour it got worse. I used to get "patch" or "multi-coloured swap shop" from the TV programme at the time.'

Around the same time the racialised taunting became more creative and Chrissie's skin colour shifted from brown to white, he came across a photo of his father hidden in one of his mother's drawers. The secret she had been keeping about his parentage – and his identity – devastated him.

'I was thinking, why would an adult blatantly lie?' he said, his soft voice rising slightly for the first time in our conversation. 'Here was a picture of a black man who was obviously my father. I never said anything to my mother – I didn't want her to think I was rummaging through her stuff – but it drove a wedge between us. After that point we were never as close. People were saying I was mixed-race – I was getting racial abuse – but then my mother was saying that that wasn't the case.'

I was totally taken aback by the parallels in our experiences: the similar things we were told by our mothers to uphold and protect their reputations, the consistent sense of alienation born of never seeing ourselves reflected in the people around us, the loneliness that came from dissecting the meaning behind racial insults that as kids we didn't think were even meant for us. *No one in the family ever told me I wasn't white too*. It's exactly how I felt. Children don't question what they are told, they don't have the emotional toolkit or the worldly knowledge to unpack the stories their parents tell them; their sense of normality is constructed and maintained by what they are shown and taught at home. For both of us, working out who we were, and how we came to exist as brown-skinned children in white worlds, was something we did by ourselves. Despite the endless nurturing and stability Chrissie and I received from our parents, the taunting and the questions and the misidentification we endured, all because we looked different from our family members and weren't told why, were deeply traumatic at times. I'm not a parent and I won't pretend that I fully understand all the decisions my mum and dad made for me – the sacrifices, the homework help, the late nights spent reading bedtime stories to me, as well as the more difficult choices around discussing our differences – but I know they did their best. I also believe that full disclosure around heritage and paternity would have saved both me and Chrissie from our own private heartaches as adults.

Racial denial and cultural whitewashing is confusing, cruel and impossibly hard to validate. A therapist I once visited called it a type of 'psychological brainwashing', and I remember the immediate shock and impact of those words as I sat in his office sobbing a few months after my dad had passed away. My mild-mannered mum and gentle, loving father, who devoted their lives to raising me and my brother, surely didn't mean to do that? My dad could have left just as soon as he realised that his baby did not resemble him, but he stayed and showered me with more love than I knew what to do with. But I'll never get the chance to discuss why our differences were simply too difficult to tackle.

Even though Chrissie was loved by his mother, his home was corrupted by an internal anguish related to where he fitted in, where he came from, and whether the person he trusted most in the world was lying to him – a fear which later turned out to be true. His mother obscured some basic truths about who Chrissie was, casting a grey film of disruption over his life and leaving him constantly unsure of himself. She died in 2018, before the pair discussed the impact her decisions had had on his childhood.

As we discussed moving inside because of the cold, Chrissie

turned and asked whether I wanted to trace my biological father.

I winced at the term 'father'.

'It's something I'm interested in doing,' I replied, slowly. 'But it feels sort of . . . disloyal.'

Chrissie nodded. 'I get that. You have had a great dad.' He paused. 'It's funny, even though now I've found my father I still don't feel like I fit in anywhere.'

On the way out of Pop Brixton, Chrissie and I took a selfie – me grinning and shivering without my jacket, Chrissie beside me in his bomber, beaming too. I studied it on the way home. He had almond-shaped, almost-black eyes like a squirrel, but stripped of his pigmentation there was very little visible evidence left that would tie Chrissie to his Jamaican heritage. It seemed he'd pretty much given up trying to justify it, so worried was he about being judged or disbelieved. At the heart of Chrissie's story I see the ridiculousness and fragility that underscores our common understandings around race. When we talk of race being a social construct, it's often as a phrase that is weaponised to discount or diminish the realities of minority ethnic people, but when applied to very select cases like Chrissie's, the way in which race can be seen as fluid is clear. A racial identity is crafted by both nature and nurture, but it is also undoubtedly affected by the way in which you are perceived – not just by your family, but by friends and membership of wider communities, and of course, by yourself. If all of these things aren't cohesive, if how you see yourself doesn't match up with how your family and the rest of the world sees you, then Houston, we have a problem – a rather large, identity-related problem. Chrissie was raised white, ethnically, and encouraged to ignore the lived experiences of his blackness, the effect of which had him believing he was, actually, white. I get that totally. But then he turned white in the physical sense, and so where did that leave him now, if he continued to be read as a white man? Like Chrissie, I have worked hard to unlearn insidious thoughts that have disfigured my black identity but I remain in the body I was born with, meaning that once I was old enough to understand it, my existential experience matched the world's perception of me. But although Chrissie has changed states through no choice of his own, his mindset remains tethered to the identity he was born – who knows if it will always be so. Vitiligo robbed him of his original mould and despite stable relationships, a fulfilling job as a counsellor and a loving partner, isolation has characterised his life.

Stories of transracial upbringings are layered and complex and often, but not always, take place within the boundaries of sadness and solitude. I left the meeting with Chrissie thinking that his life had placed my own in a more nuanced framework. I understood my parents' choices a little more because I understood those of Chrissie's mother, too. There is certainly no monolithic black experience, but after meeting Chrissie I was more confident than ever that the colour-blind parenting approach as opposed to colour-conscious, is a form of identity theft.

Transracial children, and indeed mixed-heritage individuals as a whole, are often viewed as a paradox, the person onto whom many others project their own expectations, hopes and fears. Racism is over, our very existence suggests to some. Our skin colour challenges the idea of a mono-racial society, our place in white families disrupts the traditional notion of belonging and kinship. This can be seen as transgressive – we are the connection between multiple cultures – but it is also exhausting, living under a microscope. We must start to embrace the complexities that come with not fitting neatly into one box. Society is changing, so our attitudes towards mixing must shift too. To expect certain cultural identities to correlate with certain skin tones is damaging and reductive, and we cannot police the behaviour or cultural affinities of those in transracial families. The cultural identity I have now as an adult is a hodge-podge mixture of British and Irish – gifts my parents have bestowed upon me and that I shall treasure for ever – and is imbued with a strong sense of what some would call a black consciousness, which holds still at my very core, shaping my sense of justice and belonging as well as my outward appearance. But unlike most black people I know, this consciousness has not originated from one specific country and was not nourished by my proximity to any black relatives – it will always be something of a work in progress. But I also see myself as one of the tiny, scattered pieces of the African diaspora, and that is something that today, I can say I am staunchly proud of.

White parents who raise children of colour don't necessarily have to subject them to an accidental lifetime of social discomfort and othering if they simply speak to them about the realities and beauty around their identities early on, if they instil in them a sense of racial pride, and also explain that systemic, pervasive issues of inequality will undoubtedly map themselves across the trajectory of their lives again and again. Parents might say that it's up to their children to find a way to deal with and overcome those hurdles, but as parents they will be there for them, listen to them, defend them to the death, and help them work it all out. Discussing racial differences as a family won't entrench divisions and separate parents from children, but ignoring them will. Chrissie and I are proof of that.

I left him that day thinking of the search for my biological father, where he could be from, whether we look like one another. But then looking down at the image of my actual dad, smiling on my phone screensaver, quietly reminded me once more that the biggest imprint on who I am will always come from his love, his nurture. It did not matter that our family photos had not made sense; my father is in me, always.

Being yourself is easier once you free yourself from the baggage of other people's expectations, when you look in the mirror and accept that the person staring back at you is a culmination of everything you have always wanted to be.

5

My Lot

It was love's absence that let me know how much
love mattered. I was my father's first daughter. At the
moment of my birth, I was looked upon with loving
kindness, cherished and made to feel wanted on this
earth and in my home.

BELL HOOKS, *All About Love*

My parents had never been super-social people bar the
odd BBQ with friends, but when my dad became sick
in 2014, our house transformed into a strange new show-
home, a place where someone was always coming and going.
During that summer I could almost pretend to myself it was
for different reasons, that it was great to have my dad on the
sofa all the time, that there were so many faces in the living
room or garden because we were in a perpetual state of par-
tying, of celebrating, that when he was sitting with someone
I didn't recognise it wasn't actually a health worker, or priest,
or someone to install the disabled access in our bathroom, but
an entertainer, or a new work friend. In this mirthless land

of make-believe I could almost block out the macabre and insist that we were just having one long, continuous family BBQ and my dad wasn't actually dying. Only ... he was. Cancer was carving my dad into a scarecrow at an alarming rate, reducing him to an imitation of himself. And while my brother could block out the images of Dad's new walking frame or pill box or medication when he came home from university, retreating to his room for long periods of time or refusing to discuss the components of our terrifying new life, I could not. It was anticipatory grief for me, the type that gripped me by the throat on day one of the terminal diagnosis. Grief is like a snowflake, each one special and unique. But long before a loss, our own pattern of mourning is hard-wired within us, imprinted on our insides, waiting to be released when one day, the inevitable comes. The timing and type of loss are simply the catalysts for what has already been pre-determined. From birth I was gifted a love like no other from my father. And so, I was pre-destined to grieve monumentally. My grief was rare, *sui generis*: nothing else, and nobody else's could compare. From the moment he was diagnosed, I was despondent, in a stupor, a walking, mourning zombie.

There's stuff you can't ever prepare for, like how imposing cancer adverts on the TV feel when you're living it, or the sight of your father using a zimmer frame at the age of fifty-four. All of it was a crass middle finger to the hardest-working man I knew. Soon after the diagnosis, we learned the disease had seeped into his bones. Getting to and from the loft conversion he shared with Mum was suddenly too much of a mission, so Dad moved into my room on the middle floor and I moved next door to our spare box-room. He lost his mobility quickly and soon needed a portable toilet in every room. Dinners and family conversations would be interrupted with near-comical displays of Dad's freckled bottom in the corner as he turned the air sharp and sour with a millisecond's notice. 'Sorry, lads, I need to go,' he'd laugh as we vacated the room with the efficiency of a military evacuation and my mother went to help him, leaving the dinner I'd cooked for us going cold. Then there were the occasional mornings Dad couldn't get out of bed because he was crying, and all those lonely nights he spent in hospital on his own with no one around.

There is something particularly disturbing about seeing a father, the strongest person you have ever known, crumple up with fear like a child in your arms. I often think about the words I used to try and muster up, something in the shape of comfort, whether they meant enough, whether he heard me. Right before my graduation from the University of Warwick, Dad was stuck in St Helier Hospital with a nasty chest infection, the cancer feeding off his lungs.

'I'm going to make it out for your graduation, doll-face,' he said two nights before. And I believed him – but he didn't. Mum's family friend drove us up with my brother in tow. We all felt the force of his absence that day as we struggled to move around the campus without his lead, his energy; the weight of what was missing pinned us down. I saw my dad everywhere – where he parked the car when he helped me unload my things for my first day three years before, the campus pub where he took me for lunch. He would have found the graduation gown queue faster than me and my mum who are equally useless with maps and direction, he would have been the one taking the photos, heaping his plate full of free canapés. Our day was totally disfigured without him, but the worst part by far was knowing that this was just a mere taster for the rest of our lives without him, that this was the beginning of a sick new normal. I caught the train straight back to London with my brother after the ceremony

(Mum went to stay with a friend near the university) to be beside him in the hospital. We took photos on my phone, Dad was sat up in a chair beside his bed posing gleefully with my bottle of champagne, me leaning into him while perched on the armrest holding my certificate.

'I'm very proud of you, you know,' he smiled at me after a nurse had photographed us.

'Dad . . . I'm proud of you too.'

'You better get going, it's late. Just help me into my PJs before you leave will you?'

'Yep.'

By now it was a ritual I was used to, although Mum did it more often. Dad's navy night-time bag for hospital stays lay on the dresser next to his bed. I helped him brush his teeth, get dressed, and slowly, gently, climb into his stiff sheets, the standard parent child roles reversed. I left the hospital late that night and went to a friend's house, desperate to round off the day with some level of normality, but I couldn't quite shake off the day's sadness, it was in my clothes, had seeped into my blood.

As anyone who has had their life turned upside down by a parent's sudden illness will know, everything around you becomes warped into an unrecognisable imitation of your old life – seemingly overnight. You long for the humdrum, the days when things were held together by the banal and the monotonous: Saturday evenings spent laughing at crap singers on crap talent shows; the jangle of keys in the front door when they returned from work and shouted 'I'm home!', as my father did every day without fail; the back and forth, the to-ing and fro-ing, the fetching and carrying they did for you and everyone else – lifts, errands, shopping, doctor's appointments, airport pick-ups, emergencies and favours; the sound of things being taken care of as you drifted off to sleep – doors being locked, bins being emptied, dishwashers being turned on and off. All that goes away with a terminal diagnosis. All that disappears with a cruel, carnivorous cunt of a disease like cancer. Roles switch. You, the child – selfish and conceited to your very core – must morph into someone who is suddenly strong and selfless and mature. You don't know how. You *don't know shit*. You fall apart. You waste precious time.

I kept going to my internships at Dad's encouragement. I landed a position at a women's magazine after winning a writing competition, but I was a nervous wreck and the nerves manifested themselves in my body. Sleep was not my friend; I spent hours lying still and afraid in that spare room, listening to the sound of my dad coughing up his lungs. In the day I suddenly started scratching myself, non-stop; my whole body flared up like it was on fire and the compulsion to claw at my skin was overwhelming: on the train into work, on my lunch-break, in the office loos, and on the journey back home again. On the surface my skin appeared normal, but every few hours it would feel as if someone had doused me in petrol and set me alight, but when I looked or asked others to scan my body, there was nothing to see. It wasn't until my father told me he suspected it was stress-related that it clicked (of course he was still looking out for me even in the midst of his illness). I didn't even know there was such a thing, and when I mentioned it on my third trip to the GP I finally received a soothing cream that offered a little respite.

But inside, too, my spirit was shrinking. The man who had spent every weekend at home with us cooking and doing DIY was withering away right before my eyes. Death was coming. And beside the constant, ominous anxiety and permanent sense of trepidation, the question of my heritage suddenly plagued me like never before. I knew that if my father died without me broaching the subject of our relationship then I'd live to regret it; but a large part of me felt selfish for daring even to think it. How could I even consider adding another layer of despair over the worst time in our lives? We had spent years avoiding the topic of our difference and to tackle it now, in a time of such incomprehensible pain, felt misplaced, selfish.

Nonetheless, after discussing it with Aisling, I ordered a DNA test shortly after Dad's diagnosis, before the chemo had robbed him of his mobility. One evening, as music by the Buzzcocks, the Ramones and the Clash (his favourite band of all-time) floated out from the speakers of our home computer as Dad revisited his youth, I slowly explained that I needed to tackle this topic before it was too late.

'I've always had questions,' I explained. 'And I know that one day soon, you won't be here to help me answer them.' I stopped, my voice breaking.

Dad swivelled around on his computer chair in the corner of the room.

'All right, sweet pea, I understand why you'd want to look into that,' he began. 'But I know that you're mine.' He looked me in the eye and smiled. His favourite Clash song, 'White Man in Hammersmith Palais', blared out behind us. 'I get why you would be worried but you're mine, Georgina. I know that.'

And in that moment, his reassurances were enough.

I don't know whether deep down, Dad believed we were biologically related, as I had spent my life insisting to others, or if he meant to emphasise that I was, and always had been, claimed by him regardless of how we looked together. But in that moment, it was enough. I let his words delay the impact of another high-speed collision. I hit the brakes. An unexpected DNA test result could be catastrophic – I knew that.

And so it was easier to choose another year of ambiguity over the possibility of something far worse. I'd had twenty-one years of uncertainty, what was one more? I would not pile my dad's plate even higher with pain when he was already shielding me and Mum from the worst of it. I could not force a family-wide conversation about my race and paternity when our biggest concern was keeping Dad alive, and his biggest concern was establishing a safety net for all of us while he was still able to do so. And so the DNA sample remained in my room, tucked away at the back of my dressing table, but always in the forefront of my mind. I would find the courage to process it only after he had passed away.

For all he was going through, Dad maintained his eternally optimistic disposition throughout his illness, making jokes with us and having a laugh with his doctors and nurses.

'Any hallucinations with this medication? You seeing any bugs, spiders, or creepy crawlies?' a female doctor asked him gravely upon one hospital visit.

'Nope, still waiting for those,' he would laugh while wiggling his eyebrows.

He told everyone around him not to worry – he was fine, he felt totally fine. He always thanked his visitors for the stuff he started out enjoying, like digestive biscuits and herbal tea and cake, but which he soon found himself barely able to stomach because the chemo had taken his taste buds and stolen his once huge appetite. At random points in the week he staged mini life lessons for all of us. He'd call me or my brother or my mum and explain how to load ink into the printer, or clean the inside of the car, or slice a mango, so we'd be OK 'when I'm gone', he'd say in a ghoulish tone and comical expression. When my brother came back from university, Dad asked to be pushed to B&Q in his wheelchair so he could get lightbulbs for the house and when I was in, he was constantly working from home to stay busy: his compulsion to stay on top of everything never waned. I tried to take on the role of house chef after work, since Dad was no longer able to, selfishly forcing him to take a concoction of vitamins and turmeric tablets alongside his now tiny dinners. I'd spent hours online researching the stories of those who attributed miraculous cancer recoveries to a selection of herbs, desperate as I was for him to live, desperate as I was for him not to leave us. Even though he had another fifteen tablets to take himself every day as part of his chemotherapy treatment, he obediently popped a few more to humour me. 'Thankfully, I've got my two nurses here,' he'd say to my granny when she came down from Shropshire to help out too, and I choked back tears. Mum was his main carer. She snapped into action and held it together with all the grit and tenacity of an officer in a war zone, ferrying Dad around, cleaning up the chemo-induced chaos his body had started producing without warning, and comforting me and my brother. 'We'll get through this because we have to,' she would say to me softly when I broke down after work, or in the hospital waiting room, on her shoulder. 'Come on we've got to keep going.' All the while she continued to work in her reception job because my father insisted that things continue under the veneer of regularity while he was around. Mum told me how, on the weekend he was first diagnosed and I was at uni, my father pulled out all the files and folders in our house where he stored passwords and bills and logins, how emotional that conversation had been, the look on his face when he realised she would be doing this in his absence. Mum had never been a confident driver, so after his diagnosis Dad also organised mini driving lessons to key spots so she would know how to get there without him by her side. Later, in therapy, she told me how he'd drawn maps for her on her first day at a new job after the lessons and how he'd always defrost her car in the winter months before he went to work in his own, anecdotes that brought our therapist close to tears at the time. In the house during his illness he'd make dark jokes about her future dating life, poking at her stomach after a chocolate bar and remarking, 'You need to watch it now, you'll be back on the market soon'. She'd roll her eyes, but then leave the room so he wouldn't see her cry.

When he could still just about walk, Dad asked me to accompany him to the bank so he could make the final mortgage payment for our house, which for some reason needed to be hand-delivered. Concerned about the family's financial future, of which he would no longer be a part, he worked on getting everything in order for us during that final year of his life. He was not filled with regret, or anger. He didn't preoccupy himself with ticking off bucket-list experiences, only with making sure we were going to be all right without him. I accompanied him in a taxi that day, which dropped us off seconds from the same bank in Sutton that we used to go to when he ran errands. My dad was a giant then, a strong and soft teddy bear who scooped me up and carried me on his shoulders when I lagged behind. But that day, it was he who rested his hand on my shoulder for balance as he hobbled into the bank's waiting room. Breathless and panting, he was offered a glass of water by the staff, which he accepted, before handing in the final envelope which was to secure our home. He reached out to hold on to me once again. I helped him up and we hobbled out together to take the second taxi back to our house.

If ever I am forced to face death head-on like my dad had to, square up to it in the mirror and look it in the face every single day, I don't think I'll be able to handle it with the same grace, humility and acceptance. At his core, even in his bleakest moments, there was only love. No anger. No blame. No regret. Just love and concern and gratitude for a life with me and my mum and my brother. I cannot imagine the sheer mental fortitude it must take to push aside your own immeasurable terror and simply accept the cards you have been dealt in order to help ease the burden on everyone else. But he did that. For us. It was his final lesson to us all, not to let what was out of his control totally consume him in his last few months.

One evening, after I returned home from my internship, I went up to my old room and climbed into bed with Dad. He was now spending a lot of his time immobile and had been whizzing through the library of my old English Literature course books. I'm sure he actually read more of them than I did for my entire degree: he had always been a voracious reader and demolished his books like he had once demolished his food. When I started to tell him about my day, he was tucked up, the dusky pink sheets I had chosen years ago curled up around his chin, making him look as fragile as a newborn lamb. His glasses were resting on my desk, next to a spare basin he also carried everywhere in which to catch the vomit. Before he became ill I had never really seen him remove his glasses that much, permanently glued as they were to his face. Now they were discarded more frequently than ever to make room for his tears, falling in hospitals, our house, the shower. His eyes looked so much smaller and squintier without their usual frame-work, but also so much bluer, like tiny sparkling sapphires on a pillow of pink and white.

Dad was lying flat on his back reading my copy of *Brick Lane*, which I had bought aged fifteen and re-read for a feminist literature class at university. I was moaning about work, the people, the inane drivel I was having to write. I got out of bed and began to pace the room frantically.

'I don't know if I want to do this,' I said flatly (meaning women's magazines). 'I don't know what I want to do, Dad.'

'Don't get stressed about work, doll,' he said. 'Life's too short. Choose something that you love and make sure you *really* love it, because you're going to be doing it every day for the best part of a full day for the rest of your life. I loved my job, I loved the people.' There was a hint of sadness in his voice.

He was right, of course.

'What do I always say to you? I'm always right.'

But I was raging. Not with Dad, but the situation that had befallen him, befallen us. To watch his once-mighty 6ft 3, 15-stone frame shrink in stature, the strong arms that once lifted me off the couch and up to bed at night-time lose their muscle, and the freckled, limber legs that had kept him active diminish in robustness, was an event so cruel and disturbing, it verged on the preternatural. I was furious that this ruthless, insidious disease was ripping my father out from the middle, cell by cell, day by day.

'Dad,' I said, 'aren't you angry?'

'About what?'

'That you're sick . . . that this is happening to us. Sometimes I'm so angry I feel like I can't breathe. And I know that you're still here and I can't change it but . . . I can't help it.' Tears rolled down my cheeks, I was shaking.

My dad looked up at me from the bed. 'There's no point in being angry, doll. It won't change anything. This is it. This is my lot.'

There are albums full of photos of our early life in Shepherd's Bush. I know that I had a best friend called Kitty who lived on the floor below us – we played on the stairwell with fluffy toys, but I'm not sure if this is actually my first memory or if the dots in my mind's eye have subsequently been joined up after going through those old images. My dad's attention to detail in those albums is touching. The captions are iconic. I'm pictured crawling: *She's on the move!*; dressed up in somebody's hat: *Poser!*; then walking: *Catch me if you can! Georgina takes her first steps.* There are descriptions of me drinking juice from plastic beakers and flicking through picture books on my mum's lap. On my first birthday I'm pictured eating a vanilla sponge cake, decorated with Milkybar Buttons and pink frosted icing and fashioned into the shape of a giant number 1, twice the length of my body – a fabulously extravagant cake for any baby and one which I really wish I could remember eating. He made it for me. *Happy birthday to me!* Dad wrote in his flat, easy-to-read handwriting beneath the photo. My parents spent a lot of time photographing me, my dad especially. They smoked (Dad gave up when I was around three, Mum was on and off for years), they wore eclectic (slightly tragic) eighties shirts and shoulder-padded jackets. All of us were crammed into tiny rooms. Them, and all their (white) friends; me, the only brown face in the room. Everyone looks content, and as Mum told me many years later, it's because they were.

My parents put down a deposit on the three-bed house in a quiet cul-de-sac in Sutton when I was almost two. My brother was born when I was three and a half. During family TV nights, we used to say Dad should go on *Who Wants to Be a Millionaire?* or *The Weakest Link*, because to us he knew a lot about everything. But he'd always shake his head and smile without saying much. He wasn't an exhibitionist, or even much of an adventurer, preferring the quiet life; but he was a family man through and through, possibly because he had missed out on so much of his own family life when he was at boarding school. Dad was a doer, full of cheery enthusiasm for everything he turned his hand to, and for us there was nothing he couldn't or wouldn't do. And he'd defend me to the death in most family arguments, my mother told to 'go easy on her' (me), my brother told not to 'tell tales' on his big sister. Dad had my back, and he was the most hands-on father and doting husband, the type of dad who would give in to my childish whims and spoil me. Once, at the age of eighteen when I was wearing ridiculous, towering, black open-toe heels in the queue for a club near our house, I rang my father to ask if he'd drop off another, more comfortable pair so I could switch because I could barely walk. Of course he obliged. If life is a bumper-car fairground ride, all the dizzying colours of the world rushing by as you snake your way between multiple obstacles, my dad was the driver, steering always with gentle firmness to prevent me from crashing at the last moment.

My mother always worked part-time while running our home and made sure we were nothing other than impeccably presented for school. Dad was equally organised and the main disciplinarian, but he also had a silly, childish humour which was sometimes replaced by a temporary flash of anger if ever my brother and I conspired to push him to the point of no return (this was usually signalled by a dramatic raising of the voice and the ominous appearance of his tongue poking from the left side of his mouth like a lizard, which meant we needed to get the hell gone because he was on the verge of flipping). My parents' marriage was a happy one, and any arguments they had did not run deep. When they did row, there was no real aggression, no breaks from each other or days spent away from the house. They stuck it out, through thick and thin. They had a laugh together. I remember the time my mum returned from a Sunday afternoon shopping session in Sutton, and my father was called upon to give his verdict on her new dress. He was sitting with his back to us at the computer in the corner of the room, playing his usual war games (my dad was 'addicted to that thing', as my mum used to say) as the smell of roast chicken and roast potatoes wafted in from the kitchen, the heat from the house fogging up the patio doors. I loved those full, cosy weekends at home, freshly ironed uniforms – a checked sundress for me, a blue shirt for my brother – sat ready for the week ahead on the back of the dining room chair. 'Town was packed,' my mother said. 'Heaving,' she added. 'But I got this dress. Now isn't it lovely?' She slipped on a long black frock with long black sleeves and a white, ornate collar around the neck which resembled a teapot doily. 'Da-na! What do you think?' She did a twirl.

I was doing my homework at the dining table in between them both and promptly put down my pen to gawp as Dad spun round in his chair.

'Oh, I didn't know you'd changed religions, Colette, I thought you were Catholic,' my dad said flatly.

'What?' my mother asked with a half-smile on her face because she knew a ribbing was imminent.

'Well, you look like an orthodox Mormon from the eighteenth century in that sack of a thing. Where the hell did you find it?' I collapsed laughing. My glamorous mum, who never attended the shops without her fuchsia Christian Dior lipstick, lashings of mascara and carefully applied bronzer at the bare minimum, looked like some sort of pilgrim in this ankle-skimming 'monstrosity' as my father later called it, the sight of which was just too funny for us all. Mum duly tried to defend her choice at first, but eventually admitted defeat, throwing her head back to laugh. 'Fine, fine, I'll take it back then.'

I used to believe Mum and Dad were total opposites, but when I think about it now, they shared many characteristics and balanced each other out perfectly. If you did not know them well, you might assume they were gentle, generous, fairly reserved people whose emotional displays bordered on the stoic. If you knew them better, you'd realise they were also strong-willed and proud, with tempers that flared occasionally in the privacy of their homes, and a shared sense of quiet rebellion that ran through their core but which I think was largely muted after they had me and my brother. Still, we got glimpses into those parts of their personalities now and again. My mum was fun-loving in a defiant, do-what-I-want kind of way, a trait that I suspect was quickened by her restrictive Catholic upbringing. I remember seeing her anew on the nights when she seemingly ceased to be my mother, nights when I didn't recognise this woman who commanded the attention of whole bars, singing old Irish songs with her brothers in Clare, and dancing around garden furniture at adult BBQs with her friends from the school run. On these nights, my brother and I would see our dad dial down his behaviour. He'd join in with everyone, have a laugh but he'd crack fewer jokes, he'd drink even less. He'd always keep it together so he could take care of the rest of us.

My mother and I had a generally good relationship when I was a child. She'd play 'this little piggy went to market' with my toes, and helped me make up a song entitled 'Walking with my Eyes Closed' that comprised pretty much just that line on repeat for the entirety of our fifteen-minute walk to school every day, but would become something of a morning anthem until I became too big to need an adult chaperone. The distancing that would later strangle a part of our relationship did not exist when I could not fully comprehend the secret at the heart of us. My parents' unity and stability almost, but not quite, extinguished many of the doubts that would later take hold of me.

For all of his incredible characteristics, however, the topic of our difference was totally off-limits between me and my father. When I started piecing together the hidden parts of our history, when I forced myself to take a fresh look at my childhood through the lens of a grieving daughter hungry for answers, I started to pinpoint where things must have pained him. When I look back now, I can see my father's total inability to face up to the fact that I had brown skin, where he had white. I can recognise the blank expression and the rushed, staccato answers or long pauses as both a coping mechanism and a defence tactic. He didn't know what to do with it, the issue remained unresolved.

Whereas I have a distinct memory of my mother encouraging me to identify as white when I was nine years old, I don't recall my dad ever doing the same. But I do remember around the same time, how Dad took me for after-school swimming lessons at our local leisure centre in Carshalton. He was given a form to fill out by the lady on reception relating to my ethnic background (remember these terms are incorrectly used and the form was used to try and infer my 'race'). It was a dry, bright day sometime in autumn; I remember wearing my navy blue, winter uniform. My head just about grazed the top of the counter. I could see my dad, in his dark blue fleece that he wore to work every day (and rarely washed, much to the chagrin of my mother), deliberating for a split second over which box to tick before him. The biro hovered above the page before it was brought down beside a box on the right-hand side, next to a line that said: 'Prefer not to disclose'.

'Dad ... why did you tick that?' I asked as we headed through the barriers and up the blue-carpeted stairs to changing rooms that smelled like chlorine and burnt straight hair.

'Because it's none of anyone's business,' he replied without looking at me but holding my hand.

I don't remember pushing him for a deeper explanation, or bringing it up again at home. But I do recall that feeling of him being there, and not being there; physically holding onto me while avoiding eye contact and the uncomfortable truth between us. I actually don't think I ever discussed that moment with anyone in my life, but it is a memory that remains distinct and defined. What *was* my ethnicity? And why had my father refused to pick an option? Was I black or white, or ... what then? Despite the colossal – and badly kept – secret written all over my body and enshrined in a family-wide silence, I had deduced that something about me was somehow taboo and definitely not up for discussion. And that was a very unsettling thing for a child to contend with, and even more unsettling still when it co-existed with an otherwise happy childhood. My racial heritage existed, clear as day, for many others around me, but at home, the reality of its impact did not – unless I drew attention to it, which I had learned did not result in any meaningful discussion.

When things did get particularly rough or confusing for me, I'd come home to see my father cooking us dinner or my mum ironing my school uniform or my brother playing with his friends in the garden, and reason that whatever worries I had paled into insignificance because I had a family and I should be grateful for that. I didn't allow myself to dwell on the frightening possibility that I might not be related to someone, because what if that meant I had to be separated from my home? I had – almost – everything I needed.

When I was really young and I was told off for answering back, or my mum refused to tell me where the Mini Cheddars in our house were hidden, or my dad didn't let me win at Monopoly or Guess Who, the weight of these so-called micro-injustices would often cause me to pout, frown and let fly that well-worn retort – *'this is the worst day of my life!'* As if my childish mind actually knew and understood back then what a bad day actually looked like – ha! If only I had known. In my childhood there was no such thing as bad days – not really – only days when I didn't get my own way – and the perceived indignity of those moments made it *feel* like something truly horrific was happening. But it wasn't. I didn't truly realise what a bad day was until 12 May 2015 – the day Dad died of cancer. Then again, almost a year later, when I received the DNA test results that told me we weren't father and daughter. Those two days stand out in my memory as the bleakest in my life.

When the results came through that spring, I was at the desk of my women's magazine internship – the third I'd had since leaving university a year and a half before. I was surrounded by piles of expensive clothes, female writers tapping away on MacBooks, old covers of young, white women with gleaming teeth and perfect straight hair hanging from the walls. It was a fluffy, easy and totally incongruous setting in which to receive life-changing news about my identity. That internship had been a decent distraction, as had the two before it, all of them an attempt to mould things back into the shape of something resembling A Normal Life without my father around. Sometimes it worked, at other times everything felt futile, transient, pointless. That day, during that last demotivating stretch of the afternoon (close enough to 5 p.m. that you're desperate to go home but not quite at the point where your boss has left yet so neither can you), I was surreptitiously scrolling through Facebook when the email landed in my inbox.

It was 4.33 p.m. on 18 March 2016, and while I'd been expecting the email, I'd be lying if I said the impact of the results didn't initiate a near full-on breakdown, immediately.

I received a password-protected document, and after a slight internal panic that I'd forgotten my details while trying to keep cool in front of my boss, I was in. At the top of the page was my dad's full name underneath a column entitled 'alleged father'. Next to this was another column called 'probability of paternity', and beneath that was the figure: 0%.

Zero per cent? Zero. Per cent. *Zero*. As in ... nothing at all.

My whole world muted, like a film on pause. Zero per cent. I could feel the air take on a disturbing characteristic of being totally unbreathable as my lungs became pinched. I was choking at my desk, unable to see straight, I couldn't breathe, I couldn't *think*. I closed the window and getting up superslowly because my legs were suddenly in iron casts, I walked outside to the corridor with my phone in my trembling hands. *Zero per cent. How could this be?*

I leaned against a large pillar in the hallway and let large salty tears fall all the way down on to the floor below. Everything slipped out of focus. What the hell was going on? I had to call my mum.

'You need to tell me right now why my DNA test results for me and Dad don't match. It's the same company that does Jeremy Kyle and while I find that show highly classist, I certainly trust that the results aren't faked, so you better tell me.'

'What's wrong?' she said. 'Calm down. What test results? Why are you talking about Jeremy Kyle?'

Standing in the corridor armed with results that completely obliterated my sense of self, garbling about *The Jeremy Kyle Show* in a barely hushed whisper, was not how I'd planned to spend the last few weeks at this internship. (My next move was to nab an internally advertised role as a features writer, my rise to journalistic success would be swift, seamless.) While waiting in agony for the results, I'd looped in and out of email chains with representatives from the DNA lab over various complications (more on that much later) before receiving this set of results. In limbo for weeks due to said complications, I'd tried to maintain my composure at work each day and mentally prepare myself for any eventuality. But of course, somewhat predictably, a set of results that I had not predicted hit me like the weight of a sledgehammer to the skull.

In that moment in the corridor I wished so badly I could return to the past and change it all, travel back to a time when ignorance was bliss, delete my decision to take the test from the stratosphere. But I couldn't. And now, I had to persist. One way or another, I had to peel back the layers of this secret until I got to its messy, viscous centre. And what would I find? I tried desperately to keep my voice steady and low as I told my mum about the test I had processed in secret (a dramatic outburst would have been at odds with the hallowed halls of this pristine mag where I had no friends and very few allies), but panic was rising in my throat like warm bile, and my mascara was starting to streak down my face.

'How, Mum? *How has this happened*?' An editor from the beauty department sauntered past on her way home, shooting a quick look in my direction.

'I don't know, Gina . . . ' came the slow response.

'What do you mean you don't know?'

'Well, I can't understand it myself . . . there must have been a mistake, surely? I don't know why it's saying that about your dad. He wa—' she stopped, 'he *is* your father.'

'Are you sure? Are you absolutely *sure* that you don't know anything else?'

'I don't know, it must be a mistake,' Mum said again, faster this time.

'We need to talk when I get home, OK? And I need to talk to the DNA company again.' Mum stayed quiet, except to agree that we would indeed talk later, and that yes, I should definitely call the lab because was I sure these things were 'all above board'? I wasn't sure. But I wasn't sure of anything any more, I didn't know what or who to believe.

I wiped my face as I prepared to return to my desk. Unable to comprehend the situation I was in, I thought about my mum's tone – cryptic in its calmness. Was she in shock too?

It had to be wrong, I thought. Emboldened, and desperate, I pulled up the email again, re-reading every word beneath that column with my dad's name and the percentage. *'The comparison of the DNA profiles of Georgina Lawton and the alleged father does not support the hypothesis that James William Anthony Lawton is the biological father of Georgina Lawton. Based on testing results obtained from analysis of the DNA loci listed in the technical data, the probability of paternity is 0%.'*

Their words were clinical, callous in their minimalism. I read it again, and again suddenly understood that everything was for ever changed. I had stepped into a different world, a new timeline in which my link to Dad by birth, biology and blood was gone, pulled from the universe for ever. But, then again, it had never really existed. The similarities I'd told myself we shared, the mannerisms and features that I thought bound us together and transcended our obvious differences – they were never true. It was a fallacy, invented by my parents to protect me, and them, from addressing the truth. This test proved that my entire life had been drenched in deceit. My dad was not mine – a simple fact others looking at our family from the outside had suggested again, and again, over the years. It was so ludicrous, so crass and just like everyone had joked about all those times. I was disappointed in all of us. No, worse than that, I was repulsed. And the worst part was, my father wasn't even around to help us make sense of it all, to tell me whether he knew all along, to remind me that nothing would change between us. I could already feel myself losing sight of his love.

As I leaned over the huge circular glass balcony outside the office, a place I had wanted to work in for years, a place of female-focused story-telling, I looked down at the busy lobby – men in suits and pretty women in vertiginous heels and flowy trousers rushing across the marble foyer and pushing through rotating doors – and thought about the flimsiness of personal stories, how everything we believe about ourselves can be destroyed in a split second. Family lore is a powerful force, it can build us up and forge a sense of belonging or exclusion long after we transition into adulthood. Ideas from our parents about who we are form the backbone of our identities, the bedrock to personal truths that we can recite and remember like prayers from Church or poems from school. But they condition us in more powerful ways than lessons from any book or religion ever could. Now the tale of who I thought I was had been dismantled.

I scrolled to the bottom of the email and found the contact number for the DNA lab's customer service before frantically typing it into my phone. After an excruciating wait I was finally put through to a lady with a soothing Yorkshire accent. After explaining the situation I found myself in, I asked her about the likelihood of these results being wrong. Surely that was a possibility?

'We test everything twice here,' a kind voice offered, 'so there's really very little chance of there being a mistake, I'm afraid.' Every word was laced with sympathy, and let me tell you, every word felt like a quick slap to the face.

Tears sprang to my eyes again. 'But you don't understand,' I pleaded. 'I'm not getting any answers from my mum so . . . she said it must be you. It must be the lab because it's not right. It can't be right.'

'I know this must be difficult for you—'

'How much is a re-test? I might need a re-test,' I interrupted.

'You can pay for another test but it will be the same price as before – another hundred pounds. But like I said, there's really very little chance of these results being wrong.'

Well, that was it then. I slouched against a pillar in the hallway. I watched women pouring out of the offices of various other magazines in the building and replayed all the different ways of saying 'zero per cent' in my head. I rolled the phrase over, as if I might somehow have skipped over a meaning hidden within the letters. All I wanted was for that non-number to be wrong, for there to be something in that column that could leave some sort of margin for error. But there was no wriggle room with the word 'zero', no mistaking its value. It left nothing in its wake. Its meaning was author- itarian and absolute.

I fired off a message to Aisling and Emilia in our group chat: 'I need to meet you after work.' They'd known I was awaiting test results that day and didn't ask for more info. We agreed to meet outside Clapham Junction train station at 6.30 p.m. As I walked from the platform towards my best friends through the throng of jostling commuters, I could make out the con- cern etched on to their faces. As I approached, I opened my mouth to speak, but all that came out was a low moan like a half-dead animal. I collapsed into their arms; the girls huddled around me, a human shield behind which I could hide from the whole world, if only for a few seconds. I buried my head between their shoulders and they encased me in a protective hug. It was just us in the middle of a car park in south London; the sound of cars and buses grew quiet, everything beyond us blurred into the backdrop.

The three of us have been in each other's lives since we were eleven and twelve, when Emilia, who sat next to me in all lessons, introduced me to Aisling, with whom she took the bus to school. Our affinity was solidified during our formative teenage years with bed-sharing at house parties and festivals; we each knew how to slot our bodies next to one another after a night out, what drinks to order at the bar when the others were in the loo, how to hold each other's hair back in times of severe inebriation. Aisling and I share an intuitive bond – she is able to suss out my wavelength from a text, or even a mere look, like no one else in my life. Emilia and I could laugh until our sides split. She is an entertainer, the hostess with the mostest and forever in denial about how much she does for her family and friends. Both of them dropped their plans at a moment's notice when my dad was sick and I was falling apart, offering counsel, comfort and strength when I was turning into a totally different version of myself. Since childhood they'd understood more than most that family isn't always perfect. They had navigated their own private challenges with grace and humility, and when mine hit, they instinctively knew how to step up and support. Our bond was not just skin-deep, it was soul-deep.

As I lifted my snotty nose from their jackets, I heard Emilia say something like, 'Those results must be bollocks, I don't believe it,' as Aisling dabbed away at my face with a tissue.

'I don't know, I just . . .' My voice didn't sound like my own.

'But would your mum really lie?' Emilia started tucking one side of her shoulder-length blonde hair behind her ear. 'Why would she do that? She couldn't.'

Aisling looked pensively out into the car park, saying nothing, but an uncharacteristic frown had crept across her face.

'It hasn't ever made sense, and I've believed it. All this time. All this time that *stupid* throwback story didn't mean anything . . .' I stopped as I suddenly saw my life, past, present and future changing before me. 'I don't know who I am.'

'Yes you do. You're still Georgina. You're exactly the same person,' Emilia insisted.

'I'm not.'

I kept replaying all the needless defending of my mum's fidelity as a child, how I had grown fiercely protective over my own family without a secure story to hold on to; all the times I'd been discouraged from asking more questions, instead to accept things as they were presented to me. The silence around this secret had sat in my soul for years. I'd lost track of the number of times I'd been left on my own to ruminate over the story of my birth; and with this news I now felt unable to trust my own instincts, I didn't know myself at all, I didn't know anything any more. Then the world sharpened into focus and I realised I was so angry that I had been robbed of a large section of my life, that I still couldn't access the truth or speak to my dad about it.

'Right, call your mum now – you need to speak to her, and we need to hear what she's saying,' Aisling said firmly.

All of us sat down on the sloped pavement that connected the station car park to the high street. iPhones and eye liner poked precariously from handbags and backpacks. When Mum's voice came through on the other end of the line, it was still steady.

'I don't know what to tell you,' she said again. 'Gina, the test must be wrong.'

This response did not implicate my mother, it was not an admission of fault, nor an apology. There was not a lot I could say. It barely suggested the possibility of knowledge and so kept me in purgatory. I sat there with Aisling and Emilia on the floor, until it got dark and our bums went numb as we discussed a strategy for obtaining answers. My pink pinafore dress had picked up a thin coating of dust, and we'd attracted more than a few furtive glances from passing commuters, but no one had suggested going to a pub or café: to make ourselves more comfortable in such a profoundly uncomfortable situation seemed strange. I couldn't drink; I couldn't even think clearly. Finally, close to 8 p.m., we left each other with another parting hug as we headed back into the station for separate trains.

'We love you, OK?' Aisling said. 'Just go home and tell your mum how much you need to know. She must know something.' I nodded.

'We're here, mate. Just call us any time,' Emilia reassured me, as I finally disentangled myself from their arms and walked away.

As I rested my head against the train window, I watched the houses of south London roll by in the dim glow of the orange street lamps, lighting up the vast plains of a violet sky: first the four-storey Victorian red bricks in Wandsworth and Balham, dissected into expensive flats, then the Edwardian homes on quiet roads in Selhurst with their pointed roofs and white-painted walls, and finally the stout terraced houses with long gardens filled with toys and tiny trampolines and patio furniture in Sutton and Carshalton. This was all I had known. But the bricks and mortar that had formed the foundation of my early life were crumbling beneath my feet; the buildings around me which had once felt safe and familiar were now mocking and false. The world as I knew it had been obliterated, smashed into a million tiny pieces after that email. It was the second crash in a year, and I knew that whichever way I tried, things would never arrange themselves back to the way they had been when Dad was around. I would never be the same person, breathe the same way, move through these places the same way. I was for ever changed. My childhood had ended swiftly and cruelly on the day of Dad's terminal diagnosis, but my connection to him had been maintained by *not* processing that DNA test. I had told myself that I should be happy straddling the frontier of two opposing worlds, one foot in the familiar places in which I'd always stood out, one foot in another world where making up far-away identities appeased others. Finally, though, the protective veneer of my heritage had dissolved, and all that remained was the truth – raw and unwavering and exposed. Those test results left no room for error and so I had to face up to the fact that my entire life had been a lie.

When I walked slowly into the front room, I found my mother staring blankly at the TV. Her eyes were fixed on the images of shiny faces from a reality TV show which neither of us watched. They lit up the room intrusively. We exchanged hellos and I realised that she was waiting for me to speak over them. Why wasn't *she* doing all the talking? Why hadn't *she* scooped me into her arms and told me that everything would be OK just as soon as I had come home? This wasn't looking good. I took my place on the second of our two dark red leather sofas, opposite a framed picture of Dad, which sat on a small table above his urn.

Eventually, I spoke. Just why had the test come back negative? Who was my biological father, if it wasn't Dad? What the hell was going on?

I gestured to his photo, but my mum's gaze stayed fixed on the TV. She repeated that she didn't know, it could be a mistake, it was the lab's fault. I may have said nothing in return. I may have started screaming.

'I don't know what to say.'

'Say what really happened. Tell me what's going on.'

I realised that my mum's near-silence was in stark contrast to all the continuous chatter I'd engaged in over the years about us, about her, about my fate and my family. She was not over-talking. She was not garbling desperately, or pleadingly, with eyes wide and round, in a tone that was high-pitched and urgent in that way characters in films behave when they're playing a guilty person who's been wrongly accused of something. She was letting me do the mental acrobatics as I'd always done. It was a role I had always played.

She must have carried on watching TV in the hope that everything around her could remain unchanged. We must have embraced. I must have cried, texted my mates, perhaps slept at some point. Maybe I ate dinner. Maybe I went straight to bed. I do remember feeling encased by a numbness that night and the nights that followed, which soon gave way to a renewed sense of loss. I tried to sleep and thought who I could be if I didn't really know. I thought about my dad, he was no longer woven into the fabric of my past in the way I had always believed; I felt as if I'd lost him all over again, only this time, I was grieving all by myself.

The difficult days which followed that initial, insane inter-action on the sofa are too painful to go into at length, but involved much of the same – only with a series of histrionic rows that left my throat sore and my blood red-hot. The more answers I demanded of my mum, the more she retreated into herself, paralysed by what I now know was fear. Fear that she would lose me after losing her husband, fear that she would have to face the actions she had long banished to the deepest corners of her mind. But I had lost my father, and now I had lost our lineage, and my connections to my biological grandparents and cousins. Our house was totally saturated in grief. It soaked the carpets, dripping through the ceiling like rainwater from a roof leak and coating me in a ferocious anger, before condensing and rising again, a red steam that wouldn't lift.

I existed in a fugue-like state at work, going through the

motions of writing pithy tweets and captions for spring coats but – unsurprisingly – I was not all there. And I couldn't tell my boss – 'sorry I'm not really with it at the moment, just had some DNA test results that have really bummed me out'. But everything felt so futile. I realised that a large portion of my time since graduating had been spent writing about chlamydia tests and Viagra side-effects (at a health blog internship that was actually in quite a nice team), or adding pictures of Olivia Palermo and Mary-Kate Olsen to galleries called 'Best Blonde Bobs' and 'Leather Looks We Love!' (at women's magazines). After the DNA test result, I was expected to update an entire gallery's worth of captions for 'Victoria Beckham's Street Style' with a selection of words that nearly always made me want to gouge my eyes out with a ruler, for an hourly rate which rarely worked out at more than £18k a year. Pulitzer Prize-worthy it was not. And anyway, why couldn't people see the trauma etched on to my face, smell it on the clothes I was wearing? Why didn't they get it? Of course, the beauty of the human condition is that we cannot possibly relate to one another all the time, about everything. Each of us must carry our own private traumas, heartaches, hopes and dreams at different points in our lives, and we click with the people with whom we have the most commonalities. If we were all dealt the same hand, went through everything at the exact same time, our lives would be dull and meaningless. I learned this at twenty-two, and recognised a callousness and a comfort in that knowledge, in realising that no matter where you are at, or what you are going through, the whims of the world will go on regardless.

After a few strained days in my house, I took a train to Canterbury to stay with Emma, who was working as an English teacher at a school close by. Emma and I met on the first day of university – our rooms divided by a thin wall in

our campus halls – and then we'd lived together for another
two years with our friends Patrick and Luke following the
obligatory move into the town of Leamington Spa. That first
term I knew we were destined to become firm friends after
we spent many a late night howling at reality TV on our
laptops (*The Only Way Is Essex*), swapping bodycon dresses
for attendance to crowded student club nights that served
cheap and nasty alcohol, and pulling all-nighters before
exams (hers Law, mine English). Emma's tactful offer to
assist with my make-up within the first few months of knowing me – 'can I just show you how to fill in your eyebrows,
George?' – turned me into devout brow enthusiast to this
day. Once when we went on a shopping trip to Birmingham's
Bullring mall with the boys from our house, I managed to
lose everyone and Emma called Bullring customer services to
enquire for my well-being (to which they replied they could
only assist if I required medical attention, but I was totally
fine – my phone had just died). Emma is from Belfast, and
possesses that winning Irish combination of symphonic tones
and a perpetually sunny disposition, the kind of friend on
whom you could drop by at a moment's notice and still find
yourself seamlessly slotted into the weekend's plans. When
I arrived at Canterbury train station I found myself pulled
into filled-baguette brunches, flat-white coffee catch-ups and
late-night pub sessions with her new teacher-trainee friends.
I spent most of the weekend trying to keep it together in the
presence of people who didn't know me at all – I hadn't told
Emma why I'd turned up – but when we found ourselves
alone on Sunday, I felt fit to burst. As we walked down the
eerily quiet streets of Canterbury, close to midnight, the lack
of breeze making the Gothic buildings and half-timbered
houses appear all the more imposing, I told Emma of my
test results. Without missing a beat, she pulled me into her

teaching library, which was open all night, so we could talk undisturbed.

'Oh God, George,' she said when I finally got to the end of my tale. 'I can't believe this. Did you ever think the test would come back like this?'

I shook my head, but thought back to the time in our grotty house share in Leamington when I'd revealed to Pat (who'd copied my uni choice and also lived with me for two years), Emma and Luke that I might one day take a DNA test. I remembered the concerned look on Emma's face – 'what if you get a shock result?' – and that I'd told her there was no way that could happen, she had nodded supportively, the boys had said very little, and I'd gone back to leaning on the story that I'd always believed – until now.

'Right, you need to keep pressing her for answers. You need to get your brother involved and keep going until you find out what, exactly, has gone on here. The not knowing has to stop. It's too much for anyone to deal with, you're going to have a breakdown.' She'd gone into full-on teacher mode and I welcomed the direction desperate as I was for someone, anyone, to take control of everything.

Like Aisling and Emilia, she reserved harsh judgement on my mum and wrestled with the idea that something awful might have happened to her.

'Like what mate?'

'Well I don't know, maybe she got attacked? That might be why she's not able to speak.'

I had rolled the idea around in my mind and then discarded it because it was too horrendous to comprehend. If my mum had been raped, if someone had taken advantage of her when she was vulnerable and alone and new to London all those years ago, then none of this was her fault. But then . . . I would be the product of a rape, a rapist's child. Is that why

I had sensed at times a hard-to-define distance between me and my mother? Perhaps I reminded her of someone she detested, someone who had caused her immeasurable pain. Maybe there were unspeakably traumatic circumstances to my birth which had sharpened the edges of our relationship. That night in Emma's bed I walked a thousand different pathways in my mind. But each one took me back to the same, predictable ending.

At the end of the weekend I left Canterbury with Emma's soothing words in my ears. When waiting for a train to Sutton, I called my brother who was still at university. He would return to our home the next day he promised, he would help me speak to our mother.

As my brother had morphed into his final mould, moving from adolescent to almost-man, he had become scarily like our father. He had the same milk-bottle complexion and hairy legs, but he was my dad in nature, too – easy-going, thoughtful, a mediator. His teenage years had ended too soon: he was only in his first year of university when Dad was diagnosed, and what had come after it had slammed the page shut on the chapter of his youth, robbing him of what should have been some of the most carefree times of his life. When I told him of the DNA test result at our kitchen table as we waited for our mum to return from work, he simply repeated that 'it didn't matter' to him and that 'nothing had changed in our family'. But in those moments I realised we had never opened up to each other about our contrasting racial backgrounds. The gaps between us had been plugged with a family lore that had kept us bound together, but in many ways also kept us further apart.

'So, like, have people ever asked you why we don't look anything alike?' I suddenly wondered.

'Yeah, they have.'

'Like who?' I was itching to know how this odd secret had affected my brother, whether he had been waging his own silent war on this issue too.

He paused. 'Well . . . my mates would sometimes say "why is your sister black?" And I'd tell them it was none of their business.'

This defensive refrain is something we learned from our parents. But of course it did little to placate our enquirers and simply made people all the more eager to draw their own conclusions as to the inexplicable nature of our family.

I was suddenly overwhelmed by the reality. 'You're not my brother in the same way any more. Now we really have to say '*half*-brother', '*half*-sister'. None of it sounded right. 'Or maybe we're not even related . . . ' I burst into tears.

My brother got up from his side of the table and enveloped me in a hug. 'You belong here with us, OK? Whatever the outcome, you're still a part of this family. We're always going to be a family.'

I had accepted my father was dead, but I had never fully accepted the idea of not being his daughter, or what that would mean for the relationship between me and my family.

That afternoon, when Mum returned from work, we were ready and waiting, the intervention planned. My brother declared it was time for a 'family chat' as my mother made herself a cup of tea – just as she usually did when she got home from her school reception job at 3 p.m. I sat at the table and watched her take her place opposite me as the warm rays of the late afternoon spring sun poured in through the patio doors, illuminating her face which, I suddenly realised, looked exhausted.

My little brother took control: 'Right, what's going on with these results then? How did we get here? Mum, you're the only one who knows so I think it's time you opened up.'

Mum glanced away as she stirred her tea slowly.

'Do you know what you're putting me through?' I interrupted. 'Do you have any idea the places I've gone to in my own mind these past few days, trying to figure this shit out? I have no fucking clue what is going on. And I feel like I've lost Dad all over again. You're supposed to be my mum and you won't tell me what's happening. This ends now. Today.'

Silence.

'I can tell you're lying – it's not good enough, Mum. Gina deserves answers. We all need answers, so you need to come out with it.'

After a long, heavy pause during which only the birds outside in the garden could be heard, Mum uttered the sentence I had waited all my life to hear.

'OK. There was ... someone else.'

'Talk – now,' I instructed, fearing that if I didn't force the words out of her in that instant, she would somehow reclaim them.

'There was a man one night, in a pub in Shepherd's Bush. But I can't remember anything else.'

Her explanation chilled the room, at long last here was the truth, as predictable and banal as so many had suspected, but it was the truth all the same. But what had he looked like? Where was he from?

'I don't know, that's all I can remember,' came the quick response. I could feel my fists balling up.

'Well, he was black so where was he from? Did he have a Caribbean accent, West African? You must be able to remember something else. What was his name? What does this make me?'

I was now pacing the room. My brother remained standing against the wall, hands in pockets, as he stared at our mum without saying a word.

'He was dark-skinned. Erm, dark hair, dark eyes,' she replied. 'But it was just one night, Gina. I don't have anything else to tell you. Honestly, that's all I can remember.'

'Dark? What does that even mean? The word is "black", Mum.' I felt trapped in a strange satire. 'You have been raising a non-white child in a white home and you have encouraged me to identify like you, and Dad, when that does not work.' I felt tears fall down my face. I got up from where I was sitting to stand above my mum who could not meet my glare. 'You have a mixed-race, black daughter, and even though you've tried so hard to erase that part of me to make it easier for you, it's not going away. Have you any idea what you've done? You've stolen my entire identity. I am black.'

It was the first time I'd ever claimed that word before my family. As soon as the sentences left my lips, I felt their purpose, their vigour.

'I am black,' I repeated, with more confidence. 'I need you to acknowledge that, Mum. I need to hear you say it, because I'm not about to go another second longer trying to be something I'm not.'

'There's nothing wrong with that, Mum,' my brother said. 'You need to acknowledge it, for Christ's sake. This is Gina's whole life, her identity.' We both looked expectantly at our mum.

'Yes, you're . . . well, of course there isn't. You are . . . black.'

I breathed a sigh of relief as the words I'd waited a long time to hear made themselves at home in my house for the first time. The part of me we had tried to ignore for years had audaciously entered the room – and I wasn't about to let anyone close the door on it again.

But I needed more. I couldn't rest until I knew everything. Why wasn't this explained all those times I had questions? Who was my biological father? Was I really expected to believe that my mum's memory stopped at the one-word descriptor she had offered me? He was 'dark', and that was all? What was I supposed to do with that?

My brother stayed at home for a few days in an attempt to mediate the situation, but neither of us could break down the emotional road-block my mother had established to protect herself from divulging more.

'You know half of where you're from. That's enough, isn't it?' she said a few days later when I tried to broach the subject again over lunch at the weekend. 'I can't keep going over this.'

Mum couldn't see that I was only at the very start of these conversations, I was only on the cusp of understanding my new racial identity. There was so much I had learned to keep hidden from her because I had been carrying my parents' carefully concocted narrative, there was so much that she didn't know about me as a result. I had mistakenly thought that the moment in which the truth was revealed would herald an immediate and irreversible journey into a new era of mother-daughter understanding, that my mum would want to hear all about my lived experience – but, alas, that was not to be.

I was an impostor in what was once familiar and safe territory, and the fury that came over me felt dangerous. Space between me and my mother wasn't just necessary, it was crucial. We made small talk but could not engage any deeper than that. If I stayed put I felt sure I would go insane. As I told Emilia on the phone one evening, I had to get out.

My internship ended a few weeks later and I decided to indulge the deep calling within me to leave London. I needed a new city to distract me from myself and to help me process all that had happened. I had decided, before I even booked any flights, that I needed to structure my trip around living in and moving through black spaces. I would walk down streets that had been shaped by communities more diverse than the ones I was used to. I would take time to work out who I wanted to be, and my first stop would be New York City. In truth, this choice also had much to do with my own clichéd desire to carve out a writer's life in the city that had shaped literary greats like James Baldwin and Zora Neale Hurston, a place where I knew havoc and exhilaration existed in equal measure, but really, any space far away enough, and where I could see myself could help me on my journey. I booked a one-way flight to JFK and made last-minute goodbye calls to friends and my brother. On the day I was due to fly, Emilia arrived at my house just as I was loading two oversized suit-cases into a taxi, and we had a tearful hug. 'I'll see you soon in Brooklyn, yeah?' Aisling and Emilia had made plans to visit when I was settled, but the same couldn't be said for my mother who stood awkwardly on the doorstep as my taxi drove up to our house. Neither of us had any idea when we'd speak again, and the impact of that realisation seemed to hit us both simultaneously as my mum embraced me one last time.

'I love you,' she said.

'I love you too, Mum.'

As the car pulled away, I turned around to watch my mum and my best friend waving from my drive, both of them fight-ing back tears. I was beginning to understand how much the secret at the heart of our family had truly affected us, how much it had splintered the love between me and my mother, and even between me and my closest school friends. But my mother was still the woman who had brought me into the world, who had hugged me close to her each and every time I had scraped a knee, who doled out Irish aphorisms when I was in need of wisdom, the woman who smugly recited my good grades to her sisters and who had claimed me, clothed me and cared for me all my life. We were bound for life, inextricably linked, of each other's flesh for ever.

I didn't know if the Airbnb I'd booked was going to work – I'd be living with literal strangers I'd only communicated with via the app – or if I'd have enough freelance work to fund a life in one of the most expensive cities on the planet, or even, indeed, if living in New York alone and with no real plan would be utterly exhausting, but I knew I felt a powerful call to step out and away from my old life, and onto a pathway that was not well trodden, but which could lead me to a bolder and truer version of who I wanted to be. I had to get out. When you are almost, but not quite, at the limit of what you can take, when things feel so incredibly bleak and dark that there seems to be no way out, you cannot sit still in the shadows, alone, and expect the light to find you. You must crack open a window yourself.

6

City is a Pity

I'm homesick, not for America but for Negroes. That's
the trouble.

NELLA LARSEN, *Quicksand*

I had imagined sipping on porn-star martinis with the black
New York literati on the sixty-fifth floor of somebody's glass
penthouse; everyone would be hanging off my every word
simply because I'd pepper my speech with casual British-isms
like 'loo' and 'mate', which everyone would find endearing. It
would be my own version of *Girls*, *Friends* and *Sex in the City*
(only more diverse and with better hair). I'd be independent
in a way I'd never been before, living not just away from
home, but away from the restrictions of an identity that did
not fit me. I'd be free to exist in a space I could carve out for
myself, but also liberated from the fear of doing things I'd
once lacked the self-confidence to do (dating hot black boys,
for one). Too long I'd been stranded in a strange racial purgatory, but no more! America, land of the free, would birth

a more authentic me, a country from which the world's most recognisable black cultural exports came in vast quantities, via sports, music, films, literature and fashion. Black American social identity was unified by the legacy of slavery, but elevated and marketed on a global stage via hyper-capitalism, so there would be no better place to begin my black education. Of course at this stage I still didn't know where my origins lay and I was cautious of overdoing it, of playing up to some tired, embarrassing stereotype of box-ticking on an arbitrary list of blackness, a paint-by-numbers sort of identity that would feel forced and weird, but I knew I wanted to exist in a place where my image was reflected back to me and where English was spoken, so Brooklyn it was.

I'd selected an Airbnb in Crown Heights, a predominantly African-American Caribbean neighbourhood with Jewish enclaves, trendy cafés and grand architecture from its 1930s heyday that I knew would make a welcome change from the homogeneity of Surrey. I took a cheap flight with Norwegian Air and arrived close to 11 p.m. on a mild May evening.

'What's the name of the cross-street?' my temperamental yellow-cab driver demanded in a gruff Caribbean accent as we began the ride from JFK airport to Crown Heights.

'Er, I just have the address with the street on it. Here it is again.' I reached over to show him my phone.

'I need the cross-street.'

Panic. 'I don't know what that is?'

He threw me a look in the rear-view mirror that said *this English girl is a fool*, and followed up with a series of mumbled curses under his breath. I quickly realised there was no alternative and if I wanted to make it to my new home safely, I was going to have to do the unthinkable and spend £10 on half a megabyte of phone data to search for this mythical cross-street. Newbie mistake number one: always know your cross-street.

When I finally arrived at my third-floor apartment on a quiet road, my new room-mates – two African-American women, Asha and Alexis, in their thirties – found my troubles amusing.

'You just gave him a street name? No wonder he was pissed! You can't do that here 'cos our streets are so long. You need to tell them what road we are in between.' The days of plugging a postcode into a taxi app were gone I realised. Asha laughed; she was short, with shoulder-length locks and small eyes that studied me intently.

The woman might as well have been speaking French for all the good that explanation did me (it took me another three months to get the whole cross-street thing). As she spoke, I surveyed the light-starved apartment; the living room/kitchen couldn't have been more than 120 square feet, but it was rammed to the ceiling with cookbooks, hair butters, oils, Tupperware containers, books and general clutter. Alexis – a tall, slender woman with curly red corkscrew curls and a bright, wide smile that would stay hidden until she decided I was worthy of its beauty – eyed me silently while Asha told me how this arrangement was going to unfold: I was to take her room while she would be sleeping on the sofa. I was to pay her direct in cash to avoid the Airbnb charges. I later found out that Alexis's early indifference towards me was because she'd had no idea she would be sharing her space with a random new room-mate from the UK until I arrived *that evening*. Asha, whose name was on the lease, was pocketing all the money ($750 a month) in an audacious act of sub-letting without consulting the one other person she lived with. Newbie lesson number two: never underestimate the level of New York City hustle required to survive.

But by way of some miracle, my six months in the apartment passed without trial or tribulation, and Alexis and I ended up forming a great friendship; she took me to my first Thanksgiving BBQ, we arranged double dates together and raved at rooftop parties in Bed-Stuy (I still remember the crowded, sun-dappled rooftop bar in which I first danced to 'Heard It All Before' by Sunshine Anderson, tapping two swaying, braided women on the shoulder in front of me to ask the name of the song as Alexis stood beside me and laughed). I was introduced to her group of friends, I attended her tap show, and we would spend long evenings discussing heritage and identity in our apartment when Asha was out working at her late-night chef job. With everyone's busy schedules, the tiny apartment, somehow, always managed to avoid feeling crowded.

'You know, your story is sorta the same as so many African-Americans,' Alexis told me one evening as she twisted her hair at the kitchen table and I told her about home. 'We don't know where we came from, we were brought here against our will, and we just have to deal with that. We have to deal with not knowing.'

'But doesn't it make you sad? Angry? Don't you want to know more?' I asked.

'I guess, but . . . this is what it is. I'm African-American. That's it. And there's power in that collective identity.'

One evening, I talked about my mother's defiant silence around my parentage as me, Asha and Alexis all sat in the open-plan kitchen/living room. Asha, opinionated as ever, piped up. 'Your mom got the good D and got confused and that's why she can't talk about it,' she said with a smirk on her face as she stirred something spicy in a large pot on the stove. I stifled a smile as I wondered how, if ever, I would translate that concept to my family back home.

Before I'd finished my last magazine internship in London,
I'd managed to persuade one of the editors to introduce me
to a colleague at their US arm. Weeks of emailing like a
woman possessed finally resulted in two face-to-face meetings at their Manhattan office: one with an editor, another
with their hiring manager in HR. Something in the shape of
excitement rushed over me on the morning of my meeting. I
was twenty-three, brimming with determination and, most
importantly, with contacts, who might be able to help me
land a job – who knew what it could all lead to? But once
I arrived at the office in the bustling heart of mid-town,
moments from the Empire State Building and the south
entrance to Central Park, I quickly learned the meetings had
probably been arranged out of obligation to the UK team. My
affiliation with the company had helped bring me before the
right people, but there were no jobs for a lowly graduate such
as myself, and certainly no internship programmes that came
with the lucrative offer of a sponsorship card. I'd managed
to prise my UK size-eight foot in the door all right, but once
there, I was let down in that typically all-American way, with
pleasantries and promises almost, but not quite, disguising
the rejection, the impact of which only fully sunk in on the
subway home. 'Great, so yeah, we'll keep you on file!' the HR
girl chirped after the briefest of meetings in which no one
from the editorial department was actually present and from
which I could interpret the meaning: *You won't hear from us
again, boo.* As I took the glass elevator down from their tall,
shiny office I surveyed the panoramic views of downtown
New York, the jostling streets and glass skyscrapers jutting
up into the sky like silver ladders, and I wondered if I really
wanted to work here, at another women's magazine at this
point in my life. The commitment to diversity was woefully
poor (I remembered there was one black female celebrity

cover out of twelve back at the UK branch and the look of brazen nonchalance when I'd pointed it out to an editor – 'Oh yeah ...'). I knew now that working my way up at a female title would necessitate writing a lot of stuff that I simply had no interest in. Back in London my editor would shoot me furtive, sideways glances when I pitched pieces on products for curly hair or the ills of white feminism in our weekly meetings, assigning me the daily 300-word celebrity stories instead or putting me on Twitter-duty because I was 'good with emojis'. Something told me that an American magazine would be a similar vibe: the physical embodiment of lip service to wokeness and women's empowerment, but totally hollow in the middle, as if leaning on the buildings even slightly would cause them to collapse in a pile of glitter and hairspray. And American office culture, with its false niceties and blink-and-you'll-miss-it annual leave, would surely be slicker and tougher than anything I'd experienced in London. New York was exhilarating and electric as if I were constantly plugged into my own private source of power while walking around, but to start at the very bottom once again, after years of interning in London, just for the prestige associated with living in New York City, might zap me of my energy. I decided to stick around anyway, allowing myself to be seduced by the drama and the chaos of the place, and landed myself a remote writing job for a women's lifestyle and trending news site. It wasn't exactly the dream, I didn't speak to anyone face-to-face except for the odd Google hangout meeting, and I largely worked in my tiny bedroom or at an overpriced coffee shop on Franklin Avenue, but it meant that I could earn money without obtaining a visa, and had access to a pool of professional editors as I continued to write. Ya girl was making it work.

I spent six months squeezing every last drop of juice from

New York City and loved it. I marvelled at the dizzying sense of opportunity everywhere I went and how I could step into a whole other country simply by crossing the road: entire neighbourhoods separated for Italians, Russians, Jamaicans, Hasidic Jews. My stomach could travel the world in global cuisines without ever leaving Brooklyn. Both London and New York share a fascinating energy brought about by a fusion of cultures, but whereas London sometimes feels reluctant to embrace the mélange, New York would simply fall apart without it. Or is it simply that London is not defined by the physical boundaries of racial separation, and therefore is a city less bothered by it? At that time though, I needed to be bothered by race, I craved conversation around its meaning in relation to who I was. One thing I knew for sure was that the difference in humour, in day-to-day interactions, was palpable. My city was sardonic and introverted, but New Yorkers were unashamedly brash and quick-witted – and they actually talked to each other. Subway carriages weren't semi-silent spaces of stilted interaction like the London tube; asking for directions, chastising someone for stepping on your foot, or discussing the far-too-regular subway diversions and cancellations didn't result in the same look of repulsion as it would back home, as if you'd just sneezed in someone's face instead of uttering a few words before 10 a.m. If New York is the centre of the world, then the subway is surely the centre of the centre; the urban nucleus which fizzes and whirs with the eclectic energy of the people conducting their lives within its carriages. As an extroverted English girl who wasn't used to spending so many days by herself, I loved the random interactions that took place there, finding that they added a bit of colour to my days. My accent also acted as an invitation to conversation which, if I'm honest, I loved. Uber drivers would bestow me with their business card 'in case I needed anything', free margaritas would appear on counters in rooftop bars – 'welcome to New York!' – women on their lunch break would tell me their life story after I had asked for directions, teenagers would tell me they liked my hair, and I'd find myself invited to parties, art exhibitions and theatre shows by people I'd just met. New Yorkers are masters of self-promotion and I marvelled at the way people defined themselves by the career they wanted to have, not the one they were in; barmen were musicians, taxi drivers were actually in real estate and, inspired by the casual self-assurance, I too began introducing myself to others as a 'lifestyle journalist' instead of the intern-cum-remote-writer that I actually was.

When Emilia and Aisling visited in June for a week, my life peaked. Here were my two best friends whose enthusiasm and encouragement affirmed that all my life choices up until this point had been correct because they were here with me, in New York City. When the girls arrived I realised how much I had really been missing that sense of familiarity. In America everything was new, but the girls brought with them old jokes, stories of home, a giant multi-pack of Mini Cheddars (at my request), and reminders of what I had left behind. I missed my mum. I wanted to tell her about my writing role, my friendship with Alexis, of the madness of this city, but we'd barely spoken since I had left. We had strained calls, when my brother acted as the conversational lifeline between us, but when we tried to address all that had happened, what would happen if I returned home, things would escalate and I'd find the call would end abruptly.

When my best friends arrived, though, I was reinvigorated. When life gets tough, or lonely, incredible friends are an energising force more powerful than any sugary snack or artificial drug. They act as nourishment for the mind, body and soul, making you feel as if anything is possible, checking your ego and reminding you of your bad bitch status when self-confidence wanes. All three of us crammed into my room that week in June 2016, rotating between a blow-up bed on the floor and the double bed, reliving the sleepover days of our teenage years. Emilia, a conversational tornado by day, was always the first to drop off after ten minutes of lying down at night whereas myself and Aisling would carry on whispering for hours. In the day we went for sticky Cuban food in Noho with the New York City heat pasting the clothes to our backs; we shopped for backpacks and dresses in the flea-markets of Williamsburg, spent hours wandering around the Brooklyn Museum and asked store assistants to dust our faces with sparkling powders under the bright-white lights of make-up counters in Soho. But the best day of all, and one that stands out as one of the most hedonistic and enjoyable of my entire life, in fact, began with my own impromptu tour around Crown Heights –'this is where I get coffee', 'this is the gym I got a man banned from because he started a fight with me in the weight section' – before taking the subway to Brooklyn bridge, where we staged an impromptu photo shoot with my DSLR. Then we headed to Coney Island, a place of garish amusement park rides and even more garish fairground food offerings (corndogs are weird). We met girls who offered us their condolences about Brexit, and boys who took photos of us for their Instagram page and later sent us the bright, shiny edits (in one Emilia is quite obviously grimacing as the prospect of posing for strangers makes her awks, but she kept the photo as her WhatsApp picture for years). Then I took the girls to Totonno's, a pizza joint that's been around for ever and where the old-school, Italian-American family servers shout at you if you take too long picking a topping or you're blocking the doorway – 'Come on, outa the way!' – but it's all part of the experience, you know? And Aisling swore that place delivered the best pizza of her life. Then at night we headed to Le Bain, a Manhattan rooftop bar on the top floor of the Standard Hotel in the Meatpacking District, with house DJs like the ones we love in London and Berlin, and which has an actual pool beside the dance floor and a pancake bar on the roof. Dressed up and feeling ourselves as we got out of the taxi that night, we were quickly confronted with a large dose of reality when we saw the huge queue snaking around the block. The pavement – sorry, *sidewalk* – was filled with people shuffling slowly forwards, like cattle lining up for an abattoir. In that moment my heart sank – before my inner Rihanna jumped out, that is.

'OK, ladies. Head back and strut,' I informed my friends.

'What?' laughed Emilia.

'I said strut mate.'

Without missing a beat, the three of us threw our heads and shoulders back, sauntering past the bouncers like we were walking the last-ever New York Fashion Week in existence. I noticed heads turn, then . . . nothing. We joined the back of the line. One minute later, there was a tap on our shoulders and we found ourselves escorted to the front – 'come with me' – alongside a handful of young blonde girls in tops and skirts who stood cool and indolent, while we, in typical British fashion, began thanking the bouncers profusely. (I'm sure Emilia might have said she'd thank them by way of writing a review lol.) That night we were high off the fumes of our youth, dancing and drinking until the early hours as Emilia and Aisling, who were both in relationships, broke the hearts of a thousand different, persistent men in the politest way possible. It had been the type of day when nothing could bring us back down to earth, the unpredictable mixing with the exhilarating in a city that whirred with constant possibilities.

But being in North Crown Heights, a neighbourhood which is around 75 per cent black, beneath Bed-Stuy, the birthplace of hip-hop legend Biggie Smalls, was also the perfect place to indulge my identity. I loved the Caribbean bakeries selling doubles (a curried chickpea flatbread from Trinidad), the fresh-food markets packed with complex ice-cream flavours and overpriced leafy vegetables, the novel sight of rabbis spilling out of synagogues in traditional dress in the dead of night as I made my way to bars wearing shorts and pumps in my Uber. This slice of Brooklyn served as a constant reminder of who I was, bringing me closer to myself by reflecting my own brown skin back to me, showing me every day as I walked through diasporic communities, that I was no longer one of the only people of colour I knew. That sense of being hyper-visible, of standing out, was something I had left at home. Blending into the backdrop everywhere I went felt like a warm embrace, like coming home to myself. It's no wonder that during this time in the city, I ended up dating someone black – for the first time. I don't think it was a conscious choice (I certainly wasn't scrolling through dating apps and filtering people by race – we met through mutual friends) and it didn't last very long (a few months tops; this bird isn't meant to be caged), but it perhaps represented a departure from the feelings of self-loathing I had internalised around my identity when living at home.

Being in the States in 2016 developed in me a social consciousness that had been brewing for a long time in my teens, but which I had never been able to access. In not knowing who I was, many of my beliefs were stunted but now, liberated from the lie that had defined me and living far away from home in a city in which blackness was not merely a descriptor, but an irrepressible cultural force, I felt I could look back at my past and use it to teleport myself to a better future, where many other parts of myself would also grow: compassion, determination, ambition, forgiveness. My own personal awakening was happening at the same point in which political landscapes around the world were shifting irrevocably, too. I watched as Black Lives Matter reached its first apex in 2016, the city shutting down to accommodate the protests that were more than just a rallying cry for justice on Twitter, but a living, breathing movement which was spawning copycat versions all over the world. The day after the UK voted to leave the European Union in June 2016, I was with my friends, all of us despondent at the way our country was making headlines around the world. I watched on TV as an unprecedented wave of political discussion and dissent took place back in London and wrote articles about what Brexit could mean for the minority communities back home, of which I could finally see myself a part.

That summer I also attended Afropunk festival with my friend Chris, a native New-Yorker who I'd met through mutual friends and who let me use his bank account for a gym membership (the US banking system, may I add, is trash – why are people still using cheques and what's with the lack of digital banking apps and instant payments?), and with whom I spent rum-fuelled evenings at his apartment reciting rap lyrics (Skepta, Frank, Chance). Chris was from Queens, but lived in Bushwick via a stint in Brixton, south London. With a black mother and white father, Chris is mixed-race, but his green eyes and freckles don't immediately give this away and to anyone not really looking, he is white-passing. In Chris I recognised a duality of being. He's a people person, adept at bringing groups from varying backgrounds together, but I noticed how his black friends and his Bushwick bros rarely interacted, how political conversations could be dialled up or down depending on the company he was in. Chris was comfortable in his cultural identity in a way I envied, but was also adept at code-switching, he understood that his African-American heritage was not always easily detected. At the festival, I asked him about passing and whether he felt exhausted in constantly having to explain a part of himself of which he was staunchly proud.

'In terms of identity and what I am, I'm proud of my blackness and it's at my core,' he told me as Kelela blasted from the speakers at the festival. 'I feel it in a visceral way with how upset I am with how things are in my country'. He paused. 'But to act like I don't have white privilege would be a farce. Years ago when I lived in Brixton, you had the black nationalist papers and the guys handing them out only gave them to black people, and I remember one day, it must have been summer and I had a tan, the dude looked at me, gave me the head nod and a paper. Then in winter that motherfucker would look right past me,' he laughed.

'And you know, I just accept it. That's what it is. Looking the way I do I get a lot of passes. I get an insight into how white people talk and microaggressions and I also get that not all black people will know I am mixed – I might present as another white person to them – and I'm not mad at that, you know.' I had not passed in the same way as Chris had, but as I began to realise, I had passed in other ways; culturally, and as the daughter of my dad.

Music helped immensely in that period. Like many others, I found a common sense of purpose with so much incredible black art and music that emerged from the period, roughly between 2014 and 2016, and which kickstarted something of a modern-day black cultural renaissance. I had watched an exciting resurgence of grime music unfolding back home while Frank Ocean's *Blonde*, Beyoncé's *Lemonade* and Kelela's *Cut for Me* mixtape all formed the soundtrack to my early twenties. But it was Solange's nuanced exploration of black female identity, grief and healing which resonated with me the most during that period. Her fourth album, *A Seat at the Table*, worked like a sweet, soothing balm on my worries, taking me to a place where I was so sure her messages were meant for me, so perfectly timed was that album's release with my own experiences. I immediately recognised her coping mechanisms when she detailed her own methods for escaping an innate sadness: running, singing peacefully and purpose-fully about shopping, travelling to escape grief and naming the existential struggle and mental acrobatics that so often characterise being black and minoritised in a white world, the balancing act that is required to reconcile the private self with the political construction of one's self and the weariness this elicits: 'Man this shit is draining/I'm not really allowed to be mad' she laments on *Mad,* an elegy to black rage. Her words helped me process a lot of my own pain, but also to celebrate the many rituals of black femininity – such as my hair. I had braided it for the first time in New York, and taken the time to care for it properly, revelling in the endless amount of prod-ucts available in those stores. I had finally accepted that I was part of a sisterhood that had recognised and claimed me long before I had chosen it myself, a sisterhood that transcended language and geography, an extension of many who had come before me. If I could remember that, I thought, then I could return to London any time. But I did not want the culture shock to end. After six months I received an offer to write, unpaid, for a celebrity in exchange for legal sponsorship; I decided against it because at the same time I had received an offer to attend a press trip . . . to Vietnam! It was on behalf of the website I was writing for and I wasn't really supposed to accept press trips as there was a whole section in the site's staff manual about how invitations should be forwarded to your assigned editor, as freelancers could not represent the brand and so forth, but do you think I was going to forgo the offer of getting *flewed out* to Vietnam in the name of journalistic transparency? Hell naw.

I was suddenly presented with two incredible offers; an unending red carpet of opportunity had extended before me, and all I had to do was decide when to walk it. In New York I'd spent months being the British beg-friend, desperate for the city to notice me, and just when she had begun to spill some of her secrets to me, I was suddenly distracted by someone else. But I am of the opinion that nothing that is truly for you can ever pass you by. Whenever we find ourselves presented with a seemingly impossible series of choices, before we even vocalise it, we already know which one will serve us best – we just need to be brave enough to follow through. I had always endeavoured to work for myself, to tell stories, to write only about things that interested me, and travel. I knew when that internship offer came through that celebrity news and fashion would never be my portion, but that if I turned it down, I would not be able to afford to support myself in a menial freelance writing role. And so I accepted the press trip with plans to continue travel writing elsewhere afterwards. I would leave New York City and begin a life on the road. The city had gifted me incredible experiences, but if I couldn't secure a visa for a job I loved, best quit while I was ahead.

Vietnam was an indulgent affair; a jam-packed ten days with a group of seven other American female journalists. We wandered through the ethereal town of floating lanterns in Hoi An and learned how to cook traditional Vietnamese dishes like pho (a broth of rice noodles, herbs and meat) and rice pancakes, using locally sourced fresh produce from a nearby market during a cooking course. From the frenetic capital of Ho Chi Minh we took a day trip along the River

Mekong, watching vibrant markets bob somewhat precariously along murky waters, and stopping off for food in a restaurant on the bank surrounded by long grass and flowers that seemed to stretch up to the sky. But it was on a spectacular cruise through Ha Long Bay, one of the five natural wonders of the world, when the reality of where I was and what I was doing finally sank in. As I stood on the deck of our private yacht beneath a totally cloudless sky, I watched the jagged towers of limestone rock in azure blue waters glide by. I had stepped into a mirage. So much of the sorrow and anguish I had been carrying around from the previous two years seemed to melt away, and in that moment I felt totally at peace as an infinite realm of choices and ways of living made themselves known to me. I could return to New York if I wanted to. I could go back to London. I could call my mum. No matter what choices I made, they would always be mine and mine alone, and so there could be no such thing as a wrong decision; everything would work itself out.

7

Did You Lose Your Comb?

'Just a little burn,' the hairdresser said. 'But look
how pretty it is. Wow, girl, you've got the white-
girl swing!'

CHIMAMANDA NGOZI ADICHIE, *Americanah*

On one of my final days in Vietnam, I found myself in
a small house among evergreen hills surrounded by
women I did not know and bundles and bundles of freshly
chopped hair. I looked on in amazement as 400 kilograms
of ponytails swirled around my ankles on the floor like thick
black snakes. The air was damp with the smell of hair, it was
everywhere. Four women sat side by side, legs crossed, on a
linoleum kitchen floor, sorting and counting the bundles,
occasionally rising to weigh each one on an electronic scale
close by. Two others perched on a low blue sofa opposite,
waiting to sell their hair; they would have it cut off and hand
it over in a transaction that would last just a few seconds.
I'd contacted Vietnam's largest hair factory so I could write
a piece tracing the hair extension journey from scalp to shelf

during some free time on my press trip. It was an article I had more than a little personal interest in, because I'd spent years wearing hair extension weaves myself, yet had no idea where they'd come from. I began sourcing extensions from Peckham aged seventeen, taking the forty-minute train ride from my house in Sutton with a friend who bought packets of long, straight brown hair. Peckham was always the cheapest hair-buying option, followed by Brixton, followed by Mitcham which was just ten minutes from Sutton, but which we did not frequent because prices increase the whiter the area. My foray into the world of weave was birthed in Peckham. I wandered into a black hair salon near Rye Lane and found a nimble-fingered Nigerian woman chewing gum indolently, who installed a straw-like, sweetcorn-coloured, Beyoncé-circa-Baby-Boy 24-inch number. I remember going to sixth form the next day to present something in front of the whole school and feeling that my lustrous new head of hair felt totally alien on my scalp. But I would keep that look for another four years and gradually, I began to look forward to the transformative process that came from sourcing Rapunzel-esque locks in pockets of south London, and of course, to the final completed look, which I viewed as *far* more chic than my natural head of curls. A weave had an uplifting effect; I felt more attractive, more sophisticated and I (foolishly) believed that I blended in more among family and friends.

I'd met owners and brothers Nguyen and Phan, whose client-facing names were 'Jack' and 'Tom' (lol), for a tour of both their factory and a village from which they apparently sourced their hair. After a quick exchange of pleasantries in their sorting office in Hanoi, where I'd been given a complimentary bundle of unprocessed curly hair (which I actually still have in a drawer somewhere), I'd climbed into the back

of their car for a journey of almost two hours and enjoyed a
lengthy nap. When I woke up it was in front of a large house
made of concrete blocks off a busy main road. I had no idea
where I was, but was told it belonged to their Aunt Tu. As
I followed the brothers into the house, which was adorned
with bright family photos and red calendars, I realised I had
stepped into the very humble beginnings of the very lucrative
world of hair trading.

'Our aunt, she finds the girls and arranges the cutting of
hair, and we come and collect hair every few weeks,' Nguyen,
a slight man with glasses, told me as I sat down on a faded
floral sofa opposite several women who were sorting and
weighing hair while positioned on tiny blue plastic chairs
that were extremely close to the floor. I was quickly given a
hot cup of lemon tea to sip by Aunt Tu which was tasty but
almost cloying in its sweetness. I was told Tu employed others
who drove through remote villages in the mountains adver-
tising their services by shouting prices through megaphones.
Impromptu haircuts were set up beside the trucks, and the
hair was transported back to Tu, who sold it to her nephews
for an agreed price. It was a full-scale operation, for which
the young women selling their hair rarely received fair remu-
neration. Yet the brothers told me that for locks between 28
and 32 inches long they paid a generous £60 ($75)! And that
hair of 16 to 27 inches could sell for £35–£45 ($50–$60)! In
a country where the average monthly wage was less than £150
($185), these prices sounded somewhat unbelievable, and I
later discovered that £3 ($5) per ponytail was a lot closer to
the national average price. The global hair trading market is
notorious for its lack of regulation and, as I read later, often
exploits women from farming backgrounds and those who
live in abject poverty. But with only the brothers who run
this business to translate and provide prices, that day in their

aunt's house I smiled and took photos on my camera, thinking back to all the packets of hair I had once purchased; how they end up smooth, silky and severely marked-up in price once they leave this house in Hanoi. On the shelves of hair shops from Tottenham to Tooting, one 14-inch, 100g pack of 'remy' hair (meaning all the hair cuticles have been processed in the same direction resulting in a smoother finish) can sell for around £50, the price increasing incrementally if the hair is 'virgin' (denoting its origin from just one donor). But these words are often no more than clever marketing jargon employed by manufacturers to seduce buyers into thinking they're purchasing a high-quality product. The US, China and the UK are the top three global importers of hair respectively, but each country has a hair market devoid of any regulation with buyers unable to detect the hair's quality, or where it has come from. I was duped many times as a teenager, buying hair online that was labelled as pure and unprocessed only to attempt to dye it at home and find that the 'natural black' colour didn't budge a shade.

My time at university was the catalyst for ditching my weaves, which is odd in itself because the University of Warwick, situated on the outskirts of Coventry with a student body living in the white-walled, riverside spa-town of Royal Leamington Spa, must be one of the UK's least diverse higher education settings. In my first year there, I was turned away from the campus hair salon because I was black. My real hair texture was hidden under my weave when I enquired about an appointment yet the Brummie-voiced blonde woman on the desk took one look at me and said: 'Oh, we don't do your type of hair here love,' smiling semi-apologetically, in a tone that conveyed her reluctance to even try. 'Maybe go to an afro salon in Coventry?' I waited until the term ended and I could return to London. In that same undergraduate year, Abi and I were hanging out in my halls after a shift at work one evening and discussing haircare tips. I realised I was so over the manual labour a weave necessitated, the cost involved, the straightening and bleaching of my own hair to conceal the attachments – but I didn't know how to deal with my curls. Abi favoured an all-black 20-inch straight number which covered her natural Afro hair, but she was also more knowledgeable about alternatives and haircare than I was, having learned the basics from her sister, her mother and her neighbour.

'You need to look online,' she recommended as we painted our nails on my single bed, in a shade of soft baby pink which she swears she has never been able to locate since (it was from Asda).

'Online where?'

'YouTube and Instagram. There's a whole black hair movement going on now. Those bloggers will have tips that even the salons won't know about. Just search for girls who look like you.'

And so the shift in mindset began. If I'm honest, I think the physical act of typing in 'mixed-race curly hair tips' or 'black curly haircare routines' into a search box, quite literally, facilitated a change in my thinking, allowing me to embrace not just a label, but the part of myself that had gone unseen at home. My 'favourited' videos and my Instagram 'suggested' pages quickly began to be comprised of brown-skinned women with afro and curly hair as I educated myself on what oils, conditioners and shampoos my particular hair type required, and gradually became obsessed with maintaining a healthy head of hair and sourcing products that produced optimum curl levels of bounce, shine and definition. It was refreshing, suddenly having access to my own portal of advice from black women via the blogs, videos and tutorials in an online discourse known as the natural hair movement, and it slowly started to shape the way I viewed myself, acting as a bridge that connected the version of me that had been constructed at home, with the one I wanted to become.

That day in Vietnam when I watched as the two women perched on sofas received a haircut in front of me, Nguyen was eager to emphasise that if a woman didn't want to lose all her hair she could forgo the blunt bob for a cut that left the outer layers intact.

'Why do they sell it?' I asked.

'Vietnam very hot, they don't want it,' he insisted.

But judging from the long, sleek hairstyles I saw during my time in the country, it was obvious that a large part of Vietnamese femininity was still associated with hair length. What social price do these women pay when they cut and sell their hair I wondered? Are they stigmatised, ridiculed?

I watched as one woman received a layered haircut in front of me while another went for a more drastic chop that left her shiny black hair barely grazing her chin. I suddenly realised this had all been orchestrated for my viewing pleasure, and became concerned that these women might not even have wanted to sell their hair today, that this was an entirely voyeuristic process totally at odds with my role as consumer back in south London. I spent over ten hours with Nguyen and Phan, including a visit to their hair processing factory on the way back, watching teenage girls in masks sort hair that seemed to be spilling up from the floors of the factory itself; they washed it, trimmed it, and picked out the greys and lice on small plastic stools at low tables. I was surprised to see that in order to create the ringlets many black women covet, they wrapped the hair around large steel rods and blasted it, not with chemicals, but with steam. I snapped plenty of photos for my article, and for my own interest, but was banned from taking pictures of the dyeing process. Afterwards the brothers took me for a meal in a swanky restaurant in Hanoi – which actually wasn't too awkward despite the obvious language barrier – and we discussed Vietnamese wedding culture (Nguyen informed me the bridal photoshoots I kept seeing in the street were of Vietnamese couples who weren't yet married but wanted wedding photos for their invitations) before the brothers dropped me back to my hotel in the early evening. I had arranged to spend the day with strangers, two Vietnamese men, in order to learn more about black beauty, and it had been enlightening to say the least. The black haircare industry is valued at an estimated $500 billion[1] and a significant amount of the hair I saw that day would most likely end up on the heads of black women like me back in London, with most of the profit being held by the male gate-keepers of the industry: shop-keepers in Tooting, factory workers in Hanoi. For poor Asian women, long hair brings wealth and opportunity; for the many black women who purchase and install it, this hair places us one step up in the beauty hierarchy. In Vietnam I learned that the female labour involved at both ends of the hair extension trade is largely invisible and irrelevant within this capitalist-patriarch framework. All that really matters is the detachment and reattachment of the hair from one head to another, across the globe.

After Vietnam I booked a one-way flight to Nicaragua where I ended up spending three loose and languid months. The remote writing job secured a very nominal income while I pitched and wrote articles for other brands and started my own lil travel blog. Nicaragua boasted head-turning scenery, budget-friendly prices and, at the time, a status as one of the safest countries in Latin America and the Caribbean. But it remains one of the poorest, a staunchly Catholic and conservative country in which I elicited stares for wearing short shorts in the cities, which were so hot that felt almost airless, and where peaceful protests against the government led to violent suppression and a political crisis just a few months after I left. When I was there, however, I learned Spanish in the town of Leon, full of colourful, colonial architecture and a volcano on which tourists can pay to board down. During a homestay I visited serene locations largely undisturbed by mass tourism. I spent a few days alone on the impossibly green island of Ometepe and each evening I'd watch the fiery sky turn from red to deep pink, the sun dancing then disappearing above the island's twin peak volcanoes which rise majestically out of the sparkling waters of Lake Nicaragua. On that still and verdant island I'd feel bathed in calm, as if the entire landscape – the majestic mountains, volcanoes and crystalline waterfalls around me – were in conversation with each other and possessed their own mystical healing properties, which I absorbed like a sponge.

When I finally ended up on the Corn Islands I was well rested – which was just as well because the pace of life was something different entirely. On Big Corn where I stayed, locals were lively and outspoken, with US rap, Spanish bachata and Jamaican reggae blasting on repeat from all speakers at all times. Locals lived in a rainbow of wooden houses that looped the island; they were mainly of African descent, some with a mix of Latin and indigenous roots. I felt at home on those islands, largely because they were very much in the throes of their own identity crisis too. The mainly black populace lived undisturbed by the politics of the mainland, and with their English surnames I soon learned most were descendants of slaves brought from Jamaica by British settlers and freed in the mid-eighteenth century. Life was breezy and slow, my biggest worries became working out whether to eat fresh fish or lobster for dinner, and I began dating a placid local guy whose low and slow way of speaking was soporific and soothing, and who always had a joint attached to his right hand. So relaxed, he was practically horizontal; our connection was also largely formed in that position too. I was writing and whiling away time with him, spending very little money and felt almost certain that I could embody the spirit of the island, become an *island gyal* and live in a tropical paradise for ever.

One afternoon while having a lobster lunch in a seafront café I met Sonja, a Florida native who boasted a loud and infectious laugh, long thin braids and perfectly smooth, dark skin that masked her true age of forty-something by about twenty years. Sonja had left a corporate job back home after losing her brother and ending a toxic relationship; she was footloose and fancy free, tucking the troubles from home in her back pocket to deal with later – much like me. We began bonding over personal traumas in a way that women who are alone and travelling in search of a friend so often do, but then found ourselves tethered to each other simply because our energies were in sync. I was in awe of her worldly wisdom, her nuggets of shrewd advice, her quick-witted takes on island life; she was like the big sister I'd always wanted or the woman I one day hoped to be. We hit the (one) club on the island together each weekend and swapped stories about the local men. All of them seemed to be compulsive liars; they'd implore us to go on a date with them – a beach stroll, or a fishing trip – and flat-out deny the existence of their own families, even though the island was small enough that we always knew whether they were married, or had kids, or in many cases, both. The brazen insouciance with which these married men pursued tourist women was both outrageous and highly comical, and I had to check on more than one occasion that I was not unwittingly involved in a love triangle myself. I realised that these beautiful islands were plagued with colourism, toxic masculinity and restrictive beauty standards fuelled by Eurocentric ideals, all gifts from their colonial legacy under Britain. The guy I was dating had suggested on more than one occasion I straighten my hair like the other women on the island, stop braiding in my protective style because it 'looked like an old lady' and called me a 'white gal' in front of his friends because he simply could not compute that black women came from England, and of course, a British girlfriend who was white held a little more sway. The irony of coming all the way to a black majority island with my natural hair and grandiose plans to reconcile myself to my fractured identity, only to realise that the pernicious after-effects of slavery were still hanging heavy over the region like a stubborn patch of fog, infiltrating the way the locals carried themselves and the way they related to black tourists, was simply too much.

'Girl,' Sonja started one afternoon as we sipped tequila sunrises on a long stretch of yellow sand, 'slavery on these islands has left this place in a goddamn mess.' She rubbed white sunscreen into her short, shiny legs as we watched a small boat full of fish pull into the shore, the fishermen hauling their catch from the sparkling sea as the pink sun sank into the ocean. 'That motherfucker over there told me I was too dark for him.' She gestured to a tall shoeless man at the bar behind us in a white vest: a local fisherman who was the same complexion as Sonja – a deep, rich mahogany, on which there never exists any sort of blemishes – and who, upon being rejected by her, had subjected her to a series of racialised insults. 'I'm too smart for his bullshit, that's what I am. Get me off this damn island.'

Uncomfortable myths about black inferiority had not

followed me to Nicaragua, but rather, persisted in places I did not expect to find them. Here, in countries shaped by the forces of colonialism, there were similar battles of belonging to be fought, but on different terrain.

In December 2016, I headed to Cuba on my own for a month, with Sonja following a few weeks later. When I arrived in Havana, I was on an assignment with a travel brand, tasked with writing about my experiences on locally run tours covering Afro-Cuban identity and old Cuban cars. But I was incredibly curious to see what life was like in this once-maligned and mysterious Communist country. I was soon seduced; Havana was other-worldly and filled to the brim with American tourists, in the wake of US–Cuban relations thawing. On my first evening I went for a walk and stumbled over the scattered rocks of the cobbled streets of the old town, known as Habana Vieja. I looked up at the pastel-coloured apartment blocks, stacked on top of each other, bathed in the last of the evening's lilac light, lending their dilapidated facades a distinctly romantic quality. Shirtless brown-skinned teenagers were kicking a battered football around the narrow streets, and salsa wafted from window after window, bar after bar. Everything was worth watching, each moment a scene from a telenovela. I had arrived just one month after the death of Fidel Castro, which had sparked a nine-day period of mourning. It was clear Cuba was still reverberating with a country-wide grief mixed with national pride. When it came to race, I couldn't work out what was what. A local guide on my Afro-Cuban tour duly informed me that Castro's social equality reforms had succeeded in creating a country largely untroubled by racial distinctions, and that race relations between black and white Cubans were incredible. In all my homestays and in the streets, I had noticed more blended families than I'd seen in perhaps any country ever; couples of varying shades of black, white and brown with coffee-hued children with corkscrew curls that we would describe as mixed-race back home. And each and every time I spoke to someone Cuban, they would swear allegiance to their recently deceased president, and tell me that their country was something of a racial utopia. One day in Havana I met two brown-skinned Cuban boys in their early twenties who sold second-hand books in the market square of the old city – copies of works by Fidel Castro, Che Guevara and collector's editions of Ernest Hemingway's stories, among their wares piled high in boxes and laid out on tables. In a hybrid language and cultural exchange comprising both English and Spanish, they showed me around their city, took me out to a music warehouse beyond the city and spoke to me about racial inequality under Fidel Castro. 'Racismo, you know, it's not a big deal here,' one said to me as we sauntered past an old man pushing tropical fruits and brown-tinged green vegetables piled high on a rickety cart down a windy street. 'Cuba is very equal country all because of Castro, that is why he was so popular.' But studies show Cuba is racially segregated: a 2019 report shows that 50 per cent of white Cubans have a bank account, versus just 11 per cent of black Cubans, and white Cubans control 98 per cent of the country's private companies.[2] But even though it's not spoken about, there is a general awareness of race and class inequality in Cuba. The same research showed that of 1049 Cubans asked to self-identify their race alongside an interviewer, there was not one single discrepancy between the interviewees' and interviewers' responses. Unlike perhaps some other Latin American countries, blackness is celebrated and recognised by those who have it. Afro-Cubans, who make up 36 per cent of the country, are not blind to the realities of race but the political discourse around this topic makes for difficult analysis: the term 'skin colour' is favoured over 'race' by the government, and measuring and discussing the impact of race in Cuba remains taboo owing to the widespread view that all Cubans are treated equally under Castro's Communism. But racial inequality has been a part of Cuban society since the Spanish conquest when Africans were shipped to Cuba as slaves in the sixteenth century, before arriving in even larger numbers two hundred years later when Cuba morphed into a prosperous sugar colony.[3] But like many other countries, there are few memorials to this hidden past. And as the 2019 report notes, 'ideological rationale and revolutionary rhetoric of national unity and socialist equality introduced an official silence towards race-related matters.' A silence I very much noticed during my incredible month spent there.

With Sonja by my side, I realised that being black in Cuba granted me access to a country that was not accessible to everyone. Cuba has two currencies: CUC, which is pinned to the dollar, and CUP or pesos, which is favoured by locals. With some pesos in my pocket I snuck onto buses for the Cuban price in Cienfuegos, paid local price for salsa clubs in Trinidad, and bought soggy pizza and tiny cups of coffee for a fraction of the tourist cost in the street. Passing for Cubana meant I could hitch-hike in cars meant only for locals – I didn't know it was against the law for tourists to do this though, and one time we got checked by the police. I was told to keep quiet by fellow passengers, much to my confusion, but when the officer found a Lonely Planet guide in my bag, the jig was up! We were all hauled to the station before being released a little later, the driver claiming he didn't know I was passing as a local, me apologising profusely to everyone in broken Spanish. Passing as Cuban meant I observed a genuine camaraderie between people at every level; the parlance, the openness with which they related to one another, the eagerness to help each other make a quick buck from the burgeoning tourist indus-try, is all down to the political system of unity and equality. But I also realised being a black tourist, in a country where blackness puts you at a statistical disadvantage, and images of black women and wealth are not synonymous, also produced challenges. One time Sonja and myself were mistaken for prostitutes when dining out with Dutch friends we'd met in our homestay, then again in the streets of Havana at dusk as American tourists hissed at us, then finally once more when we were almost refused entry to a well-known hotel lobby to use the wifi. Speaking, or protesting loudly, was our saving grace, an act that returned our foreignness to us, a welcome safety blanket. But speaking also blew our cover when we tried to travel inconspicuously, restoring our status to tourists when we did not want it. My time in Cuba reminded me that racially stratified societies are simply inescapable. Even in a country which seemed at surface-level almost devoid of interpersonal racial tensions and with a political system com-mitted to egalitarianism, racial categories and their impact could be seen, felt and measured. After a month Sonja and I parted ways, and I headed to my next stop: Santo Domingo, the capital of the Dominican Republic, where I learned more in a month about my place within the sprawling matrix of the African diaspora than I had in a whole lifetime of living in Sutton.

Santo Domingo is a truly gorgeous but extremely complex city. The people are direct and vivacious, the food is hearty and pork-heavy, and the national struggle with identity, race and hair is often difficult for an outsider to decipher. Being there reminded me of how far I'd come on my own personal journey of self-acceptance six months after leaving home, and three years after first learning how to care for my own natural hair.

I had found a cheap flight to the Dominican Republic from Managua in Nicaragua but had nearly missed the connection in Florida because I was sleeping in the airport lounge, caught between time zones, and my phone clock had not readjusted itself. Oops. I begged airline staff to let me board last-minute, along with a bunch of women on a hen-do who were attempting the same thing. They were in possession of a load of luggage that needed to be checked in, whereas I had just my cute pink backpack which could be stowed as hand luggage, so after further pleading (never underestimate the power of the British accent in the States), I was eventually granted access to my plane on condition that I threw out my liquids – which included *all* my hair products. This was an entirely distressing notion as my stash was NYC-obtained and had therefore looked so impressive, but with the alternative looking like a hotel stay and a brand-new flight, I had no choice. *Everyone's black in the DR, I'll be able to replenish my stock there*, I thought. How very wrong I was.

When I stepped off the plane in February 2017 I entered a world of historic buildings, melting sunsets, vibrant street art and toe-tapping salsa. But I had also stepped into a country that was drenched in a thick coating of racial tension, a tension that was evident in the national obsession with straight, sleek hair, despite the almost entirely black populace. My first lesson in this came on day one at the local supermarket in Santo Domingo, seconds away from where I was staying. To my alarm, the curly-hair products I expected to see in abundance were nowhere to be found. Instead, texturisers and chemical relaxers – which strip afro hair of its kinks by breaking down hair proteins and re-forming them to result in straight hair – lined the shelves. The sweet-smelling gels, curly soufflés and waxy hair butters I'd need to keep my shoulder-length curls poppin'? No ma'am, not here, apparently. As I surveyed the shop, lapping the hair section once, quickly, then more slowly a second time to check I hadn't missed anything, I couldn't shake the profound feeling of having stepped back in time. I was in a Spanish-speaking Caribbean country where most of the women around me could pass as a close relative, a place where everyone came in various shades of glorious brown. But most of the women sported a shoulder-length silky press, or a long, wavy weave not unlike that of the late singer Aaliyah in the mid-nineties. Had I, by some odd twist of fate, been transported back in time? Just when I was about to leave the shop, I spotted a large head of voluminous bouncy ringlets on a small female, bobbing along in the leche (dairy) aisle. Those corkscrew curls! That sheen! And just *how* was it so defined? I approached this mysterious figure with a gentle tap on the shoulder, hoping my Spanish was good enough to elicit this girl to share her product list with me.

'Hola. Um, necesito productos por mi pelo como ti? Erm, me puedes ayudar?'

My accent was far from perfect and my Spanish was peppered with give-away fillers like 'erm' and 'uh'. I'd also found the loose and fast Dominican Spanish, which regularly dropped the 's' sound and was filled with country-specific street slang, near-impossible to understand. So I was fully prepared for this girl to turn on her heel and walk off with a bemused smile, but instead she quickly switched to perfect English and proceeded to direct me to a minuscule section of products I'd missed.

'Sure! Curly products are right over here. It's not a lot but if you need more it's best to go to a specialist shop.'

I thanked her profusely, and the two of us started talking. Her name was Sara, she was just a year younger than me, and although she'd never left the DR, she'd learned her impeccable English from her many interactions with tourists over the years. Sara is the kind of girl whose natural warmth instantly makes you feel seen, and right after that impromptu supermarket meet I knew I'd have a friend for the duration of my time in her country. She was eager to hear all about my life in the UK and took me ice-skating in the city rink with some Polish friends she'd met online, as well as to a traditional Dominican restaurant where she introduced me to 'mofongo', an Afro-Puerto Rican dish of fried mashed plantains, garlic and pork chicharrón, which traces its roots to the West African staple food 'fufu', and which is mouth-wateringly good.

One evening I joined Sara and her friends in Zona Colonial, the historic centre of the capital city, filled with locals and tourists drinking, chatting and hanging out beneath palm trees in that particular way that's embedded in the cultural fabric of Caribbean and Latin countries – and which is nigh-on impossible to do in a British climate. We began talking about her country's obsession with hair and I was told that when applying for jobs in the DR, women like Sara had learned to read the ad requirements for '*buena presencia*' (good presentation): coded language for 'good hair', meaning hair that is straight. In the Dominican Republic, hair is policed in a strict hierarchy, with tightly coiled hair deemed to be '*pelo malo*' (bad hair) at the very bottom. It is not uncommon for women to be offered job roles on the basis that they accept a complimentary chemical straightening treatment first, and college and university interviews often come with unsolicited beauty advice: iron your curls if you want to get ahead and nab a place at a high-ranking institution.

'Curly hair is associated with an artistic, rebellious nature in Dominican society, or you're seen as less put together,' Sara told me as I watched groups of young Dominicans congregate on benches, sipping plastic cups of dark rum. 'At my bank job in the beginning, my curls were seen as an issue, even though I am doing the same work as my straight-haired colleagues. There was a lot of gossiping about me getting fired though. My mom said, "You should do your hair in case you lose your job." In other roles, supermarkets and business jobs, they still pay the women to go to the salon. I actually haven't seen any women in the supermarket with curly hair.'

The idea that supermarket chains are paying for the chemical straightening process of their female workers' hair still blows my mind, and it didn't take me long to realise how straight hair is tightly woven into the national dialogue on race and identity in DR. I was forced to take an interest in it when I was unwittingly dragged into the discourse myself. Just walking around, minding my business in that country as a single black female traveller, was enough to elicit unwelcome comments about both my hair and skin. Yep, *totally random* strangers began hurling comments at me in the street, and after a while it really started to freak me out. Thankfully (for all parties involved, may I add) my Spanish wasn't good enough to clapback, the words sank into my brain slowly and individually – minutes or hours later when I realised that I had actually been dragged. The first time it happened I was strolling lackadaisically through Zona Colonial, where the scorched stone streets were alive with markets selling bric-a-brac and elderly *abuelos* playing checkers in the shade. A man attached to scaffolding above me kindly chastised me for walking in the sun, lest I obtain a tan and – shock, horror – possibly grow darker. At first, I thought I'd misunderstood him and I'd also made a promise to myself looong ago never to waste energy shouting back at wastemen in the street, and so his words didn't register until later. A week later a similar incident occurred when I was in the centre of the city during a street party celebration: a girl on the back of a motorcycle, holding tightly on to the waist of the male driver in front, twisted her head back to shout something about my curls before erupting into a high-pitched cackle and speeding off before I had the chance to respond. I was distracted by the dancing, the carnival parade, and was mid-bite into an empanada, but I managed to pick up on a couple of words before she disappeared: *trenzas* (braids) and *arreglar* (fix). This girl was telling me to sort out my hair, which was down and natural, by way of getting it braided. How kind of her to offer unsolicited beauty advice, right?

But what happened to me is fairly routine in the Dominican Republic for Dominican women, and it was happening to me precisely because people assumed I was a native. Straight hair is a valuable social currency and hair which conforms to Eurocentric ideals is routinely awarded praise, with women who do not perform these beauty rituals paying the price of societal beauty shaming. In 'Good Hair, Bad Hair, Dominican Hair, Haitian Hair',[4] Katie E. Saunders examines the dialogue around hair on the island of Hispaniola, noting that Dominican beauty has been constructed in opposition to Haitian-ness and that *donas* (elderly women), and other members within the local community, uphold these rigorous hair standards by way of chastising those who do not. Community members critique others for their supposedly shoddy appearance, the insinuation being that their appearance is somehow less Dominican as a result. Commonly heard insults from her study include:

'Perdiste el peine?' (Did you lose your comb?)

'Pareces como una Haitiana peinao así.' (You look like a Haitian with your hair like that.)

'Esta te queda feo, alísate!' (That looks ugly on you, straighten it!)

As Saunders adds: 'Insults are usually yelled from the street corners or kitchen windows. The insults do not just reflect an aesthetic preference for straight hair, they also articulate a connection between bad hair and Haitian-ness . . . by manipulating their hair [women] attempt to hide racial blackness, avert the Haitian label, and assert a Dominican identity.'[5]

The warnings I received to tidy my hair and avoid tanning were part of a complex history of anti-Haitian rhetoric within which darker skin was also associated with prostitution or Haitian voodoo practices, and curly hair an undesirable lack of European blood. DR and Haiti may share the same island of Hispaniola which I found out only when I arrived at the airport – geography is not my strong suit, OK? – but the two nations have had a fraught relationship for centuries and the micro-level street prejudice seeps into government immigration policies and back again. A year after I left the island, in 2018, the Dominican government removed birthright citizenship for Haitians, leaving thousands stateless.

But despite my natural hair occasionally provoking comment, I blended in fairly seamlessly in Santo Domingo. Haggling with locals in the markets was easy if I just pointed and said little, and on nights out in noisy bars I could pass as a dominicana until my clumsy footwork and poor sense of rhythm gave me away. But during my time in this sticky and sensual country, I thought once again about how black beauty-shaming is so much more prevalent in places wrought by the forces of colonial rule. Countries like Spain, France, Portugal, the US and Britain have impressed their cultural norms upon Latin America and the Caribbean, leaving emotional wounds as well as economic scars that are embedded, bone-deep, in the bodies of these places. I wasn't angry that people kept offering me unsolicited beauty advice in the DR – I understood why – but it was strange and sad that I'd spent so long trying to alter my hair back home in Britain only to come to a black island, bursting with life and brilliance, and find my appearance was under even more intense scrutiny here. I'd arrived in a country where I was no longer a visible other, but I had also walked into a contentious world shaped by a fusion of oppressive beauty ideals that were born of European influence and enforced by the Dominicans themselves.

It's easy to think of hair-related insults as an issue that is fairly low down in the racial pecking order, a minor problem that plagues poorer countries and has no bearing on our lives back in Europe. I remember telling Sara that I could not imagine forcing my hair through an irreversible chemical process at the insistence of my boss, or being told that the hair which grows naturally from my scalp renders me incompetent for a role for which I have qualifications. But of course this sort of thing *does* happen and has *been* happening for many years in societies we like to think of as progressive.

For black women, hiding our natural hair texture with weaves or straightening treatments that more closely resemble a European aesthetic has simply been expected, certainly up until the mid-2000s. At work, or at school, failure to conform to these pressures quite literally results in sacking, expulsion and discrimination. By now many of us are familiar with numerous examples of this happening. In 2018, twelve-year-old Chikayzea Flanders was placed in isolation on the first day at his secondary school in Fulham after refusing to cut his dreadlocks. In 2017, in New York, a young black woman working at Banana Republic was told by a white male manager that her braids were 'unkempt', 'urban', and she would be unable to obtain shifts until they were removed. And back in 2016 during one of my first internships, I recall watching incredible video footage from Pretoria High School in South Africa where black teenage girls, fed up with being asked to chemically straighten their 'fros to fit in with the former whites-only school uniform code, picketed gates and brandished signs demanding that their teachers 'deal' with their 'nappy' hair. I watched in awe as these incredible young black women fought to reclaim control of their bodies at their place of education – in their country, *in Africa* – which has been routinely committed to their erasure and oppression. It was nothing short of extraordinary, and after global pressure, the school was forced to amend its racist policy code. In the same year, when I was still at the start of my own natural hair journey and not doing anything half as radical (other than trying out avocado oil), a young girl in the Bahamas called Tayhha Deleveaux sparked a viral campaign known as #SupportThePuff when she was suspended from school for wearing her hair in its natural state. I was writing an article on black hair at the time and reached out to her mother Kessa on Facebook. 'I still cannot comprehend why someone's natural hair that grows from their scalp should offend anyone,' she said to me at the time. 'It warms my heart to see so many women of colour embracing their natural beauty regardless of what society dictates. Natural hair should never be an issue.' And she's right. No other group of people bears the burden of hundreds of years of racist, exaggerated hyperbole about their features, other than black people. It has been normalised as such – that to be black means to be pre-judged on our work abilities, our politics, our class and social standing simply because of the texture or styling of the hair that grows from our heads. And the issue with haircare and uniform policies is that they are often made with our exclusion and discomfort as a central premise. Instructing black children to chemically straighten their hair, or banning styles such as braids which keep black hair neat and healthy, is a way of imposing Eurocentric beauty ideals upon those of us who do not look European – which is undoubtedly racist.

We live in a world where black hair – its type and texture – holds significance for a person's life outcomes (particularly if you are female), and as Emma Dabiri, the academic and author of *Don't Touch My Hair*, argues in her book, the treatment of black hair can be read as a continual battle for social and political emancipation all around the world. Black bodies have been stigmatised, politicised and criminalised for centuries, and myths about the inferiority of our hair have been propagated to justify the denial of our rights as human beings. As early as the 1700s, black hair was routinely compared to the wool of sheep by white slave-owners, and by the middle of the century, when black indentured labourers could work for their freedom, the law changed in America and the justification for slavery became race-based,[6] with a far greater focus on our supposed physical differences – one of which was hair. Thomas Jefferson discussed why it would be unfeasible to incorporate African-Americans into a free America in his book 'Notes on the State of Virginia', published in 1784, explaining that whites and blacks were separated by differences that were 'both physical and moral', including the lack of – wait for it – our 'flowing hair', of which Europeans boasted 'a more elegant symmetry of form'.[7] Judges in Virginia's courtrooms in the antebellum South also used hair texture and type to designate racial classification when ruling on cases that centred on a person's claim to freedom. In 1806, when anyone with a drop of black blood could be enslaved, the lawyer St George Tucker declared that a more reliable way to distinguish a negro from other races was to examine his 'flat nose and his wooly head of hair', noting that 'the latter of these characteristics disappears last of all ...' and that the 'woolly' hair of the African was such that 'a man might as easily mistake the glossy, jetty cloathing of an American bear for the wool of a black sheep'.[8] It can be seen that skin colour alone has never been a reliable measure of blackness. In America, racial categories were protected through litigation, with ancestry testimony, medical examinations and hair analysis required to see who was black. By assessing an individual's proximity to African heritage via their hair, as well as their skin, white property rights were protected and these racial determination trials in the political sphere formed the bedrock to racial essentialism in the scientific world. And the effects of this legacy reverberate through black communities to this day. The definition of colourism has expanded to include the preference for not just lighter skin shade, but looser curls that possibly speak to a European heritage. Black women with curly, not afro, hair are seen far more frequently across mainstream TV shows, adverts and social media. And there remains the prevailing expectation that certain textures belong on certain groups. Mixed-heritage or fairer-skinned black persons are not expected to possess afro hair, while comments barely concealing surprise and shock follow darker-skinned women who defy limited expectations with 'long' hair or ringlets. Powerful messages about what type of hair black women 'should' have persist online and in mainstream media, it will continue, dripping into our discussions and institutional dress codes, from a time in which black hair was deemed a determining factor in assessing our humanity.

There is no clearer window to the chaos of the soul than a woman's hair. To paraphrase the American writer, editor and fellow curly-girl Elaine Welteroth, if you want to know about a woman's spiritual and psychological state, take a look at what's going on atop her head. And if you'd met me at four-teen and seen the state of my barnet, you'd have realised there was an identity crisis of dire proportions going on not so deep within. For most of my life my hair was unfamiliar with the specialised moisturising, paraben-free creams and condition-ers that now form the backbone of my curly-hair routine. In fact there was little to no moisturising going on until around the age of fourteen, bar the odd Aussie serum. Back then it was definitely a case of: oil? Don't know her. Black hair requires oil and/or a greasing agent to keep it healthy and moist. Our hair is particularly prone to dryness due to the shape of the hair follicle; the tight coils prevent the natural oil, sebum, from sliding down and coating the hair shaft. This is why straight hair gets greasy; chemically straightened afro hair (when treated properly) appears to retain length a little better because it doesn't 'snap' off which can happen with curly hair, as it breaks more easily. I can safely say that I have only ever been troubled by greasy hair once or twice in my life, when, as an emo-girl, I would forgo washing it for weeks in order to keep my poker-straightened locks in place. But even nowadays I wash it fortnightly at most, and even though my particular curl pattern grows down – as well as out – my hair goes drier than a piece of toast without butter, if I don't seal in my moisture post-shower, with oil and cream. Over time I have worked out what suits my hair, but I remember for the first ten years or so of my life simply using the shampoos and conditioners my parents chose each week at the local supermarket, and although I think Mum knew that John Frieda, Aussie or TRESemmé did a slightly better job than, say, Head & Shoulders, I don't recall having discussions about whether we could seek out products from specialist places, because that would have sparked difficult conversations.

Looking back, though, when it came to my hair there were glimmers of recognition that suggested my parents were aware that they were raising a black child, even if they weren't entirely tuned into it. I remember my mum sourcing a white wide-tooth comb at the recommendation of a stylist in Sutton when I was seven or eight. That beloved, trusty tool lasted for almost twelve years, and was used by me, and my parents, on my hair until one day it just snapped in half. I was gutted. I lost my comb. The only one that worked on my hair. I remember how my mum and dad used it post-bath, combing the conditioner through section by section and tow-elling me dry afterwards. My hair was always washed, clean and knot-free – but it was never fully *done* – as in styled, to the high level that I later noticed was the case in other black families. Dad dealt with it sometimes, but mainly my hair was my mum's domain. She was meticulous when it came to her children's presentation – could not let us attend school with 'a hair out of place', uniforms perfectly ironed, book-bags clean, lunches packed. But funnily enough, most days I ended up coming back from school very much with my hair out of place. In the morning, my mum's styling process involved wrapping a wet finger around a couple of tendrils to temporarily tease them into a defined curl, before 'damp-ing down' the rest of my hair with water and parting it into two bunches or twists. Now this would inevitably expand in volume by the time 3.30 p.m. rolled around; my hair was a puzzle that none of us could ever solve. The hair-defining, strong-hold product of my mother's choice – H_2O – was not enough to tame my relatively low-maintenance coils, and after a day spent running and tumbling and playing at school, they would always revert to their original condition, a candy-floss-type fluff.

As is the case with most children, I got lice from school

at least twice when I was four or five. I'd be scratching my scalp on the way home, and Mum would inspect my head, cursing the lice as she did so – 'those little feckers' – before running me a bath after dinner and drowning my head in a shampoo that stung my nostrils with the pungent stench of tea-tree oil. Fixed on a chair beside me, she'd laboriously pick through every strand of hair with a smaller, nit-killing comb and remove each critter from my head one by one as I slowly drifted off in the cool murky water of our tub.

'A-ha! Got one!' she would announce, triumphantly. When it was over I'd beg her to massage my scalp with her long nails as she soaped up my hair, then hugged me close to her with a towel. I still recall that strange childhood cocktail of drowsiness, dread and excitement that came with staying up far past my bedtime to be bathed and preened, my mum sighing as she cradled my head: 'Oh, it's like doing two heads of hair.'

At home, years later, when my blonde weave had shed and felt flat, I'd enlist the help of my father, who was a great seamstress, to add additional layers of hair when I felt like my look was lacking a bit of va-va-voom.

'Please can you sew in some hair?' I'd ask while sat at the dining-room table watching him play on our giant computer in the corner. He'd sigh, pause the exploding mines and mini soldiers, but swivel around in his chair.

'I don't like doing this,' he'd frown, needle in hand, but he would always take the hair and sew it in, piece by piece.

In July 2017, a few months after I returned from the Dominican Republic, I wrote about my parents' interactions with my hair in the *Guardian,* which provoked an epic and emotional response, especially the online comments related to my father. *What a guy,* people wrote in emails and Facebook messages. *My male relatives wouldn't be adding hair to my head, needle and thread in hand*, said another. *Your dad was special*, someone else told me. And he was, although teenage me certainly took his weave-sewing skills for granted.

My mum tried her best too. The nit-picking was a repeated and necessary act of love, and symbolised my mum interacting with my hair as best she could. She made do, she ensured my curls were clean, without ever talking about where the hell my two heads of hair had come from. It would be many years before I would understand the racialised significance of these mini salon sessions in our home, because really at the time, that is not what they were. My parents and I never spoke about how I viewed my hair, or my decision to mask its texture and colour, but they offered assistance when required without interrogating the larger issue it was causing. Our differences remained undisclosed in verbal terms to each other, but in repeatedly doing my hair for me, my mum and dad displayed the strength of their love, which could almost override any racial discomfort beyond my home. The weave and the extensions may have been my attempt to fit in with the world around me, but my father's needle-and-thread hairdressing skills and my mother's combing were their own ways of reassuring me that we fitted together as a family, and that the bonds of association between us, although partially invisible, were completely unchanging and totally unbreakable.

The online discourse on natural hair has undoubtedly led to some big changes, contributing to a shift in the beauty paradigm in recent years: the stick-thin blondes are out, and curvy, pouty, racially ambiguous wavy-haired women are in. But normative beauty standards remain fixated around white ideals, meaning darker-skinned black women still pay the greatest cost for failing to sufficiently meet such standards while white women who successfully emulate these trends (hello blackfishing) receive the greatest praise. We need to remember that what is beautiful is always constructed by whoever controls the capitalist agenda. There is no escaping the idea that beauty is whiteness, simply because the capitalist-patriarch always has been white too, and the colour of beauty is the colour of power. From our Hollywood actresses to our soap stars and beauty queens, we have spent years defining beauty as one set ideal. Now we're living in strange times when an increased awareness of black beauty and issues of social inequality coincides with an extraordinary backlash against our progress. And so the battle against black hair continues: it is still being discriminated against in workplaces and schools, and certain hair textures are more likely to be stigmatised. Under the UK Equality Act 2010, afro hair is not a 'protected characteristic' like religion, colour and ethnicity, meaning black people can still be discriminated against. But a campaign led by Emma Dabiri to amend the Act and stop hair discrimination gained traction in 2020, suggesting that a societal shift is taking place, if not at a glacial speed. And in the States, hair discrimination has been so pervasive that California and New York passed laws in 2019 that ruled it is illegal to enforce 'race neutral' grooming policies which disproportionately impact persons of colour. So we move (albeit slowly).

When I was nine I remember how my mother and I were turned away from a white hair salon in Sutton, but without further exploration into what that meant, we simply took the bus into Croydon where there were black stylists who trimmed my hair and who could encase it in products that would leave it formed in miniature springs for a few days. But even back then, in the early 2000s, I don't remember having access to any products that were really suitable for mixed-race hair, and there was certainly no one around to point me in the right direction. At first Rochelle from S Club Juniors was someone I wanted to emulate, or Hilary Banks from *The*

Fresh Prince of Bel-Air. But these women had springy and defined curls that I just couldn't achieve, and everywhere else I looked straight hair was pushed as the ideal. In the rare instances I switched on British TV to see a dark-skinned black woman, they were usually straight-haired, like Angelica Bell, Keisha Buchanan and June Sarpong. By the time I was twelve all I wanted was bone-straight hair and luckily the GHD straightener obsession came at just the right time. Heat protectant spray, was, thankfully, provided by my mum, and I remember spending hours gliding the hot plates over my curls with a satisfying sizzle that imbued me with a temporary confidence – which of course lasted only as long as the dry weather did. My emo phase, around the same time, also necessitated straight hair. The confused mixed-race child that I was, I loved the macabre space where I could channel my angst into an all-black wardrobe, drowning out the screaming void inside my confused teenage heart with actual screamo music. I crafted an identity around the musical cult of the saccharine, downloading albums illegally from Limewire and attending mosh-pits where I was the only brown face. Ironically, though, the subculture of emo was, to paraphrase Jay-Z's verse in Drake's song 'Pound Cake', 'whiter than Katy Perry's face is'. The look required a chalk-white pallor, skinny jeans (with an even skinnier physique) and, of course, choppy, straight hair, under which you could avoid eye contact with other humans and disguise your most non-white features. The emo world was entirely undisturbed by kink, coil and wave, straight hair was a prerequisite. (FYI, I only recently found out that the lead singer of one of the era's biggest bands, Pete Wentz of Fall Out Boy, is actually of Jamaican heritage. If I'd known that at thirteen it may have saved me.) To reduce the wrist-killing action of manually straightening my hair each day, a lady came to our house to apply a relaxer, which would transform my hair texture from the root. It burned my scalp but helped maintain an utterly woeful block fringe with less effort. Of course the hair still didn't make me the romantic interest of my male friends, all of whom were white, because every room I walked into, my mixed-race heritage shouted louder than any vocally stretched lead singer of a screamo band could.

I certainly don't think my parents realised how much the invisible weight of society's expectations, and the unspoken pressure of being in all-white environments, led me into a constant war where disguising my hair's natural state became the ultimate goal for many years. My parents certainly told me it was beautiful, that I should style it how I pleased, but fundamentally as a child, I wished for hair like theirs. Historically, the pressure on black women to conform to societal expectations has been overpowering, and existing in the private spaces of white families for many, can add another unconscious layer of pressure.

Take the case of Kelsey Rickards, whose hair texture is very similar to mine, and who was adopted into a white family in Liverpool shortly after she was born in 1994. To avoid having to purchase specialist products, Kelsey's hair was kept shorn for years while her white adopted sister was allowed to have long hair. This led to bullying at school and a gender identity crisis – she was often mistaken for a boy. In an online essay for *Refinery29* in 2019, Kelsey described challenging her parents over their decision to shave her hair after taking control of her curls and starting an Instagram page dedicated to mixed-race haircare as an adult. In her piece (which was largely free of any criticism or anger), she wrote:

> It was always a money excuse. Once, my dad told
> me that he didn't see the problem and that it's 'just

hair'. But it isn't just hair. It's my black hair identity, and I felt as though I had been robbed of it all these years ... Now they finally understand. However, my grandparents don't. Sometimes they tell me I look like I've been dragged through a bush, that my hair looks like a bird's nest, or they tell me to brush my hair to make it look neater, but they don't understand that you can't brush curly hair! I simply roll my eyes at it because I know it doesn't work like that. This is my hair and it's never going to change.[9]

I'm not sure how you successfully navigate a healthy relationship with your family under the weight of loaded assumptions about your hair. And the question soon becomes: well if you hate my hair, what do you really think of me? Interrogating your care-givers over these issues, especially when you are adopted, fostered and plagued with fears around rejection and belonging, as well as the constant reality of being the only racialised other, is no mean feat. Hair is a fundamental part of black female identity, in large because it has been rigorously policed for centuries. The desire to 'manage' or 'control' black hair is an allegory for the way black women have been denied autonomy over their own bodies, not just through the systemic rape and brutal subjugation that occurred in slavery,[10] or the many instances in mental asylums, prisons and camps where women's heads were shaved to strip them of their identity, but in the post-colonial dialogue around female eroticism, and the way in which black women's bodies are routinely failed by the health-care system in the West (one in 2500 black women died in pregnancy in the UK between 2014 and 2016,[11] whereas for white women it was five times less; and in the US, infants born to black mothers die at twice the rate as those born to white mothers[12]). There are many depressing, proven disparities in how we treat black and white bodies, so it must stand that because hair is an extension of ourselves, not all hair is treated equally, either. For black women in white families who have been denied agency over hairstyling due to their care-givers' perception that the texture or type is too 'much' or too 'difficult', there exists the disturbing message lurking not too far beneath this that somehow you as a person in your natural state, are also just a bit too much for them to handle.

Black women are estimated to spend around six times more on haircare than other demographics, and the global hair extensions market is expected to reach over $5 billion by 2024.[13] In the UK, most of the black hair shops in London are owned by South Asian families. Walking into one of these hair shops today still feels a lot like returning to the land that time forgot: the carpets are stained and cobalt, the packaging outdated, the shop assistants often woefully misinformed about the product specifications. But black-owned alternatives, online marketplaces such as The Good Hair Club, and swish retail spaces like Peckham Palms, have sprung up in recent years to cater to women who are after a more tailored hair experience. Someone else who understands the importance of black hair presentation within white families is Gina Knight, a 37-year-old wig-maker and hair blogger from London who was fostered, or farmed, by a white family after a decision made by her Nigerian single mum. We speak after I have returned from my travels, and the Dominican Republic is just a distant memory, a dot on a very cold British horizon. Gina's story is one of a transracial upbringing too, and I'm eager to see if there will be shared reference points in our stories.

'When my biological mum came back to visit she would do my hair because she thought it was picky, and then it was a source of pain,' Gina recounted to me over Skype one cold September evening in 2019 as she reclined on her bed wearing black-rimmed glasses. Her head was shaved and looking moisturised. 'But when it was my foster mum my hair was a source of embarrassment.'

Gina was placed in the care of a white family in South Norwood, south-west London. The motivations for black mothers farming their children out to the care of white families are varied, but usually it is done to buy time while they earn money and set up a new home, in a new country. But when Gina was six it was decided she would stay with her foster family permanently, and her Nigerian mum visited intermittently throughout her childhood.

For Gina, the 'embarrassment' linked to her position as a black child in a white, 'low-key racist' home was exacerbated by her family's inability to care for her afro hair.

'My foster mum cut off my hair as a kid because she thought it looked cute. I looked like a kid from the Live Aid video. I learned to do my hair from about ten because I thought, "This can't go on when I get to secondary school!" I watched my Jamaican neighbours who would plait it for me, then I got myself a little relaxer during the time of the band En Vogue, then I had a fringe in my face like an emo girl. Learning to do my own hair has become my way of having something to talk about with other black women. I've always been about hair. I'm a blogger who talks about hair, and it's basically how I managed to find some black friends.'

Gina suffered with alopecia during both her pregnancies and began making wigs, which she soon found were loved by other women. She quickly turned the demand into a business. 'I never feel out of place when talking about hair with women – it's made the transition easier and it's something I know and love. Our hair is us. When we're talking about afro hair, we know we're talking about black, brown women, and there's no getting away from that.'

It's a wonderful sentiment, and one with which I agree. Discussing black hair with other women over the years has resulted in impromptu product recommendations, street-side compliments and conversation, and closer bonds with many friends. I love how hair, and our experiences caring for it, can be a testament to the resilient and unifying nature of black beauty – and black women. Despite the struggles with the straighteners, the disasters with the relaxers, the ill-fated fringes and the constant coaxing and coating of our curls and coils in creams, milks and butters designed to disguise our hair's true texture, we love the versatility and power of afro hair. There really is, as Gina said, 'no getting away' from that.

Before I left the Dominican Republic in 2017, my new friend Sara told me about her country's burgeoning natural hair movement, led in the main by Miss Rizos, a salon in Santo Domingo that caters to curly hair. Run by Dominican-American Carolina Contreras, the salon is placed on the top floor of a tall colonial building with balconies overlooking the street, and shelves full of dreamy products for curly and afro hair. When I walked in I marvelled at the curly-hair mecca I'd discovered. I surveyed the curls being carefully treated by stylists sporting long braids and hair of various shades of blue, pink and purple. I spoke with Carolina herself, who told me that the salon didn't even do straightening treatments, only curls and natural styles. She'd quickly established a global reputation as an advocate of black hair, with news coverage around the world focusing on her work. As I opted for a wash and cut and took pictures for an article that I never actually ended up writing, Carolina, with her shoulder-length shiny black ringlets and berry-red lipstick, told me she'd set up the salon in 2014 to counter the negative stereotypes surrounding black women's hair, and to put a stop to hair discrimination in the DR. She ran workshops in schools, had spoken on national TV, and had established herself not just as a curl connoisseur but as a champion for societal change. I left with neater, healthier hair, five small cane-rows braided into the left side of my head, a T-shirt that read 'I ♥ mi pajón' (I love my afro), and the warm feeling there was definitely space for curly hair to be fully celebrated in this beautiful country.

That night I ended up in a dark bar, with eclectic art and bric-a-brac adorning the walls, somewhere outside Santo Domingo. By chance I ended up on a table with Yaritza Ramírez, Miss Dominican Republic 2013 and Miss World 1st Runner-up 2016. Also there, somewhat unbelievably, was the famed African-American artist Kehinde Wiley, whose incredible portraits rcimagining black masculinity I'd seen at an exhibition at the Brooklyn Museum in 2015 which had left a profound impact on me, and who was invited to paint Barack Obama's portrait in 2017. Kehinde told me about his journey into art, his inspirations, and why he loved taking time to chill in the Dominican Republic. Yaritza, who had worn her natural curls in all her beauty pageants and made headlines around the world as a result, spoke to me about the importance of curly-haired representation in her country. We all took selfies together, swapped Instagram handles and hit the shots while I fan-girled (hard) and thought about all the things that had led me up to this point.

In that moment it felt like I was exactly where I should be, that my very bumpy journey was being smoothed and shaped by my travels to black spaces and the interactions with the stories I was hearing along the way. Despite the low-level hair shaming, I'd dared to dive into the Dominican Republic and ended up with a greater understanding of my hair, my power and the type of woman I wanted to be as a result. Oh, and I'd done it on a trip all alone, with only myself to rely on. I felt ready to return to London, to face my mum and create a new relationship between us, one that was to be based on truth and trust.

8

Shame

I am not tragically colored. There is no great sorrow
dammed up in my soul, nor lurking behind my eyes.

ZORA NEALE HURSTON, *How It Feels to be Colored Me*

At 4.30 p.m. on 14 May 2017, my plane from Morocco,
the last stop on my travels, touched down at London
Gatwick with a thud. I was home. I shed silent tears in
my window seat as the jet slowed to a halt against a bleak
concrete-grey sky. Drizzle lined the outside of the windows.
Yep, I was definitely back in London. I felt simultaneously
disconcerted and excited by everything English again; the
writing on the street signs, the stoutness of the buildings, the
weak and watery coffee in the airport. But the unshakeable
feeling that I had so much to do, so much to fix, immediately came upon me as I entered the Arrivals lounge. Would
I live at home with my mum? If so, would we get along? I'll
also admit the paltry rates offered in the realm of freelance
journalism didn't seem quite so appealing when negotiated

from my childhood bedroom. The image of the woman I wanted to be – successful, self-assured (and with a few Gs in the bank – let's geddit) sparkled in the mirror of my mind, a perfect vision, but reaching out and recreating her might prove trickier than expected. And what I didn't want was to revert back to frustrations that had led me to leave; I would not allow myself to sink into inertia, I would carve my own path in London one way or another.

My mum and brother met me in the airport lounge. I was dragging two heavy suitcases and a backpack stuffed with pointless souvenirs from Cuba and Vietnam. I saw that my brother was holding a giant packet of Mini Cheddars as a welcome home gift beside a trolley for my bags (I have a strange, inexplicable addiction to these cheesy baked biscuits marketed as crisps, and they had not graced my lips since the girls brought over a multipack upon visiting me in New York, eight months earlier).

'Gina. Good to have you home,' my brother said with a firm hug and a big smile.

'Thanks, it's good to be back,' I said in a voice that sounded as if I meant the exact opposite.

My mum was beside him waiting to hug me too, beaming and glamorous as usual in her pink lipstick and turquoise knitted jumper.

'Welcome back, Gina.'

'Thanks, Mum.'

We had a long, tight embrace. I breathed in the smell of her Coco Chanel perfume which lingered in her hair, her neck. Whenever I caught a whiff of that scent abroad it always transported me back home, to Mum. In the hug she felt smaller somehow, or perhaps I had just forgotten what it felt like to be held by her. Since I'd reached teenhood, I'd towered over my mum; I am almost 5ft 9in, a good five inches taller than her, a fact I became more conscious of before I left the UK when I was the tall, angry shouting daughter but of course there were many, many years when I was the baby and I received ample cradling and protection. As my mum drove us out of the car park with my brother repeating all the automated sat-nav directions to her, I thought about how our roles had changed in the time since I'd lost my dad, and whether we would be able to find each other as mother and daughter again.

In the first couple of months back, a series of interesting events unfolded. Aisling and Emilia organised a surprise welcome-home party with the girls from school, which was wonderful and a total and utter surprise. Then, I landed a job as a writer for a youth charity where I headed up the site content, writing articles for young people on careers, mental health and education. It was in Old Street with a regular salary and a young team who all had their own interests outside of work, and bosses who didn't mind if I ate porridge at my desk at 10 a.m. or asked to leave work early to go to therapy. The job gave me time to manage my freelance writing, and I wrote my first feature for the *Guardian* about my upbringing, which went viral, racking up twenty thousand shares and almost 800,000 page views in a weekend. This led to the feature on black hair and the role my parents played in looking after it, which also elicited a huge online response and resulted in me being asked to write a column in the *Guardian Weekend* family section. It all happened pretty fast, but each week I found myself given the same slot to write eight hundred words on whatever I wanted; race, identity, family, dating, renting, MeToo, Meghan Markle. It was a huge stepping stone career-wise, placing me firmly on the journalistic map in a way my sporadic travel articles for smaller publications just hadn't done and imbuing me with a confidence to carry on writing. The column also became an incredible way to connect with other people around the world with whom I shared many similarities. In the middle of working all my own stuff out, I was contacted by adoptees, those in the throes of a DNA-test-induced identity crisis, white parents asking how best to navigate race with their black children, and black children requesting tips on how to stage difficult conversations with white carers. I became a sounding board for others who had been raised in white spaces, receiving several emails a week from all over the world. Sometimes it was overwhelming, finding myself acting like an impromptu agony aunt late at night, or on my lunch-break in Shoreditch, hastily typing out messages between quick bites of Korean chicken, hoping that I would strike the right balance of empathy and support. But after a while I became captivated by the sense of community unfolding in my inbox. These messages also gave me a sense of purpose, encouraging me to continue writing when I was still unsure if discussing identity on such a public platform was the right move for my career and my family. My mother hated it; she found it exposing – 'I don't want everyone knowing our business' – but I found it liberating. Writing my truth legitimised what had happened in our home, it motivated me to demand more from those around me and it helped me find my voice, both in the political and writing sense. Naming what had gone on, living without the secret on my shoulders, unburdened me, I felt lighter, brighter. It was a way to immortalise my father, to understand my mother and perhaps it would bring me into contact with the black biological family who didn't yet know I existed. Writing has always been as instinctual and natural to me as breathing, not merely as a tool for self-expression, but more an urgent means for survival. Back in London I became worried that if I stopped, I would suffocate, that the atmosphere I was in would cease to become liveable. So I didn't; I kept going.

During this period, however, a cold depression crept up on me like a coating of frost. I moved out of my home in Sutton and into a dust-filled house-share in south London with a dodgy landlord who repeatedly asked me out for a drink and turned up unannounced to collect his post (among which were several court summons and fines), and a white couple a few years older than me, let's call them Adam and Hannah, who were actually warring with the fourth housemate over the rent before I moved in. It started off as OK enough, but Hannah and Adam subjected me to so many racist jokes that I began to feel terrifyingly self-conscious about everything I was doing. I had picked the house simply because the rent was low. Adam and Hannah had seemed normal and I had (naively) believed that a shared class background and similar upbringing would be enough of a common denominator between us all – it was not.

Adam and Hannah each possessed an individual air of superiority that I suspect was always within them, but which quickened when they saw it reflected in one another, a bona fide match made in heaven. Hannah was the type to go on about her volunteering stint in Thailand and how she had been 'stereotyped' in London because of her mild regional accent. Adam, who had been in the sea cadets when younger, once knocked on my door at 10 p.m. to inform me that I'd left crumbs on the kitchen countertop, and would I mind being more careful? Living with a couple is shit. It's one opinion, one personality, basically, but two bodies and two sets of eyes on you instead of one. A few weeks after moving in it quickly became apparent that I was a racial spectacle, too. If I walked around in shorts, Hannah would comment on my 'Brazilian body shape' – whatever that even meant. When I cooked with chilli peppers from the market, Adam would feign a dramatic cough, his eyes widening in mock horror at my 'exotic' meal. I was told my 'afro hair' was 'clogging up the hoover', that I had more in common with Hannah's three-legged black cat because – wait for it – we were both 'double minorities'. Adam scoffed that the local Caribbean takeaway must be full of drug dealers, a 'joke' he claimed that he heard from the landlord, which was fine because he was Jamaican. I was living in a heightened state of daily anxiety, waiting for the next remark at my expense; I never wanted to return home after work. I now know that these thinly veiled, racist comments are microaggressions, and they are impossibly hard to call out, not least because the perpetrators will often deny that racism is at their root, while imploring you to 'lighten up'. When I finally mustered up the courage to challenge Hannah and Adam, I was met with a firm dose of steely defensiveness. One day something happened that they expected me to find funny: Adam had returned from cycling one Saturday afternoon, covered in oil smudges. 'Are you *blacking up* to make Georgina feel less alone in the house?' Hannah had laughed. I didn't call it out, I didn't even call a friend. I didn't know what I was experiencing, how to name it, what it was, and so I went to my room and sat on my bed, alone. When I requested a house meeting with the three of us, I rattled off everything that I'd made a note of on my phone. What followed was a two-against-one case of racial tug-of-war: I was over-sensitive, the blacking-up comment hadn't happened like that, and I shouldn't be offended because they had 'ethnic friends'! Attempting to make them understand the discomfort that comes from sharing an all-white house with strangers who spoke disparagingly of the black populace on the formerly working-class street on which we lived, Adam replied: 'What about me, don't you think it's hard for me too?'

Microaggressions are an insidious form of racism often found in our most interpersonal of relationships – between workmates, housemates, our family and friends. This makes highlighting them particularly terrifying for many of us as the fear of severing important ties or upsetting those close to us is real. But there is no one-size-fits-all panacea for halting them. Staged conversations with notes allow for greater preparation, while calling them out at the time requires confidence. It took me months before I challenged Adam and Hannah – I didn't trust myself or my feelings – then when I did, I was racially gaslighted. Seeds of uncertainty were planted in my mind that made me think I had misinterpreted their remarks.

Hannah and Adam eventually moved out. Their move initiated some difficult conversations with the people who had encouraged me to stay quiet. We have come a long way since then, and I count myself lucky to have family and friends who fully see and hear me, but at the time it felt as if I were drowning in plain sight with no one able to pull me to safety. The incident also caused me to interrogate my own privilege. I was from a similar class background to my housemates, we were earning a similar wage, we talked the same way, had gone to similarly good universities, mine being the best, may I add (sorry but this is the one and only time I can flex about having gone to Warwick!), yet I learned that a shared cultural background cannot shield you from racial discrimination in any space. So-called 'hipster' racism, from well-meaning, middle-class white people, is everywhere. To them, black skin comes with the weight of loaded assumptions that class and accent and education can never eradicate.

And despite each of us aiding the rapid changes in the area, playing our part in the displacement of locals, helping the rents reach eye-watering heights, I realised then I am not the poster-girl for gentrification, the narrative of which revolves

around wealthy, young (white) people moving into historically poor (black) neighbourhoods and transforming them in
the process. Gentrification brings many changes, from which
I have undoubtedly benefited, but it also brings with it a sense
of entitlement and general discomfort from the many who
cannot 'clean up' the area quickly enough. Gentrification is
about ownership and power and belonging, and is a result of
a profit-driven capitalist society in which the colour of money
is overwhelmingly white. Affluent black people, living or renting in a poor area, will undoubtedly be set apart from their
racial and class counterparts, transitioning from outsider to
insider and back again. If I were to walk into a hip new wine
bar on Coldharbour Lane dressed in trainers and a shabby
tracksuit with the old 'fro free and unkempt, my blackness
would serve as an immediate marker of my difference – I
would not meet the expected and standardised look of the
clientele in more ways than one. My presence might elicit a
worried look from bar staff at best, a complete refusal of entry
at worst. Living in that house was a constant reminder of the
contradictory parts of my identity, and it would be down to
me and me alone, to learn how to navigate that successfully.

Thankfully at a time when this was going on, I was
surrounded by friends who got it, and could affirm my experiences as valid. Outside of work and freelancing, I became
involved with *gal-dem,* the online and print magazine for non-
binary people and women of colour. Right before I'd flown
home, I'd contacted a girl whose writing had grabbed my
attention. Charlie Brinkhurst-Cuff, one of *gal-dem*'s founding
editors, agreed to meet me at a vegan café in Peckham and to
this day she remains the only great friend I have ever met on
Twitter. That afternoon we bonded over our freelancing tales
of woe, and similarly dismal dating stories; we plotted world
domination and later, Charlie helped me make sense of much

of what was going on in my life, offering support and counsel. Over the next few months I watched in awe as Charlie
assisted *gal-dem*'s dynamic and impossibly stylish founder,
Liv Little, with securing funding to turn the magazine into
a fully fledged, award-winning new-media business, publishing irreverent, provocative articles that totally disrupted the
mainstream media landscape. A brief stint working with the
team meant I was drafted in to help edit the Opinion section,
commissioned to write a piece on the DNA-testing industry
for their hugely successful *Guardian Weekend* takeover and
to meet readers at their events. Charlie, who is the hardest
working person I know, quickly became a consistent ray of
light in my London life, not just because we were both mixed-
race, into journalism and excellent at cooking, but because we
were matched in ambition and sense of fun – and it's so hard
to make (and keep) good friends as an adult in a big city, so
when you find one, you don't let them go.

Around this time I began attending counselling sessions
twice a week. Each Wednesday at 6 p.m. my mum and I
would see a family therapist called Justine; the other session
was with my own therapist, Anthea, a black woman whom
Justine recommended. At first, the joint therapy was a lot
more taxing than my solo sessions with Anthea, which
I actually ended up looking forward to after a couple of
months. Anthea helped me make sense of myself and my
thoughts in a judgement-free space. Initially she was conscious of imprinting her thoughts and views on me when I
was still working them out for myself but we talked about
my mother, my dad, things that had happened in the past,
things that were happening at the time, stories in the news,
but mainly the psychological impact of having had my race
denied within an otherwise loving home, and how that
had shaped me. For a long time I was depressed, the kind

of depression that is bad, but not so bad that you cannot function, but which feels rather like dragging an invisible concrete block around your neck. And as is often the case with an invisible illness, there is an embarrassment around naming it. I was ashamed to claim it as depression at all. I tried to keep it at bay by distracting myself: online shopping, Uber Eats, app-dating and papering over the pain until the early hours with chemically induced highs, which predictably led to some cataclysmic lows. I went to work and hit the gym hard. I met my friends. I wrote my column and journal. I maintained a life that belied a level of some normality, but in Nando's one evening in Peckham with Emilia and Aisling I had a breakdown at the table, and then afterwards I had to go back to the house-share of horrors. When counselling with my mother was also not going well, it brought on a loneliness that cut bone-deep. I missed my father immensely and I missed my old life with my family more than ever. Anthea reminded me that I hadn't had a lot of time to grieve the second loss, the one that separated me and my dad in a different way. 'I think what you're going through could be a lot of delayed grief,' she said to me one evening, at her home in south London where the sessions took place. 'You left the UK before you had really processed the loss of the biological bond between you and your dad.' She was right – a few weeks after the DNA test revelations and I was off, catching flights, with little to no regard for my feelings. There had been no conscious effort to engage with the impact of all that had happened. I had returned to London expecting everything to fall perfectly into place, but it would not unless I put in the time and work. After all, you cannot heal what you do not feel. Anthea encouraged me not to rush my recovery, and in her sessions I felt free and able to express myself fully. But the joint sessions with my mum, on the other hand, felt like a prison from which I was constantly plotting my escape; I was always slightly late, almost on purpose, as if to delay the sessions starting because oh, I don't know, unravelling the fabric of our lives together as a mother and daughter who have been bound by silence and denial, and who are united in grief for my dad but not in our show of love for each other, was not exactly something I found myself looking forward to each week after work. My mother was paying for the sessions, and so naturally took my lateness as a refusal of compliance. But even she was a reluctant participant at first, furious at having to discuss with a stranger what she had kept under wraps for so many years. I watched as she closed up like a leaf at dusk whenever she was expected to speak for more than a few minutes. My mum, who is generous and eternally optimistic, has also never been one for melodramatic displays of emotion or long-winded discussions; she would just rather have not been there.

One cold evening in November, I made my way to counselling again, my feet heavy and reluctant as I dragged them up to the top floor of the converted Victorian house tucked off a busy main road in Balham. Each room belonged to a different therapist, and I wondered that evening how many secrets this house had heard. How many *sorrys* and *I love yous* and *I hate yous* had bled into these walls and fallen into the laps of the counsellors who had tried to placate, how many lives had been pulled apart at the seams and patched up.

'So, what are we talking about this week?' Justine asked. She was seated opposite us, and my mother and I sat beside each other in matching, wooden-frame, salon armchairs with large gold cushions that were hard to pull yourself up from. In the previous weeks we had touched upon how my father's absence had affected us both, how we both needed each other more than we realised, but we had not yet analysed the origins of the secret and there were things I needed to learn, in order to better understand my mum.

'I want to know …' I started, finally. 'I want to know, Mum, how this all went on for so long. I've had to work everything out on my own and I just need to know how it started.' My tone is unwavering. From the corner of my eye I watch the drizzle run down the window and listen to the roar of the traffic and the sirens in the streets below us.

I had to know why all the adults in my life simply refused to acknowledge the existence of a mixed-race child in their midst, how my blackness became unspeakable in both my immediate family and my extended family.

My mother didn't look at me, but slowly she began to speak. 'Your father, I wish he said something now … but he never did.'

'But it was up to you to say something to him when I was born,' I interrupted. 'You knew the truth. You are the one who stopped me asking questions.' I think back to when my mum would literally walk out of the room each and every time we came close to addressing something related to the secret. 'I can't believe you're trying to shift the blame on to dad.'

'I'm not blaming him.'

Justine interjected gently. 'But you had two parents, Georgina. Your father, as much as you loved him and he loved you, was also a part of this, wasn't he?'

She paused and then asked with a slight note of surprise in her voice, 'So Jim never challenged you, he never asked about an affair over the years? He didn't threaten to walk out?'

'No, he didn't,' my mum responded, slowly. 'We really never spoke of it.'

I could see that Justine was shocked. That same week Anthea had pointed out how much anger I felt towards my mum, and not my dad. 'I'm struck by how little blame sits at the door of your father,' she said softly, tucking her long twists behind her ears. 'He met your needs in many ways, he was a fantastic father by the sounds of it, but he was also complicit in this denial, just like your mum.'

But Dad is not here, I reminded Anthea, and to criticise him leaves a lasting bitterness in my heart. Talking about my father like that feels like peeling back layer after layer of his love, and I am afraid that if I keep going I will get to a middle where there is nothing left. I need to keep him as I loved him, I want more than anything to protect that.

So I ignored Justine, and in that moment I turned to my mother. 'You're the only one who is at fault here. The lie started with you.'

There was a pause, and my mum looked down, appearing deflated, an engine out of steam.

'Well, I just mean that your father didn't say anything when you were born. After that it just sort of continued. We carried on with life. We had your brother. And we were happy, weren't we? Things haven't been *that terrible* for you, have they?'

The emphasis on those words was enough to rile me to the point of no return. I could feel the rage travelling like an inferno from inside my chest to out through my nostrils and mouth, my tongue a searing-hot weapon.

'You had two kids,' I whispered slowly and deliberately. 'And we had the same upbringing, but we didn't have the same experiences, because my brother looks like you and Dad and everyone else, and he knows that you are his parents. He knows where he belongs, that he can trust you. No one has ever spoken about why I look the way I do, I've had to work it out on my own and I have been questioning my reality my whole life. Have you any idea of the level of madness that creates? It feels like no one wants to say what I am. Almost as if . . . ' I stopped and grabbed a tissue from the small table next to our chairs; my hands were shaking, my voice was shaking, my body was shaking as tears dripped down my cheeks and on to the gold cushion. 'Almost as if you're ashamed of me,' I finally said.

My mum hung her head, then slowly started shaking it. 'No, no, I was never ashamed of you, never,' she said as she fiddled with her wedding ring.

'I don't believe it. You are ashamed of me and it's because I remind you of what you did all those years ago, Mum, I know it.'

I had spent years pleading with my mum to revisit the conditions of my birth, asking her if I really could have been swapped in the hospital like my teacher suggested, a baby destined for another home – a terrible, heart-wrenching accident that everyone would understand, and which would explain everything. In counselling, a movie of all the times my mum had failed to meet my eyes, or tried to placate me with the well-worn throw-back story as a child, played on a loop in my head. She didn't stop to think about how these possibilities were building up inside me year after year, bringing with them a sense of anxiety, short, sharp pin-pricks that pierced the love and left me feeling as if I belonged elsewhere; another family, another country, another life.

'If you didn't want me, if you couldn't deal with all of me, then perhaps you shouldn't have kept me.' My mum grimaced slightly but didn't acknowledge what I'd said.

'I'm not a bloody bad mother, I did the best I could.'

'Yes, it's all about you, isn't it? It always has been.'

'OK, let's pause here, because I don't think we're hearing one another,' Justine cut in, right before a descent to chaos.

'Georgina is saying there was a distance between you both,

a distance she thinks comes from the fact that her race went unacknowledged for so long. And I can imagine that it would be extremely hard for that not to overshadow all your interactions as mother and daughter. Her race has always been there. But it hasn't been addressed and that has led to a denial of who she is. I am guessing you were ashamed of your affair, Colette?' Mum nodded. 'But not ashamed of your daughter?'

'No, no, of course not. Never.' She shook her head.

'If you were ashamed of your affair with a black man during your marriage, how could you separate that from me, your mixed-race child?'

There was a pause and I could feel my body tensing up, preparing for an explanation that I would perhaps rather not hear. I looked around at the attic room I was in; I studied the spider plants spilling out of their pot, the mini elephant figurines on the shelf.

Our therapist looked thoughtfully at both of us. 'I imagine the shame that comes with having an affair was a lot to contend with, Colette, especially when you'd come from a very Catholic background. And an affair with a black man, too ...' Justine raised her eyebrows and looked expectantly at my mother, who nodded slowly, as if this was the first time she had ever considered the racial element to her infidelity.

'Along the way I think the two things have become ... intertwined,' Justine continued softly, her slim legs tucked to the side of her chair beside a brightly coloured wax print bag which reminded me of something I once saw at a market during a press trip to Zimbabwe. She dressed a little like my mother, they were a similar age, but my mum is far less arty and would not have had a bag like that. 'And that despite you loving her, and Jim loving her, and both of you providing a lovely home, things were different for Georgina, because who she is wasn't fully addressed. And I think anyone would pick up on what that means. You've passed some of that shame on to her, I think.'

Justine's words were delivered like a gentle shake to the shoulders; my mum seemed to accept them.

'I – I didn't mean to . . . ' she trailed off. Tears fell silently down both our faces.

But Justine was right in that the shame around my birth had been passed down, and passed along in my family, each aunty, cousin and uncle taking their cues from my parents and never once bringing up the topic of my blackness for fear of upsetting them, which indicated to me, that something about me remained unspeakable, taboo. I thought once again to the laughter my family photos induced in others, how this had developed into a trepidation around uploading any pictures to Facebook lest I received a negative comment, or a dislike; my mother not understanding why, exactly, I insisted on walking behind her in the high street at the weekends. 'People don't think we are together anyway,' I'd shrugged. I had grown ashamed of how we appeared together.

We all talked, that day, as we had done before, about the source of my mother's shame and her own feelings around 'Catholic guilt'. The phrase elicits a familiar laugh among Catholics but the concept has actually shaped Western societies for centuries, instilling in humans, regardless of religious beliefs, a deeply ingrained need to be saved. It's been the Catholic Church's preferred method of securing sign-ups: if everyone is born bad, then everyone will need redemption – clever. And the most severe bouts of 'Catholic guilt' are distinctly Irish afflictions, of that I am sure. It's not as if the Church actively encourages feelings of guilt (contrition is the backbone to all teachings) but the idea that you are born with a sin that can never truly be atoned for (yo, baptism and confession are scams), is nothing short of draining, leaving many with permanent feelings of self-loathing. Of course guilt is a totally normal feature of a personal consciousness, but I no longer subscribe to much of what I was taught growing up simply because I refuse to feel any more shame around my existence as a black woman. In those sessions with Justine, I found it hard at first to understand why my mother had allowed her own 'Catholic guilt' around having an affair to permeate our lives at home, where it festered and turned into something more sinister, and harder to unpack.

'You've kept all this secret all to yourself for many, many years. You haven't forgiven yourself, Colette. You can't see past your own shame, even though it seems your husband forgave you just as soon as Georgina was born.'

My mum started crying silently, and immediately reached for the tissues beside her. She cannot wallow in her emotions like I can, she cannot sit with them for too long. Unlike me, she is profoundly uncomfortable when her sadness is exposed, preferring to wipe away the evidence just as soon as it appears. In that moment I felt more sorry for her than I had done in a long time, my mum can't shed a tear without feeling guilty for it.

Shame and guilt are human emotions which affect how we relate to one another. Although they are cousins in self-abasement and are often confused, they are distinct feelings which drive us to behave in very different ways. June Tangney, who has studied shame for years, notes that feeling guilt is productive and healthy as it necessitates taking responsibility for our actions. Guilt can drive people to make a change or apologise, whereas shame is a lot more complex. We feel shame when we violate social norms, or act in a way others might disapprove of, and shame-prone individuals find it harder to empathise. In their book on the topic, *Shame and Guilt*, Tangney and Ronda

L. Dearing note that 'Shame is an extremely painful and ugly feeling that has a negative impact on our interpersonal behaviour ... shame-prone individuals appear more likely to blame others as well as themselves for negative events.'[1]

This analysis goes some way towards explaining why in those early sessions, when I cried and screamed and begged my mum to understand, she seemed concerned with defending herself instead of listening to the never-ending repertoire of strange things that had happened to me as a result of her obscuration. I realised that when my mum wasn't forced to come clean about everything, to my dad, or her friends and family, she believed she'd escaped judgement. But concealing the truth for all those years had led her to turn her guilt inwards, morphing it into something harder and spikier – which is shame. When I looked at my mum then and grew furious with her inability to empathise and see past herself and her own needs, Justine saw someone totally and utterly paralysed by fear, and someone who was wrapped up in a web of dark and self-destructive thoughts related to how she was perceived.

That didn't mean that I still didn't want to burst a blood vessel or flip the table every week during those first few agonising months. The ire was an acid on the tip of my tongue; drip-feeding into my words and resulting in outbursts that left me tired and sad. Leaving those sessions and stepping out into the normal world, with my heart still racing, my body in fight or flight mode week after week, was a lot. My friends gently asked me if I should stop counselling, if it was actually helping, whether my mum would ever fully *get* it. But we stuck at it, and hearing what she had to say in the safety of a room run by the most empathetic of trained professionals helped me see all of my mum and not just the bits that made her a mother. I was descrambling the pixels in her picture and found that my mother was neither a mystery, nor a monster.

'I didn't mean to, you know ... make things harder,' she said in one session. 'You were just Georgina ... my daughter. Your colour didn't matter to me.'

I was starting at ground zero with my identity, and so was my mother, but I recognised that hearing 'I don't see your colour' from your own mother was, quite frankly, insane. My mum didn't realise it then but in saying that my race didn't matter, that it was invisible, she was kind of proving how immensely bothered she was by it, so much so that none of my family felt able to verbalise how I actually looked until I asked them to. That simple action of *not* naming the part of me which held such significance for how I identified, how I moved through the world, blotted out a large part of my identity in a home where I should have been able to be completely free. It is destabilising, picking up on the mortification that your very existence causes, because in saying that you love your daughter, son, partner or friend, but that you can't 'see' their colour, what you are really saying is: 'I can't acknowledge your difference because it's too awkward for me.' You are refusing to engage with all parts of them, and that *feels* like rejection, as if you are saying: 'I can't deal with who you are, there is something inherently wrong with it.' Not seeing race is a well-meaning attempt not to appear racist by proxy but it is also a lukewarm, half-arsed attempt to paper over perceived racial differences and avoid the beginnings of a discussion on privilege and inequality. It also suggests that there is something wrong with living with a racialised identity and it has taken me a quarter of a century to realise that there is not. Afua Hirsch, author of *Brit(ish)*, wrote words that resonate deeply with me on this topic. She noted that when friends claimed not to see her blackness it taught her that 'being black is bad ... that seeing race has sinister consequences. It implied that with recognition, racism inevitably follows. So much so, that it's better to pretend there's no black people at all. It offered me a way out of blackness, a denial, on the condition that I abandoned any attempt to be proud of my black heritage.'[2]

Saying you don't see the race of your loved one is a kiss on the cheek followed by a slap to the face; it is enjoying a hot sauna before finding yourself immediately plunged into a freezing ice bath. Comfort and discomfort intertwined, love and rejection all at once.

The session ended after I explained this to my mother, and she reflected on the impact of her colour-blind parenting. We parted ways without saying much to each other – she returned to Sutton and I headed back to Brixton. I noticed how taut and tense my neck and shoulders were, almost as if I had endured a long, heavy workout. I had been entangled for years in this web of denial, each counselling session was a way of working out the knots between me and my mother, but also the ones inside my own head. Sometimes I felt lighter and more clear-headed; other times we hit pressure points that released so much tension it hurt and I wanted to stop. But stopping would risk not returning, and not returning would risk reverting to a relationship in which I was not being seen, or understood. And so my mum and I returned each week, to the same small attic room in Balham to continue our conversations with Justine.

In mid-November, a friend of a friend linked me to an article on Facebook about a man who she said had much in common with me. Intrigued, I took a look at the story, which was quickly going viral, and saw that the man in question was Andrew Lovell, drummer of the 1990s UK band M People. To my amazement I read that Andrew was raised as a black child in a white family in Bermondsey, south London, but unlike me he was led to believe that he had been adopted by the people who raised him. The origins of his birth parents were kept hushed up, until during the Christmas of 1998, at the height of his fame in the band, Andrew pressed his parents for more details. He was told that his biological mum was alive and known to him, and was in fact the mother who had raised him all his life.

Andrew's parents had passed him off as their adopted child to save the family's shame after his mum had had an affair with a black colleague, in 1964. When I reached out to Andrew he told me that although he had a large proportion of black friends in south-east London and was told his biological father was possibly Jamaican, he suppressed a lot of worries about his difference. 'There was enough variety of language, colour and music even on Deptford High Street, so I didn't feel alone but I felt different in my house,' he told me over a Skype call. When he discovered that his adoptive mum was actually his real mother, the anguish left immediate and long-lasting psychological scars. 'When I found out, I was deeply, deeply, deeply, scarred. It happened too fast, it was too much. My dad said, "We were never going to tell you but your mum, Joyce, is your real mum." I was all over the place, splintered into a billion pieces. It was great, I'd found my mum but it was like, why didn't you tell me, why did you lie to me? Did you not love me – but I know you love me . . . I snapped and it broke me. I got post-traumatic shock syndrome (PTSD) thirteen months later, shaking in a studio in Manchester.'

It's yet more proof that the longer such secrets around parentage and heritage are kept from a child, the more havoc they can wreak on families, and like me Andrew's mental health had suffered greatly when he had uncovered the truth. Andrew and I grew up in different eras, we were both loved and cherished by our families, but in being passed off as something we were not, to protect our mothers from the shame associated with conceiving a child out of wedlock, a shame made worse by virtue of the fact we were black, made us endure matching rituals of turmoil.

In early 2018 in counselling we also spent a lot of time discussing the details of the night I was conceived. I can think of very few people who would actually want, and pay for, the opportunity to hear their parents divulge the details of their conception, but listening to my mum discuss how it all went down turned out to be the existential experience I never knew I needed. It was tough for me, not for the obvious reasons, but because my mum didn't remember much about this mystery man; no accent, no first name, and I found it hard to accept at first. My conception happened in a pub in Shepherd's Bush after everyone had gone home. She hadn't argued with my father, there were no marital issues, she was simply alone in the pub and talking to this 'dark-haired' barman, who I also imagine to be a 'dark-skinned' black man. She never returned to that pub when living in west London, the only time she saw this man was that fateful night. When I expressed disbelief at all this, the lack of memory pertaining not just to his appearance, but also to all other identifiable features that might help me track him down, Justine asked me if I could 'remember the full names of everyone you have ever slept with? Their names, their faces, where they were from?' I shook my head. 'OK, and do you think you will be able to remember them all in twenty or more years' time?' she probed gently. Knowing full well there were people from less than two years ago who remained wilfully forgotten, banished to the graveyard of bad, meaningless, or one-off sex, erased from my body-count list for ever, and that admitting this before my own mother was a little awkward for me; I stopped talking. Then I wondered out loud about the man with whom I shared half my DNA; I speculated as to his origins, and tried to press my mum for more information that might help me complete the picture in my head. Was there any resemblance at all between him and me?

'It's tricky ... I can't remember much. He had curly hair, big build, tall ...'

I opened my mouth to say something, but then changed my mind. Finding this man felt distant and impossible, like plucking a star from the sky and hoping that its light would shine for eternity. But it would be good to solve the mystery, not just for my own mental health, but to know my medical history too.

'What about if he wanted a relationship?' Justine pressed. My mum looked alarmed, as if the thought had never crossed her mind.

'Nothing can replace what I had with Dad,' which was said more for my benefit than hers. But with the DNA test results from Nigeria still very much informing how I answered everyday questions about my heritage, I would, admittedly, have loved to know who this mysterious black man was, whether or not he was even alive, what attributes, if any, he might have bestowed on me.

One session when the mood in the room was one of openness and it felt as if my mother and I could hear one another, I steered the conversation to the conditions of my birth once again. I wanted Mum to tell me about the social context of bringing into the world a mixed-race child born out of wedlock, and how that had affected her decisions. Long before I had come into her life, before she was mine and before she'd met my biological father, my mum had attended the Catholic youth clubs in West Clare, where, she revealed, she had once danced with a black man. 'It was unusual,' she remarked – because in the eighties there was not yet a migration story between Africa, the Caribbean and the west coast of Ireland.

We talked about how that had been pretty much the extent of her exposure to people of colour until she moved to London, that the Ireland she had known as a young woman was more socially conservative than the one that exists today. (I still can't quite believe it became the first country in the world to legalise gay marriage by popular vote in 2015.) For many centuries and up until quite recently, the Catholic Church and Irish state ruled over schools, hospitals, media, law and the community with complete dominion, and solved the 'problem' of unwed mothers. From the eighteenth to the twentieth century brutal institutions run by nuns, known as Magdalene laundries or asylums, were constructed, with similar organisations designed to deal with the scourge of dual-heritage children. Many of these homes were still running at the time of my mum's birth in 1961. 'Illegitimate and coloured' children of white Irish mothers and mainly African students were often taken away by force and incarcerated in horrendous homes in cities like Dublin and Donegal. From the 1940s right up until the 1980s, these mixed-race children were subjected to additional layers of racialised sexual, emotional and physical abuse, and many were prevented from being adopted by stable families.[3] As Bryan Fanning, Professor of Migration and Social Policy at University College Dublin, wrote in the *Irish Examiner* in 2018, the stigma associated with sex outside of marriage was huge in Ireland, made worse by the Catholic Church's tendency to sweep indiscretions under the rug. 'Efforts to hide unwanted women and their children away from society created a climate in which abuse could take place and be covered up,' he noted. 'The children born of relationships between African men and Irish women experienced not just the stigma experienced by other unmarried mothers but also extreme racism.'[4] In 2013, the group Mixed Race Irish was established to support the mixed-race children abused in Irish homes and lobby the Irish government to recognise the specific, racialised instances of abuse, which they argued should be viewed as separate from the general mistreatment of other children. A few years before my mum was of age, mixed-race children and their 'fallen' mothers were simply seen as problems that required civilising by the Irish Church and state. My mum did not know anyone from these homes, but she grew up in the shadow of an Ireland that had normalised the subjugation and shaming of unwed women and black people. And although Ireland has come a long way since then, shame and social stigma is still very much affecting the country's women. *The Irish Times* reported in 2020, that between 1971 and 2016 thirty dead babies had been found, on roadsides, farms, train tracks, under bridges, in bogs and wrapped up on beaches.[5] These tragic stories captivated the public discourse for a short while, without much further analysis into the culture that still forces women to give birth to their babies in the most secretive and horrific conditions imaginable.

Ireland, much like the UK, is plagued with an insidious, hard-to-name racism, although in recent years there have been several incredibly positive steps forward. My mother, whose Catholic faith and predilection had led to her keeping her thoughts and feelings guarded, also seemed to be changing, opening up, the more we spoke. In counselling that day we talked for a while about the stigma associated with having a relationship with a black man in a country that, bar the collective national worshipping of Phil Lynott, often sees Irishness and blackness as distinct entities that should not mix. I also talked about the life I would have had if Dad had walked away and left my mum, an Irish immigrant, as a single parent somewhere in Shepherd's Bush. Had she been a single mother so soon after getting married, her family might have disapproved; she likely would have faced some level of class prejudice and judgement in England, but she had not married in the fifties, like Andrew Lovell's mother, when things were very different. If my mum and dad had had an honest conversation with one another when I was born, I think they would have been OK. Their marriage, even without this disclosure, was far better than OK. I thought out loud about how we would have survived without my dad. I guess there would have been little reason for my mother to reinforce an affinity to whiteness if the lie had already been exposed and we'd stayed living in Shepherd's Bush, which had a large Caribbean population. I thought about who I would have turned out to be, how I might have talked, whether I'd be the same person, into the same things. I concluded that I would not, because my father's influence on me ran so deep it made my head hurt. But of course when Dad made the choice to stay, he absolved my mum from the worst, most public form of shame that would have linked to her affair, and did me the most incredible kindness by taking me on and making me his own. We speculated about my dad's life after he was sent off to boarding school, how that early life of isolation probably influenced his decision to stay with my mum, how wanting a family was everything to him; he was hard-wired to make do, determined to make the best of his lot. His choice allowed my mum to transcend the baggage of her taboo, interracial relationship, and it allowed me to grow up in a safe and loving environment, but also, I realised it had accidentally passed the burden of deciphering what the truth was, onto me, their half-white, half-black, fully perplexed child. But discussing all this in therapy each week, I could see why things had happened the way they had, who my parents had been, the thoughts, dreams and plans they had realised for our family by simply staying together without a word. I was the product of an interracial relationship in the nineties, from a mother and father whose secluded sixties upbringing had influenced their choices. But I was their Gina, their doll-face, and nothing would ever change that.

In early 2018 I returned from a two-week holiday with Emma to Sri Lanka which had seemed to restore me back to my default mood setting. The people there all seemed to exude a particular brand of chill that I find is near-impossible to source in big European cities, simply because we are all so obsessed with being overworked and comparing houses and buying overpriced flat whites, instead of, say, eating curry barefoot on beaches and praying in temples, which is actually a lot more soul-enriching. Sri Lanka worked like a tonic on my tired body and mind, weary from counselling. Emma and I relaxed our muscles and indulged our tastebuds by eating fish curries on powdery sands in the beach town of Unawatuna, stayed in tree houses and wandered around ancient memorials in Sigiriya, and took tuk-tuks to turtle sanctuaries and vibrant markets selling beaded tops and feathered earrings in the old city of Galle. Travel had once been a frenzied, exhausting activity that kept me moving constantly in order to distract me from myself. But Sri Lanka proved that travel could once again be a meditative tool for quiet reflection, a space to reconnect with a treasured friend. And, anyway, I had learned that if you have not made peace with yourself first, all the travel in the world won't satisfy you. You cannot outrun yourself, or escape what will always be waiting for you on the inside.

When I returned from Sri Lanka I found that the worst of the depression had left my body. I had also been contacted, to my utter disbelief, by agents and publishers encouraging me to expand on my *Guardian* columns by way of writing a book! And then I met someone. Things were looking up.

The first night we met, both of us were pissed, but we still ended up kissing. I was at a dingy club in Brixton on St Patrick's night alongside Aisling and two more of our good friends from school, Claire and Shannon. It was my first night out in months, and that week I had also written an article about celebrating my Irishness alongside my African heritage. Finally I was starting to feel in control of my identity, as if it were not just a thing dictated by circumstances of birth and social influence, but a complete process of internal and external consistency. Aisling took a photo of me for the 'gram, telling me how beautiful I looked in my green Zara halter-neck dress and braided ponytail. I felt like the best version of me I had been in a long, long time. Anyway, I swapped numbers with this guy and sometime later, he arranged the first date. The conversation between us flowed; he spoke in a pronounced, lofty voice that revealed an upbringing near Oxford, he was studying for a PhD, he had a lot to say, but I also detected a hint of diffidence around the topic of family and heritage. I have never been one for small talk on dates; I want to know what is rattling around in a person's core, what scares them shitless, their hopes and desires for the future. Perhaps it is a bit intense, but I like to know what I am working with early on. But this guy expertly steered our small talk past any mention of our shared blackness, a dance I recognised all too well having done it myself for many years. Fair enough, I'll leave it, I thought after wriggling around the topic and getting nowhere. By this point I'd spent months trying to better understand my parents' decisions; I had a new-found confidence in myself having scrubbed away at all the things that had been irking me for years, I felt shiny and new. So, when my date shirked away from the topics I'd finally learned to embrace, you best believe I noticed. I wasn't necessarily put off because I'd been there, I understood – but I noticed. We began dating, with the formal food dates turning quite quickly into hastily prepared dinners around each other's houses and long discussions about work and family, before this morphed into festivals and nights out with my friends, and languid weekends spent largely in bed. I learned that my boyfriend's fears around discussing so much of himself was down to the fact he was adopted. Totally unaware of who his birth parents were, as well as their countries of origin, that ache for home and knowledge of self was rarely spoken about. Although he knew he was mixed-race like me, and had grown up with his adoptive parents – a white mum and black dad – his start in life also meant he was unable to qualify a large part of his appearance.

Now, the fact that I had managed to attract someone else who also lacked such intimate knowledge of self, at a time in which questions of belonging also defined so much of who I was, is further proof to me that we cannot escape our identities. Whether we consciously engage with them or not, our identities are powers that guide our destinies. They shape who we become, who we seek out, and they help us connect with each other in times of great solitude. We emit energies that draw us to the type of people we need at particular times in our lives – we have it in us to forge connections with people who can fulfil us, and we find them when we need them. I love the saying about people being in your life for either a season, a reason, or a lifetime. And the conversations we had during the best parts of our relationship as we tried to make sense of ourselves in our early twenties were invaluable to both of us, and helped us step beyond an existence that was, at times, hard to navigate for similarly strange reasons.

But, heed this: there is a lot to be said about trauma

bonding, and forging romantic connections based on pain. Shared emotional issues do not make a healthy foundation for a relationship, and mutual trauma does not equate to mutual compatibility. I learned that lesson the hard way.

In October 2018, Emilia, Aisling and I walked into a bar in Balham that sold overpriced cocktails, tasteless food and always smelled slightly of damp feet. It was a Wednesday, 8.30 p.m., and we were continuing our post-work catch-ups after lining our stomachs at an Asian restaurant nearby. As we dropped our bags on a table at the back of the room and prepared to go to the bar, I caught sight in my peripheral vision of a tall, attractive man in a checked shirt, seated at a table behind me who looked a little like my boyfriend. As I reached into my bag to dig out my debit card I focused my gaze on him: *wait a second, that is my boyfriend.* And he was sitting right next to a small, blonde girl I did not recognise, in a booth beside a roaring fireplace, a scene that would not look out of place in a cheap online dating show. She was drinking a cocktail the colour of fresh watermelon, he was laughing. Something stirred inside my stomach but it sure wasn't indigestion. I turned to stare right at my boyfriend, head tilted, until he met my eyes, at which point his face lit up a little too enthusiastically as he practically leapt up from his seat, standing like a one-man road blockade between me and his table as I craned my neck to see who, exactly, he was sitting beside.

'Oh, hey Gina, what are you doing here?' he asked with a wide grin.

'I'm just with the girls ... who's that?' I asked, with the casual composure of a woman who was totally trusting of her relationship.

'Just a friend, someone I know from my area.'

I nodded. The 'just a friend' refrain echoed in my ears like the eerie music from a Gregorian choir as I walked away. I could feel a sense of impending doom in the air. There was something not quite right about the scenario playing out before my eyes. On what grounds, exactly, would a friendship with someone 'from my area' be constituted? And why hadn't I been introduced? The strained smile plastered across my boyfriend's face had been verging on manic, plus he was sitting next to her, *in a booth*, when there was plenty of other chairs around that table. I'd also never had the pleasure of meeting even one of my boyfriend's friends. There had been no casual meet-ups with his PhD course-mates, no mentions of old school-mates, or drinks with people he knew. Even though he seemed awkward about the fact that his social network wasn't vast, and I'd privately expressed concerns to my own friends, it wasn't really a major red flag – you don't usually break up with someone just because they're a bit low on the old friend-front, do you?

'I'm sure there's a logical, rational explanation,' the girls said as I returned to our table across the room and we continued to watch my boyfriend, watching this girl, without so much as throwing a cursory glance in my direction. Then their pizzas arrived. In the mood-lighting I could make out the toppings: Margherita and pepperoni – OK so ... no. I was gripping my wine glass so tightly, I thought it might smash. I should approach the table, Aisling said, lawyer-like, and clear up once and for all what the hell was going on. I did as instructed.

'Can I have a word?'

'Sure,' my boyfriend said nonchalantly standing up.

'You do know what this looks like, don't you? I have no idea who that girl is,' I half-whispered as the girl scrolled through her phone. 'You haven't introduced me, you've just sat back down with her and you can't even tell me how you met. What is actually going on?'

'Babe, I said she's just a friend. And I might need a new flatmate so I was going to ask her about moving in.'

'Well which one is it? Do you take all potential new flatmates out for pizza? *Where did you meet her?*'

What followed after that point was a calamitous public spectacle, the type that is probably quite fun to witness during an otherwise dull Wednesday evening of after-work drinks, but which is actually far less enjoyable to be a part of. Aisling, with her disarming smile and warm blue eyes, snuck off to quiz the mystery girl herself, while Emilia (who handles all crises like a total boss) and I set about obtaining the facts. But as I waited for something by way of an explanation that made sense, the story changed several times: this girl was a potential new housemate; no, he'd met her in a café; actually he'd been introduced to her by someone else. Then Aisling returned to inform me the pair had met at a bar the week before – the jig was up! I'd apparently interrupted my boyfriend's date! Slotting myself into the booth four inches away from her face, as my now soon-to-be-*ex*-boyfriend hovered helplessly next to the table, I pushed their pizzas aside. While I refrained from shouting and stopped short of attributing any blame to her, I certainly made it clear that I required open and unequivocal answers. I was his girlfriend after all, surely she could do me the courtesy of letting me know what had unfolded here. But when she refused to talk, her reaction verging on hostile, I thought quite seriously for a second about swilling the pair of them and waltzing off. Granted, we had both been misled by a man so duplicitous in nature that neither one of us had seen it coming, but at that point, sis knew the sitch. She had realised her role as accidental side-chick, and as such, her presence was no longer required beyond two final tasks which should have been carried out promptly and without sass: one, tell me what you know, and two, exit stage left.

'Can someone tell me what the fuck is going on?' I scream-cried at this point, wine sloshing dangerously around the glass I was holding in my hand as I gesticulated between them both.

There is a saying which was originally coined by Mark Twain but which has been reinterpreted and repeated on forums all over the internet which goes: 'Do not argue with fools because from a distance, onlookers may not be able to tell the difference.' I realised then as I sensed strangers side-eyeing us from full tables with similar two-for-one pizza deals, that to anyone looking on without prior knowledge, it would appear that it was me who was indeed the fool. I established that my boyfriend's intentions were completely iniquitous, that he'd been texting this girl for a week since first meeting her on a night out (a day after we had returned from holiday together), and that she did not know I existed. My heart sank. I grabbed my stuff and left with Emilia and Aisling by my side, as my boyfriend ran down the street hurling empty plat-itudes and sorrys behind us. And no, I did not waste my wine on anyone that night. In the weeks that followed, apologies, gifts and promises that remained unfulfilled were offered up like biscuits with tea. But I was done. I eventually cut off all communication and allowed his messages to remain unread. I made a promise to myself then that in the future any partner who exhibited even the smallest predilection for little white lies, who had me moving like a detective over their behaviour, or who made me feel crazy for trusting my intuition would be dismissed far more quickly. I would not deal with any more deceit, any more doubt in my most intimate of relationships. I walked away and didn't look back.

At around the same time this relationship broke down, I moved home. The rental merry-go-round of horrors was not about to stop anytime soon, but it was time for me to get off. There really should be no monetary figure low enough that will keep you renting in an environment that is unsafe and unstable, but the London housing market has been constructed as such, that renters will always be at the mercy of their landlords, whose willingness to trade in human misery will always be matched by the desperation of the city's tenants. I had stayed far too long, but friends had worried that if I were to move home, my creative output would stop and I would argue with my mother; we were not fully healed after all. I was worried that without the distraction of a boyfriend who could keep me out of the house now and again, the cracks in our relationship would reappear, that life would become one long counselling session, the separation of living spaces no longer acting as a buffer. My brother was living with friends from university, and the last time I'd lived at home, walls had been dented by my fury during vicious rows. I had slowly come to resent being in the house, which no longer felt like a home with only my mum there, who had not been ready to have the conversations when I needed them. But as Justine had pointed out to us both when we discussed the possibility of me moving home again, our grief had once been red-hot and raw, and DNA tests had destroyed long-held family narratives. In losing my dad we had both lost things of equal worth: my mum had lost her husband, her marriage, her entire support system for twenty-five years; I had lost my dad and, later, a large part of my identity. The void his death had left at the centre of our world could never be smoothed over; it would never fully heal, but we had spent months discussing topics that had once been off-limits for both of us. We were now different people with a better understanding of each other; the worst of the storm had been weathered.

During a phone call from Brixton, my mum reiterated the same sentiment.

'This will always be your home,' she said. 'You're welcome back any time. You don't have to ask, silly.'

Sutton was exactly the same as when I'd left it over two years before. The high street was the high street of my memories, only a little more desolate following the closure of the small clubs and pubs, and perhaps with a few more black and brown faces than I'd noticed before. When commuting to my job in east London, I felt Sutton's stretch from central London all the more – the journey now taking more than double the time it had done from Brixton. But aside from this, being back at home was actually a very good thing, bringing Mum and me back together again after it had felt like we would never bridge the width of the invisible chasm between us. After the break-up with my boyfriend, Mum was angry for me, like I needed her to be, and she listened to my reasonings and moans and mental acrobatics in the way only a mother could, never tiring of over-analysing where it had all gone wrong, whose fault it was, what I could have done differently. She booked us into a spa in Sutton for a massage, followed by cocktails in a pub I had forgotten existed just to cheer me up, and over salmon, salad and wine, she implored me to resist when I considered taking my cheating ex back in a moment of madness.

He'd sent flowers, chocolates, written a letter. But then in a near comical display of arrogance, he'd become angry when I didn't immediately 'thank' him, confusing the relationship etiquette for a cheating apology with that for receiving a birthday present.

'You'll never be able to trust him, Gina,' my mum said slowly as she shook her head. 'And he will chip away at your confidence – leave him be, you can do better. You deserve more.'

I wanted to tell my mother that I would probably struggle

to take anyone's word on anything after the past few years, that after discovering that my family had been lying to me for years, I would probably be plagued with trust issues forever. But instead, I said nothing.

We ordered a second cocktail each and walked home together arm in arm while I thought about why exactly it is so hard to demand more from the people you love. And real love, whether it is romantic or familial, doesn't force you to shrink yourself, or settle for less. It is full and accommodating and forgiving. It adapts to the hardest of times, and moulds itself around you like Play-Doh when life changes.

I needed my mum more than ever at that stage, just to be mother and daughter again. I felt myself happily regressing into an overgrown child in the house I had grown up in, my edges softened by all the home comforts I'd missed, and by my mum's love, which had never really gone away, but which I hadn't allowed myself to acknowledge for a long time. We eased into a routine. We went to counselling together and left the sessions together. At home I cooked. We watched TV in our front room like we used to. My brother, who had moved in with friends in Leeds, joined us when he was around, relieved that we could all live together once again.

'Why does everything always taste better when you make it?' Mum lamented as she gazed at the fishcakes I'd made.

'You need to teach me how to do those,' my brother added, to which I replied I would, while knowing that he would probably not bother trying out the recipe.

Without Dad's culinary skills to lean back on, cooking at home had been an adjustment for all of us at first. Mum had mastered the perfect roast dinner, which was formerly my father's domain, serving it with a homemade onion stuffing using Kerrygold butter, which my brother and I concluded was actually better than Dad's offering, a compliment that made my mum beam with pride.

At home I had a fully stocked fridge, and a space that finally felt calm again. The biggest disagreements in our counselling sessions suddenly seemed to relate to mundane mother–daughter disagreements: dirty dishes and crumbs on worktops instead of the difficult racial dynamics of our family. Before I went to work, Mum would wake me up in the same impossibly cheerful voice.

'Wakey, wakey . . .' A coffee with milk would appear on the desk next to my bed, along with a kiss on the forehead. I was back in my bedroom, in the bed my dad had taken when he was sick. The coffee sat beside the miniature World War Two model set Dad had completed during those bed-bound months, which felt so long ago. I'd study the meticulously painted soldiers and tanks each morning as I sipped my drink and prepared for the day ahead. Dad's attention to detail had never faltered, even when he was ill; he'd never given up on trying to hold things together.

I stayed for nearly nine months. It was good to be home.

9

Time Travelling

I had worried that I was keeping too much distance
between myself and this alien time. Now, there was
no distance at all. When had I stopped acting?

OCTAVIA E. BUTLER, *Kindred*

On the day I found my first ever black relative, I was tired.
I had invited Emilia and Aisling around for dinner in
the Brixton mad-house a few weeks before I left and had
cooked my famous crème fraiche and paprika chicken casserole. We were drinking rioja and discussing work. Emilia,
fiercely ambitious as always, was changing jobs for the third
time since leaving uni, as she wanted more pay in a similar
role, while Aisling wanted to switch from corporate life to the
charity sector, her true calling. While we lamented the cost of
living in London on our menial salaries, I received an email
notification that nearly made me drop my phone.

'Whoah. I have a match.'

'What, dating?'

'A match with who?'

'I have a relative on the MyAncestry site, oh my god I actually have one.'

Ever since I received my test results in Nicaragua, my information, my test results, my DNA, had been stored on their database. That information could be used to match me with any potential blood relatives when, and if, they added their info to the site. And someone had. And she was black.

'Oh . . . wow. Who is it? Are you going to meet?' Emilia asks.

'I don't know. I've never had a black family member before . . . ' After getting nowhere with my mum's descriptor of my biological black father, I'd let go of the idea of tracing black family members, but suddenly here was a lifeline. It was a lot to process.

The woman – her name is Keji – had her full name displayed on MyAncestry, so naturally I immediately did some basic online sleuthing, pasting her name into Google and pulling up her Instagram to see if we looked anything alike. Keji is glamorous; make-up impeccably done in every photo, with large, kind eyes and a face shape not too dissimilar from my own, and long, dark straight hair with a coiffed side-fringe. We began messaging that night after my friends had left – 'keep us posted!' – and I found out she is just a year older than me and lived close by in south-east London. I sent her a few of my journalism articles detailing my personal identity story and told her I was searching for more information around my black family, although it was still weird to attribute the word 'family' to an imaginary group of people who didn't yet know I existed, and with whom I had no real relationship. But Keji was keen to help, having uploaded her own information to the site just for fun to 'see what she'd find'. She was Nigerian through and through; both parents were Yoruba. 'I'll tell you anything you want to know,' she responded on the site before we swapped numbers.

Later I discovered that we shared 66.2cM (centiMorgans) of DNA, my largest match on the site, a closer connection than anything I share with the Keanes, Gallaghers and O'Gradys on there – all distant relatives from my mother's side. In general, the more DNA you share with a match, the higher the cM number will be and the more closely related you are. 66.2cM means Keji and I could be anything from third to fourth cousins. We continued to message back and forth for months before the conversation went cold and life continued as normal. Then, I was commissioned to make an Audible documentary on DNA testing, called *The Secrets in Us*, focusing on my journey through the industry alongside that of others whose identities and families had been affected by surprise DNA test results. Suddenly, with the safety and support of producers, it felt like a good time to meet Keji. Grateful that the meeting would not only be recorded, but also overseen by my excellent producer Tamsin, I felt a little less nervous as the meeting date approached; it would be taking place in the confines of a work-like environment, with recording equipment and a planned set of questions, which for some reason made me feel safer. Friends kept asking me if I would like to find my biological father, whether my connection to Keji would mean it would be possible, and although Keji solidified my link to Nigeria, being part of another entire family still felt surreal, almost as if the whole thing was an elaborate prank. I told friends that it was exciting to see this trail of breadcrumbs actually leading somewhere, but also terrifying because every clue, every match, took me further and further away from the father who raised me. And somewhere within, a tiny part of me wanted this biological figure to stay in the shadows, so as not to dim the light from my dad.

I need not have panicked. Debbie Kennet, a genealogist whom I contacted for the Audible programme, analysed the strength of this new DNA match. Keji and I were not close enough matches to determine who my biological parentage. 'You need a first cousin to triangulate with some accuracy,' she said to me in the University College London café where we met one rainy Wednesday afternoon. 'She's too distant a match, but if you're third cousins then that means you shared a set of great-great-great-great-grandparents, and the fact that she's Nigerian means that it's likely you do have some Nigerian heritage.'

I'd grappled with whether or not to tell enquirers I was, indeed, Nigerian, after discovering that DNA ancestry tests, the type which claim to tell us our 'ethnicity', are not based on rigid science. Mark Thomas, an evolutionary biologist I met when writing about DNA testing for the *Guardian* in 2018, thinks the terms 'race' and 'ethnicity' have no place in the DNA-testing world. 'Ethnicity is an idea of group belonging that is usually socially constructed. It's something that's decided by the individual, and can be in negotiation with peers, but it's not based on any biological component. The term "race" is a term we don't use in genetics any more because there's no genetic support for the concept of races; it's hierarchical and has a disgusting, ugly history we all know about,' he said to me at the time in his office at UCL. Mark had also told me my biological father could technically be from anywhere, and that my Nigerian DNA test results would not necessarily have meant he originated from that country. The reasons for this are numerous. When you take an ancestral DNA test, you are sending off your genome, or DNA, to be analysed. Scientists compare thousands of chunks of your DNA, known as markers, or SNPs, to that of many other people's. They cross reference your markers with entire groups around the world. If you have many markers that are similar to those from Spain, you'll be told you are a certain percentage Spanish. But – here's the kicker – markers can be shared in many different groups, in many countries, and they change over time too. So just because I have some markers that are specific to Nigerian people doesn't mean that my biological father was necessarily Nigerian. He could have been from anywhere, Mark Thomas told me, or have 'broad genetic similarities to Nigerians'. These companies are also only looking at very recent DNA samples, from a relatively small group, in one specific database, which is often made up of mainly European samples. This skews the results for black and brown people. It's quite possible a DNA ancestry test with three different companies could give you three different ethnicity estimates; this has happened to many people who have tested this theory. And for people wanting to know the origins of their ancestors, all these tests are really saying when they estimate that we are 12 per cent French, 45 per cent Eritrean etc., is that we share some markers, or SNPs, with contemporary populations who have been defined (or self-defined) as French and Eritrean – not that our ancestors were from there. The markers in the genome of someone who is 50 per cent Egyptian will not necessarily match the markers of an Egyptian from two thousand years ago who existed during Cleopatra's reign.[1]

Anyway, I learned all this information long after I received my Nigerian ancestry results and had started digging into the science behind them, and I was slightly overwhelmed to say the least, and very wary of appropriating an identity that was not mine to have. I briefly flirted with the idea of going back to being totally country-less, but found myself explaining my family, my upbringing, and half the information I knew on the DNA-testing industry to cover all bases each time someone asked me: 'So where are you from?' What if the test was pretty meaningless and I didn't have a biological parent from Nigeria after all? Should I stop telling people I was half Nigerian? When I connected with Keji, and Debbie Kennet told me our Nigerian connection greatly increased the likelihood of my ancestral DNA test results actually being accurate, I was relieved. My biological father could be Nigerian after all. Phew.

By the time the meeting rolled around, the pressure was alleviated. I knew that Keji was too distant a blood relative to immediately locate my biological father, so I was not expecting her to pull out a well-thumbed photo of a man whose face looked like mine from a dusty album, or make an emotional call to a distant relative, and declare that she had reunited us. Keji *was* the distant relative, and therefore I could expect nothing and avoid disappointment. When Tamsin and I arrived at Keji's 1960s-style council flat, she greeted me with a warm hug and ushered me in. There was a perfectly arranged table of snacks and drinks in her living room; oranges, chocolate bars, bottles of water. 'Would you like something? How are you? How is your writing going? I want to tell you about my family. I've got loads of pictures, you know.'

We were both dressed in matching jeans, but Keji's hair was scraped back into a dramatic blow-dried ponytail, save for her perfectly coiffed fringe at the front, whereas mine was in waist-length braids. Keji smiled as she spoke, pushing words from her mouth at an alarming rate, jumping between stories and anecdotes and afterthoughts as if she feared she would miss something. She had a six-year-old son, a boyfriend who she met at church; she wanted to be a journalist, like me, or maybe a teacher, and was back at college. We were both talkative, and Tamsin sat silently, with her microphone on a chair opposite, as she recorded the natural flow of our conversation. We got talking about our upbringings. 'I always got teased by my cousins for not really acting, you know, like them because I grew up just outside of London, near Kent, and I was just into different stuff,' she said when I told her of my life in Sutton. Then, we got onto our generous foreheads – 'Yeah we do have the same shaped head,' Keji laughed. She produced her photo albums and talked me through her huge family, there were so many cousins and relatives I couldn't keep up. Both her parents are Nigerian; her dad moved to the UK first in the nineties and her mum followed later, but then the two split up. There were also cousins who moved in and became brothers, half-sisters she had never met on her dad's side who lived in Nigeria, other siblings she was closer to who were UK-based, aunties who were not really blood-relatives. It was all so confusing, but with Tamsin's help we managed to deduce that I am related to her via her mum's side, not her dad's – but that was all we could affirm. After telling Keji more about my progress in counselling with my mum, the book I was writing, and the Audible programme she would now feature in, I took a selfie with my new cousin, before I thanked her for her time and got up to go.

On the train home, Tamsin asked if I was disappointed that we couldn't find out more and whether or not I felt the meeting had been useful. But it had; I'd met someone with whom I shared a significant amount of genetic information, and the rapport between us couldn't have been better. For the programme, Tamsin and I had spoken to an adoptee who had traced his biological family with the help of a 'DNA detective', an expert who does the arduous genealogical leg-work, tracing long-lost family members from broken family trees and distant DNA matches. I could look into that, I thought, but I also knew that the bonds of family that tie us together extend far beyond the biological. There is nothing that can replace the building blocks of an intimate relation-ship, stacked up over decades. Family is not just bloodline or a legacy, it is shared memories and history, a constant presence and fulfilled promises. Keji would not feel like family unless we worked on a relationship, simply because we had not grown up as such. I knew that I would always belong with the family I had known all my life, but the pull to see if I could also belong elsewhere, the desire to seek out that knowledge, remained strong. My only option, I realised that day, was to keep my DNA in the database, in the hope that one day it might lead me to a closer blood relative who could assist me with filling in the remaining blanks. Perhaps we would share some characteristics – a body shape, a blood type, a curl pattern, a predisposition for lateness and red wine – but perhaps not. Either way, I knew there would be no resemblance strong enough that would immediately bind me to a stranger. The title of 'father' had to be earned, and in my case the position had already been filled.

My experience with the DNA-testing industry had been somewhat eventful to say the least. In 2019 I reflected on my journey with my therapist, Anthea. I had made the leap to go fully freelance to work on my own projects – the Audible series had imbued me with a renewed sense of purpose. I was meeting and interviewing so many other people whose experiences through the world of genetic testing were just as surreal as my own. Those who had discovered they were donor-conceived via test kits taken for fun; adoptees who had located long-lost parents; a man whose surprise results led him to a large inheritance; a woman whose blackness was also denied by her family until affirmed via ancestral analysis. Some interviewees had contacted me after reading my work in the *Guardian*, others were found by Tamsin. Staging these conversations via Skype, or in person, felt urgent. I endeavoured to conduct each interview with empathy and compassion and without centring my own story, but I found that in many cases, people were only too eager to map their experiences over mine, having believed that no one else could relate to them. I was grateful to find a place in these little communities online and make my own too, where conversations about belonging and identity could unfold freely and without reprisal.

Between 2016 and 2019 I took four consumer DNA tests – one sibling test, one paternity test and two ancestral composition tests with MyHeritage and Ancestry – in an attempt to shed light on my genetic story. Each one initiated a shift in how I viewed myself and my place in the world, forcing dark and dusty skeletons out of my family closet and fast-tracking those closest to me through a myriad of racial understanding checkpoints.

But these DNA tests have also left me exasperated, angry, confused, disappointed, distraught and lost. They've told me of my true relationship with my dad – a pill that has not only been bitter to swallow, but which nearly choked me. They've left me in no-man's-land with regard to my own immediate black biological family but have connected me with so many others around the world with whom I share similar points of reference.

For many people of colour who don't know their racial background, and those within the African diaspora whose personal histories have been marred by the trauma and highly inconvenient logistics of slavery, there exist more specific risks and complications than those related to long-lost family. Genetic ancestry DNA tests are being used for nefarious ends by insurers and government bodies, which indisputably hits those of minority heritage the hardest by correlating biological traits with racial or ethnic labels. A phenotype is an observable trait, influenced by genes as well as the environment, such as skin colour, eye shape, hair texture. Within police work, forensic DNA phenotyping (FDP) is an emerging technology that seeks to infer a person's characteristics from their DNA in order to assist with criminal investigations. But while there are merits to this type of work, critics argue that it elevates the argument that there is a genetic basis for phenotypical differences between groups. And there is evidence that FDP is already producing results that implicate black people, or those of African descent,[2] and endangering indigenous and colonised populations who are most vulnerable to the misuses of data in forensic DNA profiling.[3] The African-American geneticist Rick Kittles even blocked his research from being used by scientists to inform marker technology in the forensic world, explaining that he 'didn't want to help them put more black people in jail'.[4] The misuse of our genome by institutions we didn't even know had our data is also becoming more of an issue. In 2015, a study of 228 DTC (direct to consumer) DNA tests found that 48 per cent of the companies allow genetic data to be disclosed to third parties and 25 per cent state that they may disclose data to law enforcement agencies.[5] This information is often hidden in complicated privacy agreements online. At this scale we can see that genetic ancestry and family tests aren't just a cute Christmas gift from a rich aunt, or a fun way to assuage a middle-class family's interest in their German or Scottish lineage – in many cases they are political kryptonite. Using DNA tests for ancestral analysis could also be helping to entrench the status of the dark and foreign 'other' in Western societies, inciting fear and helping ground laws that result in the denial of freedom and quality of life for minority groups.

And what it leads to is even more personal, political and poignant for the same groups whose histories have been blurred by trauma. As I already explained, the conclusions drawn in company ethnicity estimates are not always accurate and can dismantle cherished family histories, without any explanation of the limitations of the science.

It is estimated that the global DNA-testing industry will be worth £45 billion by 2024, and in 2018 more people took DNA tests than in all previous years combined.[6] With such an exponential surge in popularity around consumer DNA testing it's not a case of wondering *if* stories like mine will be replicated, but *when*, as hushed-up secrets are thrown to the forefront of family discussion. For barely the cost of a mid-range pair of headphones, or a cinema and drinks date for two, these DNA tests promise to tell us, in granular detail, exactly who we are, accentuating a part of the human condition that has fascinated us for centuries: our search for belonging and identity. Finding our tribe, our people, our shared resemblances, discovering what makes us whole in our search for self, shapes our affiliation to the present-day communities we find ourselves in, and in some cases, it can totally change the group identities that have been constructed for us. DNA testing can provide our lives with meaning and purpose where it may previously have lacked.

The first DNA test I had ordered was a paternity test, but it had not been processed simply because I had not wanted to upset my father during his illness. Despite obtaining his DNA sample, it had sat untouched in my room. A year later, I opted to purchase a sibling test with a company called AlphaBiolabs. Companies like AlphaBiolabs work largely with government agencies and large companies (the Home Office, courtrooms and the now-defunct Jeremy Kyle Show) instead of consumers, to provide family DNA test results. They are different to the major players like Ancestry and MyHeritage which focus on ancestral and health tests for consumers, and have seen an exponential surge in popularity over the last seven years or so. My thinking behind ordering a sibling test at the time was simple, a little selfish, and mainly motivated by fear. I feared that Dad's sample might be unusable after so long sitting in my drawer – almost twelve months. There was also a deep-rooted fear that the test would come back negative and the results would be something I'd have to tackle alone. Starting with a sibling test seemed softer and easier somehow; I knew that my brother would willingly offer not just his sample, but his support too. But the sibling test result came back as 'inconclusive'. I remember calling up the company in tears during a lunch-break on my internship at the magazine, demanding to know why they hadn't included a more comprehensive explanation of the likelihood of that happening. I later found out that although companies like AlphaBiolabs don't shout it from the rafters, inconclusive results can happen fairly frequently: on their website they note that such a result occurs in around 40 per cent of sibling tests nationally, but in their lab that figure is far lower at 24 per cent. The reasons for this are varied. Whenever we take one of these tests, we are asking for our genome to be cross-compared with the person with whom we are trying to determine the relationship. The markers analysed can also be found in much of the general population (we share 99.9 per cent of our DNA with one another), and as such cannot be relied upon to provide enough evidence to determine a biological relationship with certainty. Other times, there are fewer markers shared than expected, due to the random way relatives inherit DNA from each other. But ... none of that info is easily identifiable on these sites. After a tense phone call with a representative from AlphaBiolabs when I argued that the inconclusive result had caused me undue stress, they agreed to test mine and my father's DNA in one of their paternity tests – for a reduced fee. A year later and I was in Nicaragua, taking an ancestral test with MyHeritage.

In lacking such intimate understanding of self, there is always a gap inside you that cannot be sealed up. It is your own personal enigma which can never be solved; you carry it with you always. I don't know what it's like to be raised in a household in which everyone is united by their missing ancestral knowledge, as is often the case in the US with African-American families, but I understand the frustration and anger that comes with being denied something so personal. In the States, however, there is a power in this, black people bound together who have forged a collective identity which the rest of the world looks up to. But in the UK, of course, it is far more unusual for black people not to know their history – I discovered long ago that nearly all mixed people know their mix; black friends and colleagues now proudly claim their 'first gen' or 'second gen' status in their Twitter bios. I have always been looked at strangely for not having an answer, or a parent, to explain that part of my identity, and despite the privacy concerns, DNA testing has helped me immensely.

Our global obsession with DNA testing is a window into an increasingly heightened racial discourse. It's no coincidence that the boom in the testing market from 2016 to 2018 coincided with the end of Barack Obama's presidency, the start of Trumpism, a global increase in populist governments in Brazil, France and Russia, and Brexit. In terms of cultural production during this period we've been spoilt for choice and enjoyed an influx of black narratives in Hollywood and in the publishing world. For African-Americans and those within the African diaspora who have been denied access to their lineage, an increased access to the DNA-testing world alongside the visibility of these stories is particularly powerful, offering us the opportunity to locate ourselves in a personal and historical narrative which had been hijacked by those who should not be telling our story. DNA tools that previously felt inaccessible and overpriced have been democratised, benefiting the identity-impoverished the most. Alondra Nelson argues that black interest in genealogy began decades ago. In her comprehensive work on African-American genetics *The Social Life of DNA,* she notes that Alex Haley's *Roots* – a 1977 television series based on the story of Kunta Kinte, who is sold into the slave trade after being kidnapped from his African village – was integral in starting a national dialogue around African-American history, explaining that it allowed the US to address its overlooked history on slavery and helped establish the first genealogy framework that was later adopted by DNA-testing companies. She says:

> Haley's account of the Middle Passage, in which millions of Africans were shipped across the Atlantic as part of the slave trade, and its consequences, became an urtext, a primary narrative source of African diasporic reconciliation for a generation of Americans. The story provided a narrative about slavery and its afterlives on the 200th anniversary of a nation that had never fully acknowledged its past. In place of a presidential apology for slavery, or a national discussion on racism, or the promise of reparations, we had *Roots.*[7]

Nelson describes how 'root-tracing kits' containing family-tree templates and fill-in-the-blanks genealogical charts on 'imitation parchment' made their way on to the mainstream market in 1970s America, popularising ancestral tracing for a group of people who had never before seen themselves and their histories laid out on mainstream TV. *Roots* was born of

Haley's own internal desire to gain access to a past obscured by the horrors of slavery, and in an incredibly arresting separate non-fiction account of his journey to Gambia, he explored the role of the oral tradition in preserving African genealogy. Although he'd traced his roots to a particular village, Haley had exhausted all written documents and historical records available to him until he located a 'griot' – a walking, living archive of oral history in many African cultures. With this man's help, Haley's ancestral past was illuminated, and he discovered he was the great-great-great-great-grandson of a slave named Toby who was forced from Gambia to Maryland, USA, and whose original name was none other than the Kunta Kinte who was later immortalised in Haley's work.

The oral transmission of family information, cultures, traditions and folklore has been fundamental in preserving African identity among displaced and traumatised peoples of many ethnicities, but in the times of antebellum slavery, Africans who were stripped of their identities, renamed and prevented from reading, writing and keeping family histories intact by colonial masters, were also forced to transmit information on a grand scale in this way. Haley's account quite literally gave me goosebumps when I read it, and his work continues to inspire generations of African-Americans to seek themselves out in their own continent. His repeated trips to Gambia echoed those of the African-American civil rights leaders W. E. B. Du Bois, who moved to Accra in Ghana in 1961, and Malcolm X, who also visited the African city several times before his assassination in 1965. These journeys and the boom in DNA testing for black people laid the groundwork for a global movement of self-discovery. In September 2018, Ghana's president announced that 2019 would be the 'Year of Return', a year-long programme of events designed to attract tourists and expats alike and which covered art exhibitions, networking events for returnees, performances from Cardi B, visa assistance and the music festival Afro Nation. Although my personal journey has felt like an isolated mission at times, I'm grateful it's taken place against a backdrop of renewed interest in African genealogy through which I could trace myself.

But DNA-testing companies have taken advantage of the desperate need for personal history within the diaspora, using racially ambiguous models in their marketing and producing tone-deaf adverts. In 2019, Ancestry landed themselves in hot water with a 'love' story TV advert featuring a white man and a dark-skinned black woman in costume from antebellum America. 'Let's escape to the North ... will you leave with me?' he asks her breathlessly. Although the shock on her face is palpable, we don't hear her response and the advert fades to an image of their marriage certificate ... in 1857. A voice-over says, 'Uncover the lost chapters of your family history with Ancestry.' It was a dangerous and spurious attempt to romanticise and rewrite the history of slavery-era interracial relationships which were defined in the main by the brutal and systemic rape of African-American women by their white owners and not by cute 'n' consensual marriage proposals. Ancestry later pulled the advert entirely.

The global increase in DNA testing and its interest for black communities can also be directly linked to the rise of Afrofuturism, a cultural movement which spans art, politics, music and philosophy and which has been enjoying a mainstream cultural resurgence as of late, 2018 in particular being a strong year (think the aesthetic of Kendrick Lamar and SZA's 'All the Stars' video, the movie *Black Panther* and Tomi Adeyemi's mega-popular young adult fantasy novel rooted in West African mythology, *Children of Blood and Bone*). From this comes the concept of 'sankofa', a sacred ancestral term from the people of Ghana which is all about invoking and acknowledging our past to create a better, freer future. Sankofa is best encapsulated in the Twi phrase 'se wo were fi no wosan kofa a yenkyi', which means 'we must go back and reclaim our past, so we can understand who we are today'.[8] As a concept, sankofa is transformative and cyclical, unbound by the linear Western concept of time. Instead, it implies that the past is all around us and must be revisited constantly to inform who we are today.[9] In genealogy terms, then, sankofa is a well-suited, enduring metaphor for those within the African diaspora who are utilising ancestral tools and DNA-testing kits as a portal to a past that was previously inaccessible. This was explored in fascinating detail in 2018 in a special collection of essays within the journal *Genealogy* called 'Sankofa; or "Go Back and Fetch it": Merging Genealogy and Africana Studies'. In an introduction, Kameelah L. Martin and Elizabeth J. West explain that

> people of African descent are consistently dispelling the long-avowed assertion that the ancestry of the enslaved in the United States and their descendants is, for the most part, unknowable. In the twenty-first century, the descendants of the enslaved are truly able to 'go back and fetch' the origins of their past in tangible ways as a means to understand the present and to move, assertively, into the future ... A focus on African American genealogy is, indeed, an exercise in the study of the Black experience.

The idea that these tests can help us restore and recollect a long-lost, collective cultural memory resonates, and excites me very much. Despite the worries related to data misuse and the inaccurate ethnicity estimates, the pull of DNA testing for those whose histories have been obscured is simply too strong to resist.

The search for self can feel all-consuming and unending when you have been denied such colossal knowledge at the starting point, but the spirit of sankofa can work like a tonic on tired souls, reminding us that a step back in time will aid us in a deeper understanding of the self. Our present is a space that has been carved out for us by ancestors. We carry them with us always, and so in many ways we have already found home.

By the middle of 2019 much of the heaviness I had been carrying with me since losing my father had seemingly dissipated into the atmosphere. I had found a peaceful home in a large Victorian house-share in Brixton, with rent far below market rate, with older housemates who were laid-back and normal and a soft-spoken landlord in his sixties who only appeared to repaint my walls and floor when I asked, or to fix the boiler on the same day it broke. When I did return home to Sutton, conversations were no longer dominated by what had gone on over the past few years. My mum, brother and I took a holiday to Rome at Christmas which passed without any incident; we toasted to Dad on Christmas Day. I managed to blag a week sailing down the Amazon River in Brazil for a travel article I was writing for the *Metro* newspaper and spent a serene, contemplative period journeying through the jungle by motor yacht. One night, as I took a canoe trip down still, glassy waters, I looked up into the sky as I realised I was enveloped by complete darkness and silence. Not the kind of night I was used to back in London, in which the murmur of traffic was constant, and the urban sky glow disguised half the stars. No, this was as close as I had been to truly peaceful isolation. Except for the low rumble of howler monkeys and parrots in the distance, there was nothing and no one around for miles. I found myself looking up at the outline of the trees, stencilled against the vast carpet of black by the silver light of the moon, and felt an immense calm wash over me. *I hope you are proud, Dad.* I stared up into the abyss. After four days in the remoteness of the jungle I headed to Rio, initially wary of disturbing my new-found inner peace by re-entering a frenetic city. But the magic of a metropolis is where I feel most at home. During the Brazilian celebrations, I saw brown bodies inscribed with feminist messages and critiques of the right-wing government; the carnival focused not just on hedonistic pursuits, but on raising awareness of the attacks against minority groups under the presidency of Bolsonaro. I was often misidentified in Brazil – but I wasn't cross about it. Locals thought I was a 'carioca' (person from Rio) and I tell you I lapped that shit up! During street parties I noticed how jiggle, wobble and overspill characterised so many of the local costumes, and brown, black and bronzed bodies doused in glitter and flowers writhed together in the searing heat, all shapes and sizes and shades, seen and celebrated.

When I got home I was preparing to wrap up my counselling – it had been two years with Anthea, more with Justine. I was talking about my father's impact on me for my Audible series, and it was bringing up painful truths.

'I am starting to realise now, as I revisit things in my work, that he was complicit with Mum in maintaining the silence around my identity. And that's weird to say out loud, but it's something they decided together, I guess.'

I was in Anthea's converted garden extension which she used for clients, sprawled out on a comfortable sofa, surrounded by mountains of cushions. 'You know, when you first came to me I do remember thinking how free of all blame your father really was,' she smiled. 'I know you had many wonderful experiences with him. He was the primary care-giver for you in many ways, but yes, he obviously also found your identity hard to address, he could not talk about it at all.'

Tears rolled down my cheeks silently in those conversations – I worried that I was somehow dishonouring his memory, that with each assumption I was chipping away at another bit of our love for each other.

'But why couldn't he?' I asked. 'What was so wrong with just speaking the truth, for just naming what I am? Sometimes I wonder if he *really* did, you know, love me.'

'From what you have described between you and your father, he loved you very, very much, Georgina, and he showed you that every single day. You can't fake all that.'

I left the sessions thinking that over the years Dad must have said something to someone about our relationship. Did he really believe the throwback story we referenced, or was it just a way to placate me? I may never really know. I decided to contact Mick, my dad's friend who lives five minutes from us in Carshalton. I needed to go back in time and revisit my father's life through one of his friends who knew him best. Mick and my dad used to car-share for work and were colleagues for the best part of twenty years. Mick's wife is of Jamaican and Nigerian heritage, his daughters went to my school and we are of a similar complexion. Surely the two of them spoke once or twice about the shared experience of raising mixed-race daughters, perhaps as they crossed the Albert Bridge on the way to work, my father's regular punk soundtrack turned down low to allow for conversation? Or in their office with their kitchen ladies? I needed to know what had been said, so I could reframe and understand our relationship in a new context without losing sight of what existed between us. I had become obsessed with archiving the past between my dad and me, but it was the only way I could move forward.

We met in the Greyhound in Carshalton, a historic timber-lined pub with traditional decor and dark wood floors overlooking Carshalton ponds which was where we also had had Dad's funeral wake. On the morning of the meeting, my mood was melancholy, I had not been back there since the day of his funeral. It was strange, I realised, to revisit this place again and talk about Dad when it was filled with memories from the most painful day of my life.

At 1 p.m., as the rain pelted it down, Mick and I ordered drinks – a pale ale for him, a Diet Coke for me. I'd half expected him to have a moustache, as that was my defining memory of him from my childhood, but he had shaved it off many years before.

'It's not been the same since your dad left, pet, it's all about the bottom line now,' Mick said referring to work, his soft Geordie accent the same as I remembered. The conversation shifted to family – I asked how his daughters were doing, what they were up to, and then I began digging about his conversations with my Dad, when I was a kid.

'The first time I saw you, you were pegging it around a school kitchen in a mini tractor. You had an Inset day and your dad had brought you into work with him. I saw you and I thought, "Oh, she's mixed-race." And I said to Jim something like, "Oh, she's gorgeous, what's the story?"' Mick paused and smiled. 'He looked at me and all he said was: "Sometimes these things happen." That's it. And very unlike Jim actually; there was also a look in his eye which said: don't ever ask me that again. So I never did.'

'Really?' I had never heard this before.

'Yep. I didn't think there was much point pushing it.'

'No, I guess not. Did you think I was my dad's then?'

'I thought you were related to Jim, I thought you were his from a previous relationship but Stephanie [Mick's wife] always said "No she looks like her Mum." I mean I could see you looked like my kids – you were mixed-race, that was obvious.'

It was obvious, but when I tell Mick that those words were never uttered in my house, that my race was not named, he was shocked. 'Right, yeah. That must have been confusing.'

You betcha.

He recalled the time I had gone to his house and Stephanie offered to do my hair, which I don't remember. 'That was a typical black mum thing, her asking if you wanted your hair done properly. And I said to your dad, "If ever Gina wants to get in touch with her black side and get her hair done, send her over."'

'What did Dad say?' I leaned forward across the table, waiting for more.

'He just looked at me and smiled knowingly, but that was all.'

This image of my father was slightly at odds with the picture painted by my mum, of the man who took on the throwback story with complete blind faith. This version of my father was that he was very much aware of the social expectations around discussing the anomaly which was our family, but like my mother, his defiance resulted in a racial stagnation in our home.

'I remember asking Dad to take me for a doctor's appointment to find out the truth when I was really little. Then when I got older I mentioned a DNA test, but of course I didn't know how to get one.'

Mick smiled but didn't say anything.

'Why do you think Dad didn't follow through with helping me sort all that out?'

''Cos he loved you. And also he would have had to come to terms with the idea that you weren't his, pet. And if he didn't talk it through with your mam, there's no way he could have done that with you.'

'Yeah. I just wish they had, you know, talked it out.'

'He was great, a great man your dad, but by god with this he was idiotic!' Mick laughed. 'He just couldn't face up to it.'

We tucked into lunch – a chicken pie for him and a vegetable casserole for me as I was trying to be healthy, but which I later regretted as it was not filling enough. I am a firm believer that deep emotional conversations require deeply calorific foods for sustenance. We parted with a hug near Carshalton station as I rushed off to take the train to see Anthea for one of my final sessions.

To obtain a reliable picture of the past, you must find more than one reliable source. I had resurrected my father's memory through Mick, and it had illuminated many more parts of him that I did not know. My father's decision-making process and his style of parenting were illogical and frustrating at times but they were rooted in a tenderness that came from deep within him. They weren't perfect, but neither are we, and I suppose we cannot expect love to be perfect all the time, either.

10

Passing

People thought that being one of a kind made you special. No, it just made you lonely. What was special was belonging with someone else.

BRIT BENNETT, *The Vanishing Half*

Before I'd gone freelance, I'd received a long message from a businessman called Ben who lived in London, and after scanning its contents I realised there were, once again, too many eerily similar coincidences in our lives for us not to meet. After some sporadic back and forth over many months, we eventually chose an All Bar One in Moorgate, close to where Ben worked and just a few seconds from my office, for a drink.

It was a blazing hot August day, and all I had to go on was Ben's tiny avatar from Gmail. I ended up lapping the place once, then twice, before deciding to sit down outside like a spare part and send him a message. London was pulsating with the heat in a way that was making everyone excited; the pavements were packed with city workers loosening their ties and clutching their ciders in Finsbury Square where I went on my lunch-breaks. I watched disgruntled cyclists fly past busy commuters, and busy commuters bump into imposing para-sols. I realised, in a way that was rather unlike me, that there was a small flutter of anxiety sitting somewhere in my core. Ben and I were about to turn parts of our lives that remained hidden inside out, like the lining of an old coat pocket – an awkward enough thing to do with someone like a therapist or partner, let alone someone you've never met in person before. I really didn't want to embarrass Ben, or myself, by saying the wrong thing, or worse – crying in public.

Suddenly I was spotted. A tall man wearing a white col-lared shirt, open at the neck, strolled confidently over to my table and shook my hand. Ben immediately offered to buy us drinks, despite the fact he was the interviewee, and two min-utes later he returned with a Diet Coke for me and a bottle of mineral water with ice for himself.

After a quick smattering of small talk, we got to it. Ben was straight-faced, direct, with a clear low voice.

'Lots of what you talk about happened to me, too,' he said as he relaxed into his chair in the shaded spot where we were sitting. 'And because I read your article around the time I was asking my mum questions, I thought we should meet.'

'What part of my writing resonated the most?' I was curious.

'Well, the throwback explanation was something I clung to myself. My dad's mother was called "Spanish", and in photos she does appear almost mixed-race, so apparently that's what we said caused my appearance. And also hiding family photos from my friends and even girlfriends. I did that.'

Ben was born in 1973 in Paris, to white British parents. When he was a few months old, the family returned to Marylebone in London, where Ben was raised alongside his younger brother and sister who, like his parents, were white in appearance. When he was six and a half, the family moved to Buckinghamshire, a county to the north-west of the capital and the place where Ben described feeling the impact of his difference for the first time.

'Older kids noticed that my parents were white and people would ask, "Are you adopted?" I didn't know what it meant, but I blurted this out to my mum one day and she said no. Still, though, I didn't have a concept of race. It got to a stage, I don't know when really, where I realised it was unusual but still it didn't get spoken about. Something clicked and I worked out it wasn't normal. If people pushed and asked, I'd tell them there was a black ancestor somewhere in the family. And you know, I never felt like I wasn't part of the family – my dad never treated me differently – but I never spoke to my siblings about why we looked different. It was just this thing in our family that we didn't discuss.'

As Ben spoke, I realised that to others we would look like relatives; cousins, siblings, a dad and daughter even. Ben had a caramel complexion a couple of shades lighter than my own, salt-and-pepper hair that was closely shaved, and in which, to trained eyes, a loose curl pattern could be spotted, and serious, dark brown eyes. He was business-like and did not waste words, often wrapping up and moving on from the most interesting parts of his reflections before I could dive in and ask him to elaborate. Ben explained that, like me, he was in the middle of a difficult period with his mother after seeking answers around how his race went undiscussed for over four decades. Ben had two young children with his wife, who is of German ancestry, and after their birth he was faced with a renewed sense of anxiety over what he didn't know. He didn't want his children to know the contours of identity conflict; he wanted a smoother, easier ride for them.

'My youngest is three, and it had become a bit of an issue with my wife, as she was growing very frustrated with my mum. So I talked to a counsellor about strategies and things, and we discussed that my sister would be a good person to get on board. I'd never spoken to my siblings about any of this at all, but we managed to engineer it so my sister was at our house with my mum, and my wife took my son out. I said I wanted to talk to her about something, but then I sort of broke down, and my sister filled in the gaps. Eventually my mum said it was "an African chap" she'd met in Paris. After waiting so long for an explanation, those are words I won't forget in a hurry.'

'There was no denial?' I chipped in, remembering just how long it took my mum to open up and silently noting how close relationships with siblings can avoid the tricky terrain of race for years.

'No there wasn't, actually. But we probably talked it through for no more than an hour, then she claimed that she didn't know who he was, what his name was, where he was from. And we went around in circles a bit, asking her, "Are you sure?" And that was it. And she went back to acting as if nothing had happened. She said she'd tell my dad about it but when I phoned him a few days later he had no idea so I had to blurt it all out. It wasn't pleasant, doing all that on the phone, as we hadn't talked about this for forty-two years. But then the next day he came over and was great. He had believed the story until I was seven, when he'd found out the truth from my mum. Up until then he thought it was the Spanish ancestor throwback thing. He said it was his job to keep the family together, and that's what he did.' Ben looked down, straight-faced, before sipping his water.

Our scenarios were startlingly similar, and I wondered once more if my dad had truly believed that I was his, just as

Ben's father had for the first few years of his life, or if both men had known the truth but had sealed off the parts of themselves required to engage with that in order to keep the family whole.

'My wife was very glad that we'd had the conversation, but she was pretty gobsmacked that my mum went back to pretending everything was normal,' Ben continued.

'That part sounds familiar.' I explained how my mum had immediately reverted to her stance of silence after I uncovered the truth. I sipped my Diet Coke and asked Ben if he thought his mum knew more.

'I don't know,' he admitted. 'My mum has an amazing memory, you see, and shortly after our conversation she started talking about a film she'd been at in 1964 with my father. My wife was sitting there thinking, "How can she go over those details from fifty years ago, but claim not to know anything about your biological father?" There's still an underlying tension there as she thinks her mother-in-law is denying her children, and me, the knowledge we should have. I discussed it with my brother who lives in Switzerland and he was great, but we still haven't discussed it as a whole family, and I don't know if my parents have talked about it.'

There is something so powerful and contagious about a familial silence, enacted to protect or preserve a difficult reality. Both of our families froze collectively like statues in near-identical poses when asked to qualify our appearance, and neither Ben nor I ever spoke with our siblings about our differences until the truth came out. I asked Ben if he'd consider counselling with his mum, and explained how much progress I had made with my own mother.

'No, I don't think we could. It would be ... very difficult to get her to open up.'

'Is it weird referring to the brother and sister you've

known all your life as half-siblings suddenly? I found that hard,' I said.

'We use the term, but it doesn't change anything. Your parents and your family are who you grew up with. I'm very much a nurture rather than nature person.'

We chatted a little more about Ben's plans to keep quizzing his mother and he told me how he planned to turn his attentions to genealogy and the DNA sites that I had already used.

'I've already received my ethnicity estimate and it says I'm forty per cent "West African", which is interesting but also a bit useless because it's so bloody broad.'

Another odd little affinity.

On the packed and sticky tube home two hours later, I remained weirded out by how many of our childhood and modern-day racial experiences were shared, but then again, the stories I had been privy to over the past couple of years were evidence enough that identity erasure is far more common than many of us would believe. It occurs in soft and safe homes in cities and the suburbs; its after-effects can be measured in individuals who are seemingly balanced and functional. Ben was very different from me – works-in-finance-smart, started-his-own-business-smart. He had life experience I lack, is two decades older than me, and has been married for years, whereas the longest relationship I've achieved is with Virgin Media (seven years and counting). I find it oddly reassuring and strangely sad, then, that this level-headed, suit-wearing city worker fought the same battles of belonging twenty years earlier in a suburban upbringing not too dissimilar from my own. Both of us benefited from time-generous parents in homes where food was always on the table, yet both of us had been unable to qualify the essence of who we were in these very same safe spaces, which had left us feeling just out of reach from the people who loved us the most. In Ben's case, he may never be able to access this part of his life with his wife and children, a fact which I could see was causing him emotional turmoil and adding a layer of tension between his mother and his wife. Unless he manages to stage conversations with his parents and siblings, the way mixedness and blackness is navigated in Ben's family may continue to be shrouded in secrecy and tension for another generation.

This got me thinking more about the complex nature of passing. Like me, Ben was left to construct an identity from the ashes of an absurd story that had burned at the core of his parents' marriage. Ben said his father had been preoccupied with keeping the family together, and his actions were noble and generous, but as I thought after our meeting, surely a loving home could have been maintained without sacrificing the development of Ben's identity? Why was overlooking his blackness the only way to secure family cohesion? In each of these stories, why does blackness have to be something that is tolerated or forgiven? Since my own revelations have come to light, my mum swears that she and my father never spoke of my race or the fact that I might not be his, and I was celebrated as their child, in many ways. But why was my identity not celebrated too? Ben had expressed nothing but gratitude to his amazing father, but the love intertwined with the denial muddied the waters, adding another layer of confusion to the betrayal. Anthea's words ring in my ears when I try and weigh up the impact of a loving upbringing, enshrined in secrecy. *'It was both.'* There was both love and denial, celebration and toleration, colour-blindness and, to some degree, colour consciousness. It wasn't always good and it wasn't always bad. It was both. Sometimes at once, sometimes one more than the other.

Were these family-wide silences proof that neither set of

parents ever worked past the feelings of hurt and disloyalty our mothers' affairs had brought about? Or do they also indicate an awkwardness around our blackness? Because if they were attempts to protect Ben and me from difficult truths, they have had somewhat the opposite effect, coming at the cost of our mental health and sense of self. That silence, the things that have remained unsaid for years and years, led us to believe that we were the biological offspring of both parents, which as kids we thought made us fully white. That silence is both the most fantastic and the most damaging thing that has ever happened to us. It is both.

Passing is about deception, but there is more than one way to pass as something you are not. Each of us will be misassigned a role at some point in our lives – the boyfriend instead of the brother, white instead of dual heritage, the help instead of the customer (funny how that one always affects the black and brown folk). And as intersectional identities become increasingly common, the definition of passing has expanded to include other experiences, such as gay men and women who are often misidentified as straight. Passing as white, straight, or in some cases as both, can still offer protection and safety for many minority individuals, but it also speaks to the omnipotence of straightness and whiteness as identities to which we are all encouraged to aspire, despite many advances in civil and gay rights.[1]

Passing is not just related to the racial. Teresa Kay Williams, Professor of Sociology and Ethnic Studies at UCLA, supports this theory noting that passing extends beyond 'phenotypical ambiguity', and can exist in various forms. (Remember eye colour, hair style and skin colour are examples of phenotypical variants.) Williams writes, 'Passing can occur based on physical appearance, cultural display, or both. The participants, their intentions and motivations, and the social context within which passing occurs, must all be interactively understood because "passing" does not necessitate taking place objectively, consistently, or even rationally.'[2]

In my case and Ben's, it was apparent that we were not white, so logically we should not have passed. But our family's silence, combined with our ability to learn and replicate the social cues of a white suburban family, helped us pass within our homes and occasionally, as children, beyond them. Once we began to doubt our identities however, we were left at a bewildering junction: how to demand the truth from a family that had embraced us, but among whom an element of our appearance also seemed to incite awkwardness.

However and wherever passing happens, when you knowingly pass as something you are not, a little slice of the real you goes missing along the way. Sometimes it is lost for ever. To me, there exist two very distinct types of passing: those who knowingly pass, and those who have been unwittingly passed off. In both cases for passing to be successful it can never truly be acknowledged. If you are deliberately and consistently passing as something you are not, then you must deceive the group to which you're trying to gain acceptance, largely for certain advantages, as was the case with racial passing in America in the eighteenth and nineteenth centuries, or for any gay people whose sexual identities remained covert for safety. If you are being passed *off*, such as children unwittingly being raised by fathers who aren't their own, it brings the deception to a whole new level. Being passed off requires a 'passer' (a parent) to make the choice for the 'passee' (the child). The passee is denied agency in this process at first. Being passed off also requires participation from a range of others to uphold the story and this can inflict a whole heap of psychological confusion on the passee, whose world is warped as others play pretend, too. The passee's interactions with others will be disfigured, as they will all be asked to suspend belief and sustain false realities. When Ben and I realised we couldn't pass as white, the depressing conclusion meant that we couldn't pass as the son or daughter of our white parents. Accepting this meant deconstructing not only our personal identities, but the world into which we passed.

Being passed off has brought about substantial benefits too; Ben and I have benefited from a large amount of white privilege; we have anglicised names and surnames; we were born into white families untroubled by the economic hardship that often comes with being a first- or second-generation immigrant; we understand how to code-switch and navigate whiteness; we blend in during family events, because we have been accepted. In being passed off, we have had our identities sacrificed, yet found solace and acceptance. We have lost one community but lived quite happily in another. We have much to be grateful for.

A few weeks after meeting Ben, I visited my dad's family. I knew that my grandparents and my dad's sister had read my articles over the years, but we had never really discussed what they meant, or what it was like for them when I was born. For my grandparents, how have I passed as their son's daughter, and their granddaughter, for so long when I am black and they are white?

Dad's family all live in Shropshire, a quiet county of astounding natural beauty that borders Wales to the west and Birmingham to the east, sitting above the Black Country. Every year when my dad was alive, our Christmas ritual began with the five-hour pilgrimage from our home in Sutton to my grandparents' house in Church Stretton, the car loaded to the brim with presents for all the family, sailing up the motorways and later down winding country lanes until we landed at my grandparents' home. Church Stretton is a small, soporific market town of butchers, bakers and antique shops, nestled among misty moorlands and dramatic highlands. We'd visit for four or five days each December and spend the festive season making snowmen with my cousins, tucking into mince pies on my granny's fancy blue china plates, and unwrapping new toys by warm fireplaces, a large grandfather clock ticking away in the background. There'd be a spread at my auntie Celia's, or at my dad's brother's house. After a period of prolonged eating, someone would suggest a hike on the snow-capped hills of the nearby Long Mynd, or we'd attend a carol service at the Protestant church where Granny always seemed to have about seven different organisational roles. Shropshire is green, pleasant and serene. But now Dad is no longer with us, it has taken on an eerie, menacing vibe in winter. Being there at Christmas felt a lot like getting to the ominous scene in a movie – there were too many ghosts waiting for me in my grandparents' house and I wanted to skip over the entire experience. Winter there without Dad simply became too bleak and so I decided to visit in the summer instead.

In grief, people go one of two ways when it comes to maintaining special traditions without a loved one: you either return religiously to the sites you once loved, trying desperately to pay homage by doing things in exactly the same way because someone who wasn't as close to them will say It's What They Would Have Wanted, or you can branch off and start anew. In my opinion, the death of a loved one is such a cataclysmic event, no matter what you do, things as you once knew them have ceased to exist for ever, so there's no point trying to recreate anything. Like the BC/AD dating system, your life is forever cleaved in half, into all the living you have done before and after their existence. Trying to force old traditions when their death has brought about a completely new way of living is a bit like trying to plug an Android charger into an iPhone – no matter how hard you try, it just won't work. Sometimes when the grief is raw, keeping to old habits helps because dreaming up new ways of being requires extreme a mental dexterity you just won't be able to muster, and in the first year after Dad's death, returning to Shropshire helped me, my mum and brother feel closer to him, but it was also shockingly difficult. So I'm a big advocate of establishing new forms of being when you feel up to doing so, and I am good at adapting to change because I have had to be. Visiting Shropshire that summer helped propel me forward, instead of feeling as if I was stuck on loop with the ghosts of Christmas past.

The first time I took a trip alone, I stayed at my auntie Celia's a few miles from my grandparents' home. After some hillside walks with Celia's dog and my cousin Jim (who visits me often in London for weekends of mischief and some sightseeing), I finally mustered up the courage to ask my aunt what she'd thought when I was born. As Celia drove me from her house to Church Stretton, and verdant hills, heather-covered at this time of the year, rolled by outside, she recounted the early reactions to my birth, and I recorded our conversation.

'We first saw you when you had jaundice in the hospital, and I said out loud, "Ooh, they've kept you under that lamp for quite a while!" – I just thought you had a good suntan. And nobody said anything. Actually, Vin said "shut up" and kicked me under the table.'

I started shaking with laughter at the way my auntie told me this. Vinnie, or Vin, is Celia's husband, a warm, bald-headed, no-nonsense man who rarely joined in with the family board game dramas each Christmas, preferring instead to excuse himself and walk the dog or take a nap after dinner.

I imagined he'd realised sooner than his wife that I was a little more than just 'tanned'.

'I thought that was an ideal opportunity to say something, as we were all there, with Granny and Grandpa, but nobody said a word.' I realised this obviously meant they'd all cottoned on quite quickly then. 'It wasn't our place to say, there in the hospital. And from then on it was just accepted. James, your dad, didn't even speak to our mum about it, but he did ring up before Granny saw you and said something about you having "very dark hair". You kick yourself a bit now and I think, should we have pushed a bit more? But your dad, he was very good at brushing things off and just making a joke about something, wasn't he? And he didn't open up to anybody.'

'Yep. This is true.' I thought of Dad, a man who was profoundly deep but who I think avoided deep conversations at all costs. I told Celia how sad it made me, thinking of how he must have wrestled with the decision to stay or go in his own head that day in the hospital, and ultimately coming to the conclusion that he didn't want to be a single man without a family, that he would unflinchingly take on this child who did not share his bloodline.

'Yes, and me,' she said, looking ahead at the empty road as I stared out of my window at the steep fields of green, dotted with sheep the colour of porridge oats.

I thought about all the times I'd made this trip, sitting in the back of our car while Dad dutifully ferried us to his parents' house each year. It dawned on me once more how many difficult things my father had dealt with on his own, inside his own head. Dad was equally stoic when sick, rarely breaking down to protect everyone else from having to comfort him. The mental fortitude, the tenaciousness and courage it must have taken to seal off all that pain to protect us from having to deal with the worst of it, blows my brain to dust when I try and quantify it.

'Your dad accepted you without question, and we did too,' Celia continued, eyes still fixed on the road. 'Perhaps he was just frightened of losing your mum. Maybe he thought she might have disappeared with you and that would have been it? He obviously didn't want that.'

'No, yeah, I guess he didn't . . . but didn't you all think it was weird?'

'We all didn't think it was right, but as time gets on it's harder to say anything. Nothing was ever said. We all accepted you as Jim's daughter and we still do. I just wish your mum had said something sooner, to you and your dad, because these secrets – they're no good, are they?' She smiled. 'I knew you'd want answers sooner or later, I did think that. And your mum being brought up in a Catholic background, I think Catholics are a bit funny about things like that, aren't they? And then I suppose your mum has been conditioned to a certain way of being.'

Celia has a melodic, high-pitched voice just like my granny's, the type in which you can rarely detect anger or malice, and when the two of them smile, they look a lot like Dad. But her comments were at odds with my kind, eternally busy granny, who, after everything had come out, told me that she had always believed I was my dad's. My stern, generous grandpa, who had helped our family several times throughout the years, had said he had 'always known' that I couldn't be related to them but accepted me all the same. And neither of them had spoken about it with each other, let alone with my father.

The visit to Shropshire flew by in a blur of country walks and boozing in country pubs with my cousin. After my three-hour train journey home, I took a nap before waking up to write an opinion piece for an online site. Later, I was cooking a stir-fry (everyone in my house-share was out so I could sing Ari Lennox's 'New Apartment' out loud with casual indifference and pretend I actually lived alone, and not with four others). I called Aisling to tell her how the trip had gone.

'God, isn't it so strange how your grandparents had different views to your auntie Celia?' she said. 'How no one ever said anything to your dad?'

'I know. Mental. Shropshire was lovely though, I still feel very much accepted even though Dad's not here and everyone knows the truth. Nothing has changed much. I didn't expect that it would.' This was both a good and a bad thing, I realised.

'I think ...' Aisling paused. She is always measured and tactful even in difficult conversations. 'I think maybe your family just didn't know what to do when your parents stayed silent.'

'Yeah. You know what? You're right. I just wish someone had said something to me, 'cos I was drowning with this, I really was.'

'I know, George.' Aisling and Emilia, more than any other people in my life, had been privy to all the strange little battles of belonging I'd had to fight, claiming my family and denying my mother's infidelity in the face of a near-comical level of derision.

The way the obvious truth has been ignored in my family, and in the families of many other people I have met, epitomises our collective British attitude to discussing race. We don't want to name our differences in case we cause offence, so instead we ignore them entirely, in the hope that either they will go away, or we can simply overlook them. But as I know too well, this tactic is no good for anyone who lives with the baggage – and beauty – of a minority identity. It fails to grant us the breathing room to express ourselves fully, scrubbing us out, and encouraging us to cut off vital and fascinating parts of ourselves in order to fit in. When white people are forced to confront race after years of self-imposed ignorance or denial, there is defensiveness and anger simply because those who are white have functioned as the normative touchstone for all of humanity and have not lived with race in the same way as non-whites, and are, in effect, raceless. In 2018, the Channel 4 news presenter Jon Snow stated, during coverage of a Brexit rally live on air, that he'd 'never seen so many white people in one place', resulting in 2500 Ofcom complaints. We are so used to non-white people dealing with politicised, racialised identities in this country that confronting 'whiteness' also means confronting the notion that it is an experience viewed through a particular lens, and is neither universal nor objective.[3] But arguing for a world without race, or where race isn't acknowledged, isn't the answer either, because this would be, in effect, a world without any people of colour. If you dream of a raceless future, it goes hand in hand with the elimination of black people, and so we must learn to de-centre and deconstruct whiteness and white supremacy instead. Interpersonal acts of love and kindness within mixed relationships, both romantic and familial, are not the panacea for racism, but in identifying and dismantling the structures that have helped normalise the denial and erasure of minority groups, we can build a future in which a mixed family is neither taboo, nor a talking point.

Passing is pain, but it is also kindness. Getting to the truth of how and why I have passed, and as what, has felt like uncovering a family-wide conspiracy in which everyone has been asked to play a part; but I am slowly understanding that the story of how I came to exist was codified in silence only after others took their cues from my parents. My dad claimed me, and between us passing also meant love, acceptance and a life as his daughter, which I will always remember; but passing started with my mum, and intertwined with her reasons for passing me off were her feelings of shame and guilt around her affair, which somewhere along the line, were passed on to me. There is a particular mental anguish that comes from being asked to conceal or suppress a part of you within the home. It requires a cognitive dissonance to live separately from a culture that is mapped on your face, the story that is written on your skin, or flows through your bloodline. The painful consequences of engaging in racial masquerade have been documented for years in America, but the stories of those who have been passed off as something they are not remain layered, complex and obscured by embarrassment and fear within families. Passing adds an invisible tension to each new friendship and relationship but now that we are finally free of it, now my mother and I have spoken at length over many years about its impact, I feel as if we can move on.

In one of our final sessions with Justine, I decided to discuss how the Audible series was unfolding. I had told my mum about Keji, about the people I was interviewing, but I had not yet asked her to be a part of it. A recorded conversation would make the programme more meaningful, but it would also represent a huge level of growth between us. But she hated those things, did my mum. When I first began writing online, I remembered the lashing out, the embarrassment, at the way in which I was exposing us, and so I was not expecting an enthusiastic response. To my amazement, however, I found that Mum was up for an actual interview when I broached the topic.

'I realise that it's important to you to keep talking about everything and that it helps you understand more about who you are. And I'm happy for you to continue with that. I think I'd be OK with maybe being interviewed if ... if it was done well.'

I nodded slowly, barely able to comprehend what this meant for us. Whereas I was once frustrated at the way Mum's thoughts dripped like water from a leaky tap, infuriatingly slowly at times, in comparison to my own which flowed freely and without filter, I was now watching this same woman volunteer herself up for a recorded interview in front of a producer she had never met. I had struggled to understand her motivations for shirking all my questions over the years, and Mum could not understand my urgent need to discuss things so publicly. But that day marked a complete departure away from those guarded, selfish versions of us. I marvelled at where we were, who we had become, sitting in silence with a smile on my face.

'I think that's a huge shift in attitude. I've never heard you say anything quite like that,' Justine said wide-eyed, her head tilted. 'It really shows how much progress you've made, Colette. You realise that this is important to your daughter and you're prepared to help her on this journey. I'm very pleased for you both.'

My mum said nothing but turned to me and smiled; talking about our family, about my blackness, about her affair was once so taboo, but we had shed our most defensive layers and now there was barely anything to talk about in our weekly counselling sessions. The hours we had spent shouting, crying, then talking, and finally, slowly, coming to understand each other will stay with me always, the result of which is a relationship based on a deeper level of understanding and forgiveness. And there had been no better person to guide us through the process than Justine, whose kindness and empathy radiated from every atom of her being. With each session she had nudged us into a talking territory that had once been awkward and tricky, stripping away years of tension and distrust and helping us find our way back to each other. In one of our final appointments I confessed to her that when we had started seeing one another in 2017, I had doubted her ability to truly 'get' the whole racial erasure thing because she was white, and in my experience, attempting to talk to white people about the impact of that had not exactly gone smoothly up until that point. 'Yes, I can imagine,' she laughed when I brought this up. 'You probably thought: who's this white lady to tell me anything?'

I nodded. 'But how did you know? How did you strike the balance between both of us?'

'Well,' she replied, 'it's my job.'

But my intuition told me there was something more to it than just skill and professionalism. Justine understood my innate anguish at not being heard at home, but she also explained so much to my mum without patronising her, unpacking her shame and tendency to turn pain inwards – without ever isolating her.

'Can I ask you a question?' I felt as if I might overstep a boundary but there were words I was dying to say, and as always, I was not one for holding anything in.

'Yes, go ahead.'

'Do you have a mixed-race family by any chance? Or kids like me?' There was a pause, a wry smile.

'Yes. I do.' She did not elaborate.

'I knew it!' I exclaimed with more ardour than I had meant to release. I thought back to the bag, like the ones I had seen in Zimbabwe.

'How?' She looked a little concerned.

'Just . . . just an inkling.'

Justine had been the most incredible uniting force between

me and my mother, and had helped us rewrite a family script that we could both read from, but it was just on a chance recommendation from a friend that my mother had found her. She had not asked for a therapist who had experience dealing with identity, or race, and I had chastised her for not looking for a black woman. It's a family therapist's role to help bridge gaps between clients, but I believe Justine's ability to unpick racial nuances, to get my mother to understand the seriousness of what she had done while slowly, week by week, allowing me to hear and see my mother in order to forgive her, would have been particularly hard to do if she were not a mother herself, and in particular a mother to mixed-race children. It was yet again proof to me that our identities inform so much of how we interact with one another in the world, emitting invisible signals that connect us with the right people, at the right times in our lives. Justine was destined to be our counsellor, some things are just meant to be.

In the spring of 2019, I was buying a cupcake from an elderly lady with white hair, in a little tent in the outdoor grounds of a hospice in Cheam.

'That's £1 please, dear.'

'Thanks.' I dropped the money into her creased palm and collected my slice of spongy goodness.

'Have a nice afternoon, dear.'

All around me were other families waiting for the morning's memorial service to start. I saw mothers and fathers pushing tiny babies at the very start of their lives in giant buggies across the lawn. At the other end of the spectrum, others were pushing around parents or grandparents in wheelchairs. I watched people wearing fundraising T-shirts with the faces of those they had lost, shaking hands with doctors and nurses. There were nuns, healthcare workers and I recognised Father

Luke – a Dutch priest who I swear is immortal because I could recall him being drafted in for many masses at my school when I was about twelve, and he still looked the same. I was at the annual spring memorial service at the Royal Marsden Hospice where my dad passed away. Dad died on 12 May and his birthday falls on 28 April. As a result, spring makes me feel quite … sprung to say the least. The season takes on an oxymoronic meaning; what is normally a period of hope and new beginnings is also a time in which I reflect most acutely on the things that I have lost. Spring was Dad's favourite time of year (along with Christmas) and each time it rolls around I remember how he'd downplay his birthday even after mum ushered my brother and me into the kitchen to sign a secret card for him, or present him with a 'best dad' pint glass on our behalf, how he would excitedly recount how many frogs were in our pond, or dutifully point out all the flowers coming up in our garden that he tended to. But spring is also the season of change, and change as I know, is unavoidable, an immutable certainty of life. Nondescript trees I have blindly ignored for months suddenly demand my attention by sprouting pastel pink blossoms, the days grow brighter and longer, and the bars and cafés all around south London seem to hum with vivacity. Spring brings promise, is the most optimistic of all seasons. My brother and I, along with Mum, all attended the outdoor ceremony together, standing in quiet contemplation in the hospice gardens among others who were remembering someone they did not want to lose. The female doctor who I remember tended to Dad read a poem about sunflowers; another person spoke about how much they had fundraised for new equipment in honour of their father. I felt sort of woozy and unpredictable, as if I wanted to burst into tears, or let out a loud screech and disrupt the quiet, reflective silence at any moment. There were hymns and a priest too, but it's a Catholic-lite sort of service, seeing as it lasts only twenty minutes and all the hymns are actually quite upbeat. It was nice to come here and remember Dad, but of course it awakened in me a sadness I had trained myself to dampen, in order to carry on living. I saw myself in the building beside my father as he snoozed and snoozed and snoozed, his radiance dimming second by second as we held his hand and fed him ice lollies from the bed. I saw myself on the bench on which I told my brother that Dad was in what the doctor called 'the final stage of life', the exact spot where we had held each other and cried. I walked past the room in which I had tearfully, selfishly asked Dad what we would do without him. 'Just try and stay together as best you can,' he had said to me at the time, his eyes closed, a smile on his lips.

British hospices are incredible things: they offer round-the-clock comfort and care to patients, and support for families, all of which is totally free. Each year at the memorial service, there is the chance to commemorate a loved one with a miniature plastic sunflower which sits in a giant box within the grounds that function as a garden. Each flower costs £5 and all proceeds go back to the hospice. After the ceremony that year my mum and I searched for Dad's flower to take home with us. We saw not one, not two, but seven sunflowers brandishing the name 'Jim Lawton'.

'Oh, there's so many,' my mum exclaimed as she leant down to pick one up. Then my dad's friend and former colleague Mick bounded over. 'I did a whip-round and a few of the kitchen ladies wanted to contribute. So there we are.'

'That's really nice,' my brother said quietly as Mick surveyed the box and we caught up on what was a beautiful day. His once-rounded belly had flattened considerably since I'd last seen him. 'Yep, I've been watching meself, pet, cutting back on all the bad stuff you know. No more chips and pies for me!'

Mick returns each year to complete the Marsden March – a walk from the Royal Marsden hospital in Chelsea to the one in Sutton where the spring ceremony is – in my dad's name. He was always around at the house when Dad was sick, bringing tea and files for my dad to work with and even building the new bed my dad bought to ease the agony of his cancer-stricken back. Friends like that, and the friends I have kept in the most agonising parts of these past few years from home and from university, illuminate your darkest hours, shining a light on a pathway when you think there is no way out.

If I can live my life with just one smattering of Dad's values, if I can take one tiny cell of his selflessness and carry it with me for ever, then I know I will be better for it, I thought as we drove home after the event. If we do it right, the way we live our lives, the reach of our actions and the things we do for others will leave a mark on the world long after we are gone. A love like my dad's comes around once, maybe twice, in a lifetime, but its imprint remains etched onto the hearts of everyone he touched, immovable and everlasting in spite of his physical absence. You never forget the comfort and protection that a love like that brings. You spend the rest of your life looking for something shaped in its image; it never leaves you.

After the service, I returned to my house in Brixton. I had work to do, articles to write, plans to make. There is still so much I want for the relationships with my family, but as my brother pointed out at the hospice service, our growth as a family has been incredible. We had come together to remember Dad, a united, peaceful, imperfect front, a family that had stayed together, just like he wanted.

Notes

2. Restarting

1 Yaylaci, Ş., Roth, W.D. and Jaffe, K., 'Measuring racial essentialism in the genomic era: The genetic essentialism scale for race (GESR)', *Current Psychology*, 2019, https://doi.org/10.1007/s12144-019-00311-z

2 Jordanna Bailkin, 'The Postcolonial Family? West African Children, Private Fostering, and the British State', *The Journal of Modern History* 81(1), 2009, pp. 87–121.

3 https://mediadiversified.org/2018/03/02/foster-families-who-ignore-race-are-participating-in-a-pernicious-form-of-racism/

4 Jayne O. Ifekwunigwe, *'Mixed Race' Studies: A Reader* (London: Routledge, 2004), p. 189.

3. Don't Make a Fuss

1 Miri Song and Peter Aspinall, 'Is Racial Mismatch a Problem for Young "Mixed Race" People in Britain? The Findings of Qualitative Research', *Ethnicities*, 12(6), 2012, 730–753, https://journals.sagepub.com/doi/10.1177/1468796811434912

2 https://www.pewsocialtrends.org/2015/06/11/multiracial-in-america/

3 https://phys.org/news/2010-12-one-drop-persist-biracial-individuals.html

4 Lewis R. Gordon, 'Race, Biraciality and Mixed Race', in Jayne O. Ifekwunigwe, *'Mixed Race' Studies: A Reader* (London: Routledge, 2004).

5 Nikki Khanna and Cathryn Johnson, 'Passing as Black: Racial Identity Work among Biracial Americans', *Social Psychology Quarterly*, 73(4), 2010, pp. 380–397.

4. Wearing Someone Else's Face

1   https://www.runnymedetrust.org/uploads/images/SuttonScorecard.pdf
2   Jennifer R. Steele, Meghan George, Amanda Williams and Elaine Tay, 'A cross-cultural investigation of children's implicit attitudes toward White and Black racial outgroups', *Developmental Science*, 2018, https://www. sciencedaily.com/releases/2018/05/180514140821.htm
3   Harold D. Fishbein, *Peer Prejudice and Discrimination* (New York: Psychology Press, 2002).
4   https://www.medica-tradefair.com/en/News/Archive/ Skin_Colour_Matters_When_it_Comes_to_Health
5   University of Southern California, 'Black Girls Are 50 Percent More Likely To Be Bulimic Than White Girls', *ScienceDaily*, www.sciencedaily.com/ releases/2009/03/090318140532.htm
6   Gina E. Miranda Samuels, '"Being Raised by White People": Navigating Racial Difference Among Adopted Multiracial Adults', *Journal of Marriage and Family*, 71(1), 2009, pp. 80–94, https://doi. org/10.1111/j.1741-3737.2008.00581.x
7   https://www.ncbi.nlm.nih.gov/pmc/articles/PMC2366972/ Richard M. Lee, 'The Transracial Adoption Paradox', *Counselling Psychology*, Nov; 31(6), 2003, pp. 711–744, doi: 10.1177/0011000003258087

7. Did You Lose Your Comb?

1   https://www.huffingtonpost.com/antonia-opiah/the-changing-business-of-_b_4650819.html
2   https://www.giga-hamburg.de/en/system/files/publications/wp315_hansing-hoffmann.pdf
3   https://www.giga-hamburg.de/en/system/files/publications/wp315_hansing-hoffmann.pdf
4   https://ir.library.illinoisstate.edu/cgi/viewcontent. cgi?article=1014&context=mts
5   'Good Hair Bad Hair Dominican Hair', (https://ir.library.illinoisstate.edu/ cgi/viewcontent.cgi?article=1014&context=mts)
6   Heather Hanna, *Women Framing Hair: Serial Strategies in Contemporary Art* (Newcastle: Cambridge Scholars Publishing, 2015), p. 169.
7   Thomas Jefferson, 'Notes On Virginia', p. 133, http://historytools. davidjvoelker.com/sources/Jefferson-Race.pdf
8   https://digitalcommons.law.yale.edu/cgi/viewcontent. cgi?article=7841&context=ylj
9   Jacqueline Kilikita, 'Being Adopted Into A White Family Cost Me My Black Hair Identity', *Refinery29*, 2 May 2019.
10 Emma Dabiri, *Don't Touch My Hair* (London: Penguin, 2019), p. 6.
11 https://www.bbc.co.uk/news/uk-england-47115305

12 https://www.americanprogress.org/issues/race/reports/2018/06/05/451647/
    mass-incarceration-stress-black-infant-mortality/
13 https://www.researchandmarkets.com/reports/4847031/
    hair-wigs-and-extensions-market-global-outlook?w=5

8. Shame

1 June Price Tangney & Ronda L. Dearing, *Shame and Guilt* (New York: The
   Guildford Press, 2002), p. 3.
2 Afua Hirsch, *Brit(ish)* (London: Vintage, 2018), p. 16.
3 https://tbinternet.ohchr.org/Treaties/CERD/Shared%20Documents/IRL/
   INT_CERD_NGO_IRL_37383_E.pdf
4 *Irish Examiner*, 13 March 2018.
5 *The Irish Times*, 11 January 2020.

9. Time Travelling

1 Sheldon Krimsky & David Cay Johnston, *Ancestry DNA Testing and
   Privacy* (Washington: Council for Responsible Genetics, 2017).
2 Duana Fullwiley, 'Race, Genes, Power', *British Journal of Sociology* 66(1),
   2015, pp. 36–45.
3 Morris W. Foster & Richard R. Sharp, 'Race, Ethnicity, and Genomics',
   Genome Research, 12, 2002, pp. 844–50.
4 Fullwiley, p. 43.
5 Sheldon Krimsky & David Cay Johnston, p. 7.
6 Antònio Regalado, 'More than 26 million people have taken an at-home
   ancestry test', *MIT Technology Review*, 11 February 2019.
7 Alondra Nelson, *The Social Life of DNA* (New York: Beacon Press Books,
   2016), p. 71.
8 Carmen E. Bovell PhD, Florence Jones Calhoun MEd & Desiree
   DeFlorimonte PhD, *Walking in History: Sankofa: Our Trip to Ghana and
   Benin* (Pittsburgh: Dorrance Publishing Co., 2019) p. 4.
9 Emma Dabiri, *Don't Touch My Hair* (London: Penguin, 2019), p. 83.

10. Passing

1 Kora Beck, 'The trouble with "passing" for another race/sexuality/
   religion . . .', *Guardian*, 2 January 2014.
2 Teresa Kay Williams, 'Race-ing and being raced, the critical interrogation
   of passing', in Jayne O. Ifekwunigwe, *'Mixed Race' Studies: A Reader*
   (London: Routledge, 2004).
3 Myriam François, 'The fury of "white people" with Jon Snow shows a total
   lack of self-awareness on race', *Guardian*, 12 April 2019.

Acknowledgements

To my mum and brother, I love you for ever. Dad is always with us.

To my grandparents and Dad's family, thank you for making it known that nothing has changed.

To my family in Ireland, I will always cherish our memories together.

With much love to every one of my friends. I appreciate the laughs and the support over the last few years more than I can even put into words: Emilia, Aisling, Charlie, Pat, Emma, Luke, Becky, Shannon, Abi, Ray, Zahrah – you da best. To my dad's friends Dave and Mick, thank you for reminding me of the love.

With special thanks to Zoe Ross at United – the best agent in the world, a brilliant advocate and the person who laboured over the initial proposal for this book with me for almost a year and helped me find my voice. To my first and brilliant editor, Hannah, at Sphere, thank you for your patience. And to Fiona, Cath and everyone else at Little, Brown, I am so grateful for the way you got behind this book so fervently.

A special thanks to all interviewees featured in this book, and also to anyone who has ever contacted me to discuss the things I have written – thank you for the inspiration to keep on writing. Our stories are valid.